Pro OpenSSH

Michael Stahnke

Apress®

Pro OpenSSH

Copyright © 2006 by Michael Stahnke

ISBN 978-1-59059-476-6

9 8 7 6 5 4 3 2 1

Trademarked names may appear in this book. Rather than use a trademark symbol with every occurrence of a trademarked name, we use the names only in an editorial fashion and to the benefit of the trademark owner, with no intention of infringement of the trademark.

Lead Editor: Jason Gilmore
Technical Reviewer: Darren Tucker
Editorial Board: Steve Anglin, Dan Appleman, Ewan Buckingham, Gary Cornell, Tony Davis, Jason Gilmore, Jonathan Hassell, Chris Mills, Dominic Shakeshaft, Jim Sumser
Project Managers: Beckie Stones and Laura Brown
Copy Edit Manager: Nicole LeClerc
Copy Editors: Ami Knox and Damon Larson
Assistant Production Director: Kari Brooks-Copony
Production Editor: Laura Cheu
Compositor: Kinetic Publishing Services, LLC
Proofreader: Lori Bring
Indexer: Michael Brinkman
Artist: Kinetic Publishing Services, LLC
Cover Designer: Kurt Krames
Manufacturing Director: Tom Debolski

Distributed to the book trade worldwide by Springer-Verlag New York, Inc., 233 Spring Street, 6th Floor, New York, NY 10013. Phone 1-800-SPRINGER, fax 201-348-4505, e-mail orders-ny@springer-sbm.com, or visit http://www.springeronline.com.

For information on translations, please contact Apress directly at 2560 Ninth Street, Suite 219, Berkeley, CA 94710. Phone 510-549-5930, fax 510-549-5939, e-mail info@apress.com, or visit http://www.apress.com.

The information in this book is distributed on an "as is" basis, without warranty. Although every precaution has been taken in the preparation of this work, neither the author(s) nor Apress shall have any liability to any person or entity with respect to any loss or damage caused or alleged to be caused directly or indirectly by the information contained in this work.

The source code for this book is available to readers at http://www.apress.com in the Source Code section.

Contents at a Glance

Contents

PART 1 ■■■ Quick and Secure

PART 2 ▪▪▪ Configuring OpenSSH

PART 3 ■ ■ ■ **Advanced Topics**

■CHAPTER 8 Managing Your OpenSSH Environment 165

PART 4 ■■■ Administration with OpenSSH

About the Author

**MICHAEL STAHNKE** works as a UNIX Security Administrator at a Fortune 100 company in the Midwest. He has headed implementations of Secure Shell for his corporate IT group and provided consultation and assistance with production rollouts around the globe. Additionally, he has led several studies and projects to improve the security state of his large-scale UNIX/Linux environment, utilizing SSH, mandatory access control, configuration management integration, and automation techniques. When not devoting his time to improving security at work, Michael spends time researching and applying new open source technologies and practices on his ever-changing home network. Michael has also done contract programming to create content management solutions utilizing PHP, Perl, MySQL, and C++. Michael earned a CS degree from Ball State University in 2002. He also recently became a CISSP.

About the Technical Reviewer

 **DARREN TUCKER** is an independent consultant in Sydney, Australia. He has worked on a variety of systems and networks for over 10 years, many of those with OpenSSH and other SSH products. He has been a member of the OpenSSH development team since 2003. He likes cricket and dislikes talking about himself in the third person.

Acknowledgments

I would like to thank a few individuals who helped me make this book a reality. First and foremost, I would like to thank my wife Jaime for putting up with an absent and almost nonexistent husband on several occasions during the authoring process. I would also like to thank John Traenkenschuh for encouraging me to write down my experiences with SSH. Brian Tower also deserves many thanks for allowing me to share my ideas and for helping correct a few oddly worded sentences.

Finally, I would like to thank the open source community for so many projects that I use everyday; but I especially want to thank the OpenSSH development team, including my technical reviewer Darren Tucker, for delivering a high-quality, secure connectivity solution at a price that everyone can afford.

Introduction

What Is SSH?

In 1995, Helsinki University of Technology researcher Tatu Ylönen learned that system passwords were being retrieved through network monitoring, resulting in a compromise of the university network. Simple tools allowed adversaries of the university to gain access to several account names and passwords. Mr. Ylönen responded by creating the Secure Shell (SSH), a security solution intended to resolve the deficiencies of legacy protocols by encrypting data, account names, and passwords while they are in transit, thus rendering network sniffing useless.

Mr. Ylönen's creation resolved many issues that had haunted legacy protocols for years. The initial release of SSH quickly became popular at his university and throughout the Internet. Users from around the globe were soon asking for copies of the software, support on that software, and of course new features. Later in 1995, he founded SSH Communications Security (http://www.ssh.com). With this new tool, security/system administrators could replace legacy system access applications such as rsh, rlogin, rcp, Telnet, and FTP with secure alternatives. SSH could also provide solutions for many common user-friendliness issues—for example, through simplifying passwords by moving to digital credentials in the form of public keys.

According to http://www.openssh.org, Mr. Ylönen released his SSH originally as Free SSH, but it contained a few proprietary libraries and licenses that prevented it from being widely adopted by major projects. As the Free SSH project progressed, newer versions came with more restrictive licenses. Some early licenses attached to Free SSH forbade developers to create Windows or DOS versions. Later licenses restricted the use of Free SSH in commercial operating environments.

In 1999, Björn Grönvall, a Swedish computer scientist, created a new version of SSH called OSSH. When the OpenBSD project became aware of Grönvall's work a few short months before the scheduled release of OpenBSD 2.6, the decision was made to include an SSH implementation in OpenBSD. The OpenBSD community forked OSSH to enable rapid development and control over the project, and continued developing and refining it on a very rigorous schedule—upon release, the product was renamed OpenSSH. Shortly after the release of OpenBSD 2.6, Linux advocates and other UNIX programmers saw the need for SSH on their systems. OpenSSH was then split into two versions: baseline (for OpenBSD systems) and portable (for Linux, UNIX, and other operating systems). OpenSSH is freely usable and redistributable by everyone under a BSD license. It has since been included in nearly every major UNIX and Linux release, and is regularly integrated into embedded devices and appliances.

OpenSSH creates value in a network of any size by protecting data. In the enterprise, UNIX administrators will find using key-based authentication allows them to perform tasks and script as quickly as with rsh/rlogin, but with added security and logging. Security administrators will be happy to remove legacy clear-text protocols and applications.

Auditors can streamline their workflow as they will only require understanding of one service instead of several. The list of benefits for implementing OpenSSH is long, and this book provides instruction on many of the benefits and best practices.

■**Note** http://www.openssh.com is the official home page for OpenSSH. You can find the latest source code, FAQs, credits, history, and goals of the project there.

Who Should Read This Book?

This question has been foremost in my mind since the onset of this project, as my goal is to compile and offer the right information for the right audience. While architecting and deploying OpenSSH implementations for Fortune 100 enterprises and home networks alike, I have referred to SSH resources both online and in print, and I came to the conclusion that most information on the topic is scattered, disorganized, or pretty dated. This presents a problem to most overworked system administrators. Maybe you are looking for an immediate response to a security incident, or perhaps you need practical information you can use now—not security theory or outdated implementation details and obscure encryption trivia—if so, this book is for you.

Maybe you are a stressed system administrator responsible for UNIX security, stuck in endless Sarbanes-Oxley, HIPAA, or compliance audit du jour meetings; inundated with conference calls, procedural reviews, and emails at all hours; and even forced to carry the support pager off-shift. Like you, I needed immediate answers to the problems with the plain-text protocols, and searched to learn concepts and best practices that helped me make the most of OpenSSH. The time you spend weighing and ultimately implementing this transition to SSH or improving your existing SSH environment should not be wasted, given the importance of this security solution. If you share my sentiments, I think you will find this book valuable. Along the way I will draw upon my experience implementing large-scale SSH systems, and provide real-world examples, scenarios, and best practices.

How This Book Is Organized

Secure communication is not a new goal among information technology professionals, but as new topics, tools, and exploits are created, new measures are taken to obstruct the adversaries and provide assurance of risk mitigation to management professionals. This is where the Secure Shell protocol comes into play, and in this book I will discuss OpenSSH, the most popular implementation of that protocol.

If you are system administrator, security professional, or home user of UNIX/Linux, then this book will provide value to you. Chances are if you are picking up this book, you have some idea what OpenSSH is and what you can do with it. Your exposure to OpenSSH certainly will not be a hindrance as you continue to work your way through the book. Whether you have introductory knowledge of OpenSSH or are simply looking to hone your skill set in a certain area, I am confident that by the time you complete this book, you will be able to piece together an effective, secure SSH network solution.

Part 1: Quick and Secure

The first part of the book deals with introductory topics, including reasons for eliminating legacy protocols, how OpenSSH can help you do so, and basic connectivity. Installation and compilation of OpenSSH on Linux is also covered.

Part 2: Configuring OpenSSH

Part 2 of the book is devoted to in-depth analysis of command-line options, configuration files, and settings. These settings become critical when trying to achieve maximum usability while not compromising the secure infrastructure you are striving to achieve. After a detailed explanation of configuration settings, authentication is covered. Authentication in OpenSSH depends upon several complex settings and concepts, as opposed to traditional password authentication. The power of public key authentication will be introduced and explored, as well as host-based authentication, when appropriate.

Part 3: Advanced Topics

In Part 3, the real power of OpenSSH starts to take shape. Tunneling less secure but still useful protocols such as X-Windows, VNC (Virtual Network Computing), and rsync is introduced. Port forwarding and tunneling of most generic TCP protocols is covered as well.

Chapter 8 discusses best practices for securing OpenSSH on both the server and client sides. Chapter 8 relies on the knowledge presented throughout the book to build an OpenSSH secure backbone utilizing an administrative gateway as the focal point for administration. Managing hundreds or even thousands of servers in this fashion becomes a less daunting task when the right scripts and security settings are employed.

Part 4: Administration with OpenSSH

OpenSSH can be used for automating nearly every administration task on a UNIX/Linux operating system. Chapter 9 provides an introduction to scripting with OpenSSH, which includes coverage of shell scripting, Perl, and PHP options. These scripts provide a foundation on which administrators can develop their own automation processes using OpenSSH.

Chapter 10 provides a look at the SSH Tectia Server from SSH Communications Security. This popular commercial SSH implementation has some differences from OpenSSH, which are explored in this final chapter. Working a heterogeneous environment is also discussed—for example, when moving back and forth from SSH Tectia Server and OpenSSH, certain incompatibilities will arise. This chapter aims to minimize the impact of those incompatibilities and show you how to manage a complex environment.

The first appendix provides information about several popular Microsoft Windows SSH clients, including PuTTY and WinSCP. The second appendix shows you how to get an SSH server running on a Windows platform.

What's Not in This Book?

Because of my work with OpenSSH security, I am often asked questions that appear to be related to OpenSSH, but in fact are separate security topics altogether. Several security publications and books cover security from a more theoretical standpoint, which can be helpful to architects and to those interested in learning a concept at its deepest level. This book takes a different route, opting not to linger on the security theory behind OpenSSH, and instead has been designed from its inception to be a book for hard-working administrators trying to keep their proverbial heads above water. That being said, the topics of OpenSSL, IPSec, VPN, PKI, firewalls, and Kerberos are not really covered in this book. There are several wonderful publications that do cover those topics well—however, most of them do not cover OpenSSH in the detail presented in this material. These and other security topics are mentioned when pertinent to the successful implementation of OpenSSH.

Prerequisites

While this book strives to accommodate beginners and experienced professionals alike, a few assumptions are made on your general understanding. The text covers installation and configuration on Linux in the most distribution-agnostic way possible. If you are able to translate commands from Linux onto your operating system of choice, please feel free. Basic command-line knowledge is assumed, including the ability to edit configuration files and to manage daemon execution. Root access or root-equivalent authority is also a must for editing configurations and installing OpenSSH.

Knowledge of Perl and shell scripting is also certainly helpful, but is not required for learning the scripting and administration topics covered in this book.

For most examples, I connect from one system on my network to another. While all of these examples can work with only one computer, having more than one available to you will make the power and ease of OpenSSH more apparent to you.

My Network

The network used in this book is my own home network. The names of my systems are a bit odd, but I will briefly introduce them here because they are referenced throughout the material. Note that I have /etc/hosts and DNS configured on my systems so that using a fully qualified domain name is not needed. Examples in this book that require fully qualified domain names will use example.com. Table 1 describes my network naming system.

Table 1. *The Network Utilized in Examples Throughout the Book*

System Name	Description
rack	My primary workstation, which is running Linux, is named rack. It is normally at least a dual-boot system with Fedora and SUSE Linux running on it. This system is named rack because it is inside a rack-mount chassis.
www	My primary web server is named www. It runs a typical LAMP stack (Linux, Apache, MySQL, PHP/Perl/Python). It also runs LDAP and DNS services.
zoom	zoom is a Debian Linux system.
mini	mini is the Microsoft Windows XP workstation used in this book. It is in a small form factor case—hence the name mini.
macmini	macmini, amazingly enough, is an Apple Mac mini computer running Mac OS X.

Downloads

The code, configuration files, and scripts used throughout this book are available for download on the Apress website, `http://www.apress.com`, in the Source Code section.

Read On

If you classify yourself as a rookie with OpenSSH, it may be best to start at the beginning of the book. If you have basic knowledge but still want to further your abilities with keys and scripts, Part 2 is great place to start. If you have a good understanding of OpenSSH and are trying to get maximum value and security out of the tool, feel free to jump from section to section or even topic to topic. The goal for the book is to provide you with a comprehensive tool set with which you can do your work securely and efficiently.

If you wish to contact me, I welcome your comments, feedback (for better or worse), updates, and errata. Feel free to email me at `mastahnke@yahoo.com`.

I hope this book will rest near your main administration workstation and be reopened periodically, as so many system administration books I have relied on in the past.

PART 1

■■■

Quick and Secure

CHAPTER 1

■ ■ ■

Legacy Protocols: Why Replace Telnet, FTP, rsh, rcp, and rlogin with SSH?

If you are reading this book, there is a very good chance you might already be aware of some of the advantages of using the Secure Shell (SSH) protocol over traditional UNIX connectivity offerings such as telnet, ftp, and rsh. This chapter will clearly outline those advantages and hopefully enlighten you on a few more positive features of the Secure Shell protocol.

Before getting into a specific discussion about the advantages of the Secure Shell protocol, I will cover several general security-related topics that will allow you to not only better understand the UNIX/Linux secure connectivity principles, but also understand the issues that ultimately spurred the creation of SSH.

Foundations of Information Security

To understand how effective SSH is in terms of security, a discussion of how information security is measured is warranted.

According to the International Information System Security Certification Consortium, or (ISC)² (http://www.isc2.org), security has three main goals, namely *confidentiality*, *integrity*, and *availability*.

Confidentiality is gained through access control, or ensuring unauthorized persons are unable to gain access to the data. Confidentiality is almost always handled by some form of encryption if the data is in transit.

Integrity deals with authenticity of the messages. Is the reader of the message viewing the message in its intended form without any tampering from outsiders? Integrity can be achieved via strong authentication and digital signatures.

Availability is a security concept often forgotten. If the data is unavailable, it is assumed to be secure, but in that case, the data is also not usable by anyone. Ensuring availability will provide protection against failing hardware and Denial of Service attacks, and utilize disaster recovery.

■**Note** For more information about these three key security goals, check out *CISSP All-in-One Exam Guide, Second Edition* by Shon Harris (McGraw-Hill Osborne Media, 2003).

At this point, it may seem like I have strayed a bit from the goal of introducing the Secure Shell protocol as an excellent security choice, but in reality, the Secure Shell, and in particular OpenSSH (http://www.openssh.com), provide all three elements of information security, which is something that the aforementioned traditional UNIX protocols certainly do not.

The final high-level information security concept I wish to cover is the trade-off between usability and security. If a system is thought to be more usable, with less overhead, or less bureaucracy, it usually is assumed to be less secure; in contrast, a system utilizing challenge response authentication, PIN numbers, and other mechanisms is often a headache for end users, but extremely difficult to gain unauthorized access in. This trade-off will require analysis during many phases of your OpenSSH deployment.

Analysis of Legacy Protocols

To understand the distinct advantages that OpenSSH provides over legacy connectivity and administration protocols on UNIX and UNIX-like systems, it is important to understand their strengths and weaknesses.

Common Strengths in Legacy Protocols

Telnet, FTP, and the r-utilities, which include rlogin, rcp, and rsh, have several strengths that can account for their success and explain why they are still so widely used today when more secure alternatives are available.

- *Installation*: telnetd, ftpd, rshd, rlogind, and rcp are typically enabled on a UNIX system out of the box. The default installs of HP-UX, AIX, and Solaris offer these systems enabled immediately upon installation completion. Often the default settings are enough to get an administrator running with these protocols on new machines. It is appropriate to mention that most Linux systems and some of the BSD variants have these traditional services disabled after a default installation.

- *Cost*: The r-utilities, ftpd, and telnetd servers are part of the operating system. An SSH server is normally a third-party package, save for Linux and BSD systems, though it could be included on the vendor media. Using third-party tools normally implies a cost either in the form of a software acquisition, training, or support. The stock utilities have no software licensing cost, other than the fees for the operating system, and most experienced UNIX administrators will be familiar with the functionality of these utilities.

- *Ease of use*: The traditional utilities all are easy to use due to their basic authentication practices requiring a username/password or trusted host authentication mechanism. These tools allow for automation of authentication procedures by using trusted hosts/ users, which led to a large proliferation of scripts and programs relying on these systems for proper execution. For example, even today several enterprise-grade clustering solutions rely on rsh to execute failover and perform several different types of cluster administration.

- *Speed*: A final strength of these protocols is speed. A simple programmatic `for` loop utilizing `rsh` can be orders of magnitude faster than a similar script utilizing SSH. Speed is normally sacrificed to ensure security.

What Makes These Protocols Legacy?

In this context, the term *legacy* is used to describe protocols such as Telnet and FTP because there are better tools available, at least from a security perspective. Legacy also implies that these utilities have been around for a while and are working in many environments. By learning about legacy protocols, their usage and their downfalls, the need for more secure tools will become apparent. Beyond recognizing the need for secure tools, after understanding the tools SSH can replace, you will see how the SSH protocol is designed to handle each of these shortcomings.

Security Analysis of Telnet and FTP

Telnet and FTP often are grouped together as a connectivity solution. Telnet allows remote command execution, while FTP allows for data transfer. Many of their flaws are common, which means that providing protection against the weaknesses in these protocols can be done with single solutions.

Telnet

Telnet is both an application and a protocol. It was designed to replace the hard-wired terminals connected to every computer. It also allowed users at different types of computers to execute their commands on remote machines. Telnet's first and most apparent security issue is that everything, including authentication credentials, are transmitted in clear-text format over the network. This means, using freely available network sniffers such as Ethereal, you can see every piece of information passed over the network.

■**Note** For more information about the sniffer Ethereal, you can visit `http://www.ethereal.com`. Additionally, it is often included in Linux distributions. Several other network sniffing applications are freely available. In particular, for sniffing on a switched network, Cain & Abel works very nicely. This is available at `http://www.oxid.it/cain.html`.

Many administrators understand that logging in directly as root via Telnet is a bad security practice, but at the same time, many log in as nonprivileged users, and then use `su` or `sudo` (`http://www.courtesan.com/sudo`) to become root all inside of a `telnet` session. This data is easily harvested. Many consider it safe to use Telnet in a situation where the client and server computers all reside on an intranet, yet this is actually a highly insecure practice. Consider that almost every organization has someone who is disgruntled, whether it be a supplier, employee, or partner trying to exploit your system resources. If this is a home network, a friend or family member might attempt to procure your root password to look at files they should not have access to (credit card info, gift receipts, and e-mails) or to hack your system for fun.

Using Cain & Abel, I am able to sniff on a switched network. The snippet presented in Listing 1-1 is a sniffer file with just a little cleanup. The reason some characters appear twice is because I sent those to the remote machine, and for each character I sent, it was returned to the display. As you can see, my demonstration password is easily captured, along with my root password. The same principles used in this example on Telnet can be used with FTP and the r-utilities.

Listing 1-1. *A Sniffing Session from Cain & Abel*

```
=============================================
=== Cain's Telnet sniffer generated file ===
=============================================
login: ssttaahhnnkkee
 Password: goldfish
 Last login: Wed Jun  1 18:18:35 from rack
stahnke@www:~
[stahnke@www ~]$ ssuu  --
 Password: myrootpassword$
 root@www ~> uuppttiimmee
  18:21:25 up 23 days, 15:51,  2 users,  load average: 0.24, 0.07, 0.02
root@www ~> eexxiitt
 logout
[stahnke@www ~]$ eexxiitt
 logout
```

Telnet clearly lacks in the confidentiality department because armed with a simple sniffer, an adversary can watch all data transmitted between the server and your telnet client window. Integrity can also suffer by having a rogue server setup with the Domain Name Service (DNS) name or IP address of the target machine intercepting information and then forwarding it on (a *man-in-the-middle*, or MITM, attack) either as a pristine copy, or tampered to make some alterations to the intended system. In this sense, integrity suffers because Telnet has no authentication performed by the server. The only supported authentication is user-based Telnet, which is also susceptible to many classic attacks including *ARP Poisoning* (updating a switch's address resolution table with false data, often used to sniff switched networks), and several types of injection or insertion attacks.

Certain issues with the Telnet protocol can be overcome using one-time passwords, or token-based authentication; however, Telnet sessions still can be victim to an insertion/session-hijacking attack where an attacker can insert arbitrary commands and data into an existing Telnet session, or take over the session completely. These attacks sound sophisticated and complex; however, with the emergence of tools such as HUNT (http://lin.fsid.cvut.cz/~kra/) and dsniff (http://www.monkey.org/~dugsong/dsniff/), these attacks can be executed with ease.

Common organizational security policy often dictates a minimum password length with some variance of punctuation, numeric, uppercase, and lowercase characters. While complex passwords are a wonderful thing, this is negated when Telnet is in use. Even if you have created a 50-character password that is more like a large sentence, it is easily found and harvested using point-and-click tools freely available. Remember that a user does not have to be actively monitoring the output of a network sniffer. It is quite easy to look for the string password and have it e-mail someone the three lines above and below that string.

As for availability, `telnetd` commonly runs out of `inetd` (the Internet services daemon) in most implementations. Normally, this is quite reliable, but I have seen `inetd` die on systems from every major vendor I have worked with, thus leaving a Telnet connection inoperable. A walk or drive to the console (unless you are lucky enough to have remote consoles on systems) is needed to allow network connectivity again.

In summary, Telnet's biggest disadvantages come from confidentiality and integrity, with confidentiality being the easiest to breach. FTP, which is often used in conjunction with Telnet, has remarkably similar weaknesses.

FTP

FTP, or File Transfer Protocol, is much like Telnet in that it is an application and a protocol. It allows a user to store and retrieve files on remote systems As its primary means of authentication, FTP relies on a username and password, just as Telnet does. FTP's primary concern again is the clear-text transfer of data and authentication credentials. FTP opens up a new problem as well. If an FTP password for a user is compromised, the adversary can not only upload/download files as the user, but also log in to the machine interactively (via `telnet`, `ssh`, or `rsh`) because the username/password combination is the same by default.

While there are implementations of FTP daemons that allow for separate passwords or very configurable security, the inherit weakness of FTP still exists, namely that everything transmitted is in clear text.

Using FTP through firewalls can also be difficult to set up. FTP uses multiple ports for its communication and data transfer. Because of this, additional ports must be opened on a firewall. Some firewalls have specific knowledge of the FTP protocol, and can dynamically open ports for an FTP transfer, but these firewalls can sometimes be exploited by attackers spoofing an FTP-like transaction.

Tip If you are forced to use FTP for legacy applications and scripts, look at `vsftpd` (http://vsftpd.beasts.org). `vsftpd` has several advanced security options that take it a step above traditional FTP daemons, and the ability to encrypt communications over SSL (Secure Sockets Layer) has been added, making it a very nice alternative to stock FTP daemons.

Security Analysis of R-utilities

When working in medium- to large-sized UNIX environments, maintaining synchronized root passwords, updating configuration files, and installing patches can be a very tedious process. To help facilitate such matters, a collection of three utilities known as the r-utilities were designed in BSD4.2 as great features to allow administrators to remove the connectivity and configuration differences between their systems. Namely, the `rsh`, `rlogin`, and `rcp` utilities introduce a way to manage dozens, hundreds, or even thousands of systems utilizing simple programmatic `for` loops. Each is responsible for implementing a specific feature that helps administrators accomplish this goal. Specifically, `rsh` allows the user execution of remote individual commands, `rlogin` gives a terminal window, and `rcp` allows the user to store files to or retrieve files from a remote machine. Administrators and power users have made these utilities essential to their daily tasks when interacting with UNIX systems. These tools were developed in an age of computing where networks were trusted and used only by computer professionals. Networks were not connected together in situations beyond academia. Eventually, their ease of use caused these tools to proliferate into nearly every UNIX variant in existence.

However, one would be hard-pressed to find a set of tools that has more security problems than these. These tools shine when it comes to speed and stability, but when security comes into question, they obviously tip the scales on the usability side. The inherent problems from the r-utilities lie in the trust mechanism. Most setups of r-utilities involve trusting servers using files called .rhosts. If machine A trusts machine B, then Machine A must also trust the authentication mechanisms of machine B. This can lead to several interesting scenarios. Additionally, many times trust relationships were not set up by individual machines, but by IP addresses, or ranges of IP addresses, or even domain names. For example, if I have a machine running the r-utilities daemons, and I trust anything coming from *.mycompany.com, anyone who plugs into my network is now allowed to hop from their machine to all the rest of them. This becomes of particular concern with the rise of user-controlled machines that can pass the r-utilities a UID of 0 or that of any other arbitrary user.

If I am a consultant and I walk into My Company and plug in my laptop, most likely I will be assigned an IP address via Dynamic Host Configuration Protocol (DHCP), and it will probably resolve to something in the *.mycompany.com domain. Because I have root access on my laptop, I can use rlogin to connect to another system, machine B, and machine B trusts that since I have root on my laptop, I should be able to have root on machine B.

The r-utilities have a slew of other concerns that stem from trust relationships among machines, weak (in some cases, virtually nonexistent) authentication, and clear-text transmission of all data.

Again, confidentiality is lost in this setup. There is no encryption, and with many trust relationships, such as those provided with .rhosts files, there really is not even any form of access control. Integrity is also very low because I can set up my laptop with the same IP address as machine B and get all of the information intended for machine B, do as I please with it, and then relay it to the real machine B, or just keep it. This attack is also a type of man-in-the-middle attack. Availability becomes questionable and is probably less important when the integrity and confidentiality are at such low levels. If the data is available, can it be trusted?

The discussion of the downside of the r-utilities can be extremely lengthy, but overall the r-utilities are situated on some extremely shaky ground. For more information about UNIX security in general and especially problems with rsh, rlogin, and rcp, you can review *Practical Unix & Internet Security, 3rd Edition* by Simson Garfinkel, Gene Spafford, and Alan Schwartz (O'Reilly and Associates, 2003).

WHERE DO LEGACY PROTOCOLS STILL MAKE SENSE?

Using legacy protocols is a bad idea about 95% of the time. However, in my daily work as an administrator of hundreds of UNIX/Linux systems, I still do from time to time.

I use FTP heavily for patching systems via tools like rpm, apt, pkg, CPAN, and swinstall. The FTP server is configured for read-only access and only has publicly available data, so if any information is compromised it is easily replaced. Additionally, most packaging systems have a way to verify integrity such as RPMs using GNU Privacy Guard (GnuPG, http://www.gnupg.org).

Until very recently, if UNIX machines needed to transfer data to or from a mainframe, the only choice was FTP. However, OpenSSH is now available for the mainframe (`http://www-1.ibm.com/servers/eserver/zseries/zos/unix/toys/ssh.html`), and hopefully we can soon eliminate FTP as a data transfer mechanism of mainframe data.

A final usage of legacy protocols involves the use of private networks inside of High Performance Computing (HPC) clusters. I recommend using the r-utilities internal to the cluster only. Normally, two head nodes are on the intranet and the rest of the compute nodes are only on a public network. The r-utility daemons are not enabled on the head nodes, but they are enabled on the compute nodes due to speed and assumed security on a private network. Additionally, most HPC software vendors count on `rsh` being enabled. As an added security measure, `iptables` (`http://www.netfilter.org`) can be used to block the r-utilities ports on the head nodes, in case the r-utilities are ever enabled.

Learn to Replace Legacy Protocols

As network computing grew in purpose and popularity, these legacy protocols were made even more common on all types of machines. With the surge of an Internet presence in the middle 1990s by most corporations, along came their Telnet, FTP, and r-utilities for all to see. During the latter half of the 1990s, it was commonplace to read about a compromised environment, system, or corporation because of the use of .rhosts files or weak passwords. Even Fortune 500 companies with very large information technology budgets were not immune to the problems created by poor choices in connectivity protocols and poor policies covering information security.

Many organizations have created new information security policies requiring heavy restrictions on the usage of the r-utilities, Telnet, and FTP without providing a new solution; these policies are then left unenforceable, allowing virtually everyone to get some form of business exception, which allows someone to accept the risk. This is not always required, however, because a viable replacement solution exists in the form of OpenSSH.

The case for Telnet, FTP, and r-utilities made in the past is simply not viable today. These days, networks are shared via Virtual Private Network (VPN), Demilitarized Zone (DMZ), and extranet access. Consultants, contractors, and business partners are constantly onsite, devoting their resources to the highest bidder, and everyone understands that information is probably your organization's most valuable asset. OpenSSH will enable the replacement of legacy protocols and enforce information security policy.

Improving Security with OpenSSH

To replace these legacy protocols, you need a toolset that can provide terminal emulation, transfer files, and run commands remotely, all while encrypting the data, providing user and host authentication, and have comparable availability, speed, and ease of use.

Replacing rlogin, rsh, and rcp was the original goal for the SSH protocol. It has done so without relying on simple IP addresses or *.mycompany.com entries. OpenSSH also provides sftp in lieu of FTP, eliminating clear-text authentication, while still offering a very similar command set.

Establishing Security Basics

To understand the power and security embedded within OpenSSH, some key security ideas must be conceptually understood. OpenSSH relies on several security mechanisms to ensure the confidentiality, integrity, and availability of its data. This section will not explain exactly how OpenSSH uses these security mechanisms, but it will provide background information so that when a security focus point is discussed, some background on the topic can be assumed.

Checksums

Checksums are used to verify integrity of data. They are calculated values that are used to ensure the provided data matches the expected data. For example, upon login to a UNIX system, a user is prompted for a password. That password is then encrypted using a checksum and compared against an expected value in the passwd or shadow file. If the value provided matches the value in the file, the user is permitted to log in. If not, the user must try again.

Checksums are fixed lengths. If a file is 100 bytes or 100 gigabytes, a checksum will be of the same size. This can lead to the potential problem of checksum collisions. In certain sum algorithms the collision rate is high, while with others a collision is nearly impossible. The data inside a file cannot be derived by just having the hash value of a file. Checksums are sometimes called *hash functions*, because they convert data via a one-way hash.

sum

Of the different forms of checksum, the sum command is one of the least secure. It is found on UNIX/Linux systems and can be used to check to see if two files are the same; however, programs are available to pad a file until a given sum output is reached, thus negating sum efforts.

To use sum, try checking your /etc/hosts file. The output is the checksum followed by the number of blocks in a file.

```
stahnke@rack: ~> sum /etc/hosts
3705       1
```

MD5

md5 is a 128-bit hash function. It is commonly used in UNIX/Linux as the hash mechanism for password encryption. The collision rate on md5 was generally thought to be very good; however, recently several algorithms published and implemented have been able to produce collisions in a few hours. At the time of this writing, in many cases md5 is still reliable and secure, but most people are moving to another hash function.

To create an md5 hash value of a file, use the md5sum command. It is installed by default on many different system types, and is available for nearly any operating system. The following example shows how to generate a hash value using the md5 algorithm:

```
stahnke@rack: ~> md5sum /etc/hosts
f935ef656d642e4e3b377e8eba42db66  /etc/hosts
```

SHA-1

SHA-1 is another hash function that uses 160-bit checksums. It is generally thought to be more secure than md5. SHA-1 is used in some password authentication implementations on

UNIX/Linux. It also is approved for use by the United States Government. The collision rate on SHA-1 is significantly lower than that of even MD5; however, recently some theoretical attacks against SHA-1 have been presented. These, too, require weeks or months on supercomputers to duplicate. For maximum security, combining multiple hash algorithms can be used. If someone is able to duplicate an MD5 and SHA-1 checksum, the chances of a collision is believed to be impossible even using today's fastest supercomputers.

SHA-1 hashes can be generated using sha1sum. This utility is available on Linux and several BSD variants by default. It normally is an add-on for Solaris, HP-UX, AIX, and IRIX. In the following example, a sha1sum is used to compute a SHA-1 checksum of the /etc/hosts file:

```
stahnke@rack: ~> sha1sum /etc/hosts
d538de234634994b2078a34ea49c377108193ce7   /etc/hosts
```

Tip OpenSSL can be used to generate md5 and SHA-1 sums also. openssl md5 /etc/hosts and openssl sha1 /etc/hosts will provide hash outputs.

MACs

MACs, in a security sense (not MAC addresses), are Message Authentication Codes. In cryptography, a MAC is a small amount of information used to authenticate a given data set. A MAC algorithm uses a secret key in combination with the data set to create the MAC or tag. This process can protect a file in the form of integrity, because a MAC will change if the data set has been altered. MACs also provide nonrepudiation (proof of origin), because the secret key must be known to generate a valid MAC.

MACs are not normally available from the command line of a UNIX system. These algorithms are used in encryption security products, such as OpenSSH.

Symmetric Ciphers

Encryption is handled in the form of *ciphers*. A cipher can be a simple as a character substitution. For example, if a message is to be sent over an untrusted medium, the message might be, "We attack at dawn." This text is called the *plaintext*, and is human readable. Using a simple cipher called ROT13, the ciphertext, or encrypted text, is "Jr nggnpx ng qnja." This substitution simply replaces each letter of the alphabet with a character 13 places to the right of it. For example, "e" becomes "r," and "w" becomes "j." The party receiving the message then has to replace each character with the letter 13 places to left in the alphabet, which can span the beginning or end of the alphabet. These are called *symmetric ciphers* because the same key is used to encrypt and decrypt a message.

This is obviously an example of weak cryptography, but it illustrates some key points. Poor encryption is trivial to break. Replacing a single letter with another letter often takes very little time to decode. Patterns can easily be discovered in the ciphertext to assist with decoding the message. For example, if a character occurs more often than any other character, and the plain text message is English, that letter probably represents the letter "e." Attacks can be made against encrypted messages.

Encrypted messages can be sniffed on a network; therefore strong cryptographic algorithms should be utilized to thwart potential attacking efforts.

The simple substitution cipher given in this example is keyed by the number of letters to rotate the alphabet by. Because there are only 25 possible values for this key, it is about 4 bits in length, thus extremely weak. Ciphers depend on a shared key. If a shared key is agreed upon, ahead of time by both the sender and receiver of a message, the encryption is much stronger. An attacker will then need a sniffed (intercepted) ciphertext message and a key to decode it properly. Strong ciphers also produce ciphertext that will contain higher degrees of randomness than most normal written languages.

This description of ciphers is fairly high level. To administer OpenSSH, no knowledge of how a cipher is created is required. For performance optimization or security concerns, however, knowing which ciphers to choose and their key length can come into play.

There are two main types of symmetric ciphers utilized in computing today: block and stream ciphers. Both of these types of ciphers are supported in OpenSSH.

Block Ciphers

Block ciphers are used to encrypt data of a fixed length in conjunction with a shared key. For example, if a cipher is using a 128-bit block of clear text, the encrypted text would be 128 bits. The way the encryption occurs is dependent on the key and cipher algorithm. Decryption of block ciphers requires the shared key and using the decryption algorithm. Ciphers are generally a fast solution to encryption, but they present a problem of transmitting a shared key to the receiving party without it being compromised.

DES

DES, or the Data Encryption Standard, was published in the late 1970s as an encryption standard for the United States Government. It uses 56-bit keys, which at the time would have taken years to break; however, with computational power increases, compromising DES-encrypted communication is possible, and with some expensive hardware can be done in hours or sometimes minutes. DES is only supported by the OpenSSH client for compatibility with SSH Protocol 1 servers that do not support any stronger ciphers. OpenSSH does not support any cryptographically weak ciphers by default.

3DES

3DES, pronounced triple-DES, is a derivative of DES that uses separate shared keys (either two or three) to encrypt, decrypt, and then encrypt data again using DES. Because it was designed to be implemented in hardware, the structure of DES makes it relatively slower to implement in comparison with other ciphers. It has not been broken by any known attacks against it.

AES

AES, which stands for Advanced Encryption Standard, was adopted by United States Government as an encryption standard after DES proved to be much too weak. Like DES, it relies on a shared key, but the algorithm used for encryption is much more difficult to break. AES supports several different block sizes as well. Using OpenSSH, AES key sizes can range from 128 bits to 256 bits. AES performs at high speed and is commonly used in hardware and software.

Blowfish

Blowfish is another block cipher that is supported in OpenSSH. Blowfish is a fast cipher that was aimed at replacing aging DES technology. It usage has been decreasing because of the stronger security and key lengths supported by AES and other block ciphers. However, there have been no known compromises of the Blowfish algorithm. It is fairly simple to utilize in software and hardware implementations. Although the algorithm allows variable key sizes, SSH always uses Blowfish with a 128-bit key.

CAST

CAST is a block cipher created by Carlisle Adams and Stafford Tavares. CAST-128 has a block size of 64 bits and varying key sizes between 40 to 128 bits (in increments of 8). CAST-256 also exists, and is stronger; however, OpenSSH uses only CAST-128 at the time of this writing.

Stream Ciphers

Stream ciphers act on plaintext one digit at a time. They normally incorporate a key of random digits. The original key is fed into an algorithm that produces a *keystream*. The keystream is combined with the plaintext values to produce ciphertext. Stream ciphers are optimal for usage when input size is unknown. Block ciphers must use padding if a given segment of a plaintext message does not contain a full block. Steam ciphers can send data of any size. They are also normally faster than block ciphers.

ARCFOUR

ARCFOUR is a cipher compatible with the RC4 stream cipher owned by RSA Security. It is a commonly used stream cipher, used in many networking devices including wireless devices that implement Wired Equivalent Privacy (WEP), and Wi-Fi Protect Access (WPA). ARCFOUR has some weaknesses in it that are difficult to exploit, but it is not recommended for wide-spread usage.

Symmetric Cipher Summary

The default cipher used by OpenSSH protocol 2 is AES. This is for the best security/performance ratio. Normally, not changing the defaults for the ciphers is recommended, unless specific needs arise. OpenSSH also supports different modes of several block ciphers, including cipher block chaining (cbc) and counter mode (ctr). These offer some variation algorithms as described previously. Several other ciphers exist, but they are not covered in this discussion.

Asymmetric Ciphers

The SSH protocol relies on encryption in its foundations to provide confidentiality. Symmetric encryption requires that each side of a connection agree on a key that explains the decoding of the encrypting data. Asymmetric algorithms for encryption require the usage of *key pairs*. Each key pair consists of a *private key* and *public key*. Both keys must be used to decode a message.

The private key is known only by a single party, and is protected. The public key can then be distributed over public medium, because by itself it offers no advantage to an attacker. This eliminates a major concern with symmetric ciphers, which is delivering the shared key to the remote target.

If I have my message again, "We attack at dawn," I encrypt the message using a public key for the intended recipient. The recipient then uses his or her private key to decode the message. If another person intercepts the message in its ciphertext format, that person will be unable to decode it because he or she does not have the private key required. In this situation, only one party must have the private key. This is why this algorithm family is called *asymmetric*. Asymmetric algorithms are oftentimes called *public key encryption algorithms*.

Asymmetric algorithms use key lengths much larger than those found in symmetric ciphers. Where AES might use a 256-bit key for very strong protection, asymmetric algorithms oftentimes use 2048-bit encryption for strong protection. Because of this, the computational power required to decrypt a message is much greater than the power required for a block or stream cipher. These algorithms are much slower.

Oftentimes, in nicely architected encryption solutions such as SSH, an asymmetric key algorithm is used to send a shared key for a symmetric cipher. This way, the overhead of the asymmetric algorithm is only encountered during the initial connection establishment, and after that a fast symmetric encryption cipher can be used.

OpenSSH uses two different protocols. In protocol 1, the shared key for the symmetric cipher is sent via an asymmetric algorithm. Protocol 2 uses the Diffie-Hellman key exchange algorithm.

Public key cryptography also has an advantage in that it can be used to ensure a message was sent from a particular source, whereas symmetric keys require a preshared key to do this. If I encrypt a message using my private key, obviously anyone can decode it. But if I encrypt the already encrypted message again using my recipient's public key, not only is he or she the only one able to read it, but because he or she must use my public key as the second step of the decryption process, the recipient can be assured the message came from me.

OpenSSH uses public key cryptography internally. Key generation for user and host-based authentication is discussed in Chapter 6 along with more details of asymmetric key algorithms. Authentication using public key cryptography is often referred to as using digital credentials for authentication.

OpenSSH Replacing Legacy Protocols

OpenSSH encrypts all portions of the data stream, including authentication credentials, rendering network sniffers useless. Confidentiality is ensured. Integrity is kept at high levels because encryption and MACs make session hijacking or putting up a rogue server more difficult.

OpenSSH performs stronger authentication than traditional protocols. OpenSSH uses digital credentials routinely, which allow OpenSSH to assert the identity of a machine or, optionally, an individual. Digital credentials, covered in Chapter 6, are also more difficult to compromise than traditionally used username/password mechanisms. OpenSSH can also allow the running of only certain commands. This can help minimize user error and risk should an account be compromised. Logging is also much better than most legacy protocols from UNIX. OpenSSH logs to syslog at a logging facility of your choice, and at the verbosity level you desire, which is explained in Chapter 4, when server configuration is covered.

The usability level for OpenSSH continues to grow as clients become commonplace on UNIX/Linux systems, and, of course, as more tools, documentation, and applications support OpenSSH. Although still slower than traditional rsh, the difference is often not detectable to an administrator or power-user at a workstation.

Throughout the rest of the book, we will explore the functionality of OpenSSH for system administrators everywhere who need to keep systems running with maximum availability and security.

Summary

In this chapter, I covered the downfalls of traditional protocols to illustrate reasons to move to an SSH connected environment. I also discussed the goals of security, which are confidentiality, integrity, and availability. You learned about the trade-off between usability and security, which will continue to be a theme throughout any deployment of an SSH solution.

Finally, I introduced you to some key security concepts, encryption methods, and hashing mechanisms. The discussion of the advantages of OpenSSH has begun, but to have a real appreciation for its security and ability to replace legacy protocols, it's best to have it installed. Chapter 2 covers installation from source or in binary format to get your OpenSSH implementation started.

CHAPTER 2

■ ■ ■

A Quick SSH Implementation

The theory and history of SSH have been documented in technical journals, magazines, books, and Internet blogs. The goal of this chapter is not to make you an SSH historian, but to get you running with SSH as early as possible.

This chapter will cover the following:

- A brief introduction to SSH

- Installing/compiling OpenSSH

- Troubleshooting

- A quick look at some client tools

A Brief Introduction to SSH

Secure Shell (SSH) is an encrypted connectivity protocol utilized by users, administrators, and applications for secure interaction and system maintenance. SSH has advantages over traditional communication services, such as `telnetd`, `ftpd`, `rshd`, and `rlogind`, normally included with UNIX and UNIX-like systems. SSH provides a deeper level of authentication than the previously mentioned daemons do. The SSH daemon accepts usernames and passwords, but it also prevents a *man-in-the-middle (MITM) attack* by authenticating the host. Man-in-the-middle attacks are common in many technical security concepts. The premise of a man-in-the-middle attack is that the attacker sits between client and server, pretending to be the server while talking to the client, and pretending to be the client while talking to the server. For example, using `rlogin`, I could connect to host John from host Ringo. However, if someone is able to spoof the IP address of John, Ringo will not know it. This allows the *rogue* John server to obtain the critical information I was intending to pass to the real machine named John. A basic illustration of this is provided in Figure 2-1.

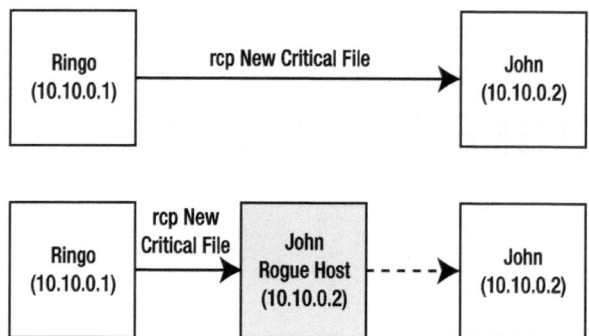

Figure 2-1. *An example of a man-in-the-middle attack via IP spoofing*

With an understanding of what a man-in-the-middle attack is, you must wonder how such an occurrence can be prevented. If you were somehow able to validate the host you are transferring data with is the host you expect, IP spoofing becomes a worry of the past. SSH provides this functionality through its use of keys. SSH uses keys in an asymmetric algorithm to prove each host is the expected host.

Asymmetric encryption (also known as *public key*) algorithms basically have two pieces, a public key and a private key, whereas symmetric encryptions algorithms have only one key. The private key of your key pair should be protected as you would protect your credit card numbers, house keys, etc. The public key, on the other hand, is just that—public. Anyone can have it, because without its companion private key, a public key is unable to cryptographically unlock a message encrypted using the public key.

Imagine that the public key is a mailbox on the sidewalk. People know the location of it and can drop letters in, but only authorized persons (the post office workers) have the private key to open it. In the case of SSH, I know (or can obtain) the host's advertised public key, when my message is sent encrypted via the host's public key; only the host with its private key can unlock it. When the validation process is complete, you are ensured this host has the key pair you expected and can begin transferring my data.

While key exchange might sound complicated, it takes place mostly under the hood in SSH technologies. The first time you connect to a host via SSH, you will be asked whether you want to add the host's public key to your inventory of known keys. This is where your client first trusts the host and sets up the host key exchange.

For example, if a connection is attempted to the machine www from the workstation rack and the host key has not already been cached (trusted), the following message is displayed:

```
stahnke@rack: ~> ssh www
The authenticity of host 'www (192.168.1.109)' can't be established.
RSA key fingerprint is d9:2f:0d:72:a9:cb:5d:07:e6:23:23:e5:cb:ba:35:3f.
Are you sure you want to continue connecting (yes/no)?
```

To verify that this is indeed the host it is thought to be, a simple command can be run from the host. This can be done on the console or through another connectivity protocol if it is thought to be secure.

```
stahnke@www: ~> ssh-keygen -l -f /etc/ssh/ssh_host_rsa_key
1024 d9:2f:0d:72:a9:cb:5d:07:e6:23:23:e5:cb:ba:35:3f /etc/ssh/ssh_host_rsa_key.pub
```

If the key fingerprint, which is a hash of the of host key, matches the key fingerprint presented by the client, the connection has been verified and can be accepted.

System administrators also can populate the host keys of remote machines to leave this process out of the hands of end users. This is covered in Chapter 8.

Note The first time you connect to a host via SSH is very important, as this is a time when a man-in-the-middle attack is possible. When you accept the key (validate the key fingerprint), make sure you are confident the host is the intended target.

After the first time you cache a host's public key into your repository, you will not see anything about keys again, unless one changes. If a key changes on a remote host, SSH will balk and wonder why. This is a good thing. Usually one of the following causes is responsible for a key change when connecting via SSH:

- Your network uses Dynamic Host Configuration Protocol (DHCP) to obtain IP addresses, and the last time you connected to this machine it had a different IP address and/or name. If you use DHCP extensively, read Chapter 5 to find a way to turn off initial public key acceptance.

- The system has been rebuilt and/or SSH has been removed and reinstalled. When a machine is rebuilt, SSH keys are regenerated. Keys can be saved and restored when rebuilding a machine eliminates this key change, but it does not often happen.

- SSH keys have been regenerated. SSH keys can be regenerated because security policy recommends it or the host's private key has been compromised.

- There is a rogue host trying to be the host you want to connect to. While this probably is not very common, this is what the host-based key exchange is trying to prevent. If you are not aware of a rebuild or SSH key change, contact your security/system administrator.

Caution Many people just click/type yes anytime a connection is made; I encourage you to think about the connection being made and ensure it is trusted or can be validated. Additionally, educating SSH users to do the same is recommended.

What Is SSH Doing?

SSH uses digital credentials for authentication in the most basic setup. In the case of SSH, you know the password to your account. On top of that, the host is providing a form of authentication via public key. If something changes about that host, SSH will balk and ask questions about that host's authenticity. Further details of authentication and keys can be complicated but essential to the advanced SSH user, and I will cover these details in Chapter 6. Right now, we are out to solve problems, the first one being this: can you offer encrypted communication to your machines? Of course you can, using SSH.

Basics of SSH

SSH has a few important components that make up the secure connectivity solution. Breaking down SSH into a few vital parts will help create a fundamental understanding of what is needed to get a secure solution onto one of your systems. The path /etc/ssh is used in most binary distributions of an SSH implementation. Actual paths may vary depending on your installation preferences.

SSH involves the following pieces of configuration material:

- *Daemon configuration files*: Commonly found in /etc/ssh, these files control all settings for the server portion of SSH. These are the files most often modified to optimize SSH in your implementation.

- *Client configuration files*: Also normally found in /etc/ssh, these files allow client settings for the machine and then can be modified or overridden by each user to tune the SSH client for choice applications.

- *Start/Stop scripts*: These scripts control the manner in which the SSH server daemon starts and stops. Very few edits should be required here over time.

- *Host key(s)*: Host keys are normally found in /etc/ssh as well, with one key being labeled private and only readable to root, and the other being public and readable to all.

- *Known hosts caching of some kind*: Known host caching can vary depending on what implementation of SSH you chose to deploy; however, all types of SSH implementations cache hosts' public keys to perform host authentication. OpenSSH caches host keys on a per-user basis, but can also have a system-wide file populated so each user does not have to verify remote host keys.

Right now, it is time to stop talking about being secure and start acting.

■**Caution** Turning off the Telnet server would normally be thought of as a good start toward security, but leaving a remote machine without connectivity can be worse. Be sure to disable legacy protocols after proper communication and testing has occurred.

Installing SSH

In the second half of this chapter, I am going to show you how to implement OpenSSH. There are other choices in SSH implementations, mainly from SSH Communications Security (http://www.ssh.com), but because at this point you likely want quick results at the lowest cost, OpenSSH seems like the right way to go. Discussion of the primary alternative to OpenSSH will occur later in Chapter 10, although a brief introduction is in the next section. For many setups, OpenSSH works very well, and the learning is valuable. Do not think the work done in the early chapters for your implementation will be undone later; chances are it will stay.

Choices in SSH

The SecSH[1] (Secure Shell) specification is at `http://www.ietf.org/html.charters/secsh-charter.html`. From this publication and other documents, different projects and companies have created their implementations of SSH.

OpenSSH

OpenSSH is deployed in venues throughout the world ranging from a small home networks to the very heart of large communication operations between UNIX servers in Fortune 100 companies. In my work with SSH, I have found OpenSSH to fit 90% of the needs of 99% of the customer base.

OpenSSH (`http://www.openssh.com/`) implements the SSH protocol and is freely available. It is the most commonly used implementation of the SSH protocol on many platforms. OpenSSH combats several known security vulnerabilities in traditional connectivity protocols through the use of encryption and message verification. Connection hijacking is prevented due to the Message Authentication Codes (MACs) used. Your systems are protected from MITM attacks when using SSH because of the host authentication that takes place. Furthermore, with OpenSSH you get secure tunneling capabilities for TCP protocols, which are covered in Chapter 7, as well as a variety of authentication methods, reviewed in Chapter 6.

Let us break this down a little to make sure you understand what OpenSSH can and cannot do. OpenSSH is free to obtain, use, modify, and redistribute. It is provided under a BSD license, which means you can download it and use it without payment to anyone. Also, you are free to change the source and under no obligation to return your updates to the open source community. Keep in mind, however, that although licenses for software are free, the total cost of ownership still needs to account for patching, supportability, in-depth knowledge, etc. OpenSSH provides a means to replace the previously mentioned insecure daemons and provides some additional layers of security.

SSH Communications Security Inc.'s SSH Tectia Product Line

Another main alternative to OpenSSH will be discussed in-depth in Chapter 10, and that is SSH Communications Security Inc.'s SSH Tectia line of products. The SSH Tectia product provides a few advantages over OpenSSH such as commercially available support and web management tools for SSH.

The cost of the Tectia product is a major disadvantage when comparing it to OpenSSH. Licensing agreements are reached with the vendor, but at the time of this writing, the list price for an SSH Tectia Server A for UNIX is $774.00 (USD); this price does not include maintenance and support fees. Additionally, free support of SSH on forums, newsgroups, and mailing lists is generally aimed at OpenSSH rather than SSH Communications Security's Tectia line.

---

1. SecSH is the official IETF acronym for Secure Shell. See `http://www.openssh.com/ssh-dispute/` for more information.

Connecting via OpenSSH

The steps to getting OpenSSH running on a Linux system are fairly simple. If you are running almost any Linux distribution, chances are that OpenSSH is already on, configured, and working just fine. To verify this, execute the following:

```
stahnke@rack:~> telnet localhost 22
Trying 127.0.0.1...
Connected to localhost.
Escape character is '^]'.
SSH-1.99-OpenSSH_3.9p1
```

■**Note** You might need to type **CTRL+]** then **q** to end the telnet session.

This banner indicates that on my machines, OpenSSH 3.9p1 is running. If you have an OpenSSH banner displayed, you can move on to "Checking Your Work" later in this chapter. If you are on a system that does not include OpenSSH by default or you want to build your own, follow right along. OpenSSH relies on libraries from OpenSSL and zlib to install properly. You can download the OpenSSH source from http://www.openssh.com or you can download a precompiled binary from your commercial UNIX/Linux vendor. For example, IBM provides OpenSSH for AIX in installp format, the package format native to AIX. Packages, of course, ease administration by allowing querying and dependency checking.

Installing OpenSSH

For this example build of OpenSSH, I will be using a SuSE Linux system. The steps I outline will be the same regardless of what platform you are installing on, but the syntax could vary.

■**Caution** If your system is using a UMASK different from 0022, I recommend setting it at 0022 for the build of OpenSSH. Having an abnormal UMASK can cause many headaches and a large amount of troubleshooting later on.

Downloading OpenSSH

Downloading OpenSSH simply involves pointing your favorite web browser at http://www.openssh.com. Navigate to portable.html if you are not running OpenBSD. Select your platform and mirror, and download the source. OpenBSD users can use the nonportable (original) version, as it is the native platform for OpenSSH.

Note The download of OpenSSH and the other OpenSSH prerequisites can be verified using GNU Privacy Guard (GnuPG) or MD5 checksums. This step can verify integrity of the download, but is not covered in the material.

OpenSSH Prerequisites

For OpenSSH to work properly on most systems, libraries from OpenSSL and zlib are required. zlib is installed on almost every UNIX type of platform by default.

Is zlib Installed?

zlib provides the compression mechanism inside of OpenSSH. In an rpm-based distribution of Linux (or if you have rpm installed on AIX or Solaris) you can simply try the following:

```
stahnke@rack:~> rpm -q zlib
zlib-1.2.2.2-3
```

Caution zlib has a security problem in releases prior to 1.2.2 at the time of this writing. OpenSSH will not compile against zlib 1.2.1 without specifically enabling --without-zlib-version-check during configure. Keep in mind that some vendors (Red Hat in particular) often backport patches from upstream developers into older versions, so 1.2.1x on a Red Hat/Fedora system might contain the security fixes required. A best practice is to keep your system patched.

If something is returned, you have zlib installed and can skip this zlib installation. You can use other package management tools to verify the installation of zlib also. Oftentimes simply checking common library directories for libz.so (libz.a static library, or combined static/dynamic libraries on AIX; or libz.sl shared library on HP-UX) is enough to verify its existence on your system also.

```
stahnke@rack:~> ls /usr/lib/libz.* || ls /usr/local/lib/libz.*
/usr/lib/libz.a  /usr/lib/libz.so  /usr/lib/libz.so.1  /usr/lib/libz.so.1.2.2.2
```

If your system appears to be without zlib, you can navigate to http://www.gzip.org/zlib and download the source. While there are configure and compile options for zlib, documenting them is beyond the scope of this book, since the default options provide you with the functionality required.

```
stahnke@rack:~> gunzip zlib-1.2*tar.gz
stahnke@rack:~> tar xvf zlib-1.2*tar
stahnke@rack:~> cd zlib-1.2*
```

```
stahnke@rack:~> ./configure
stahnke@rack:~> make
stahnke@rack:~> make test
stahnke@rack:~> su
root@rack:~> make install
```

Is OpenSSL Installed?

OpenSSL provides most of the encryption methods that OpenSSH uses for communication and key encryption.

For rpm-based systems:

```
stahnke@rack:~> rpm -q openssl
openssl-0.9.7f-7
```

OpenSSL is another toolkit that is installed on almost every system by default. To verify it is installed, you can start with

```
stahnke@rack:~> which openssl
/usr/bin/openssl
```

If a path is returned, you are ready to begin your OpenSSH compilation. If not, let us look at a few more options.

```
stahnke@rack:~> ls /usr/lib/libcrypto.so || ls \
/usr/local/lib/libcrypto.so
/usr/lib/libcrypto.so
```

This is a check to verify the library's existence. If you still are without OpenSSL, it is time to build your own. The source code is available at http://www.openssl.org. If you click "source" on the front page, the tarballs page highlights the latest version in red. You want the latest version, so this works out well for you. Please keep in mind that adding new software to a system requires root access.

```
stahnke@rack:~> gunzip openssl*tar.gz
stahnke@rack:~> tar xvf openssl*.tar
stahnke@rack:~> cd openssl-*
stahnke@rack:~> ./config
stahnke@rack:~> make
stahnke@rack:~> make test
stahnke@rack:~> su
root@rack:~> make install
```

Hopefully everything went well and you are now ready to get and compile OpenSSH.

Installing OpenSSH

If you chose to not use the precompiled binaries available for your system, you can build from source. Building from source of course provides the maximum amount of flexibility on the system and the maximum amount of knowledge. Start with downloading the tar.gz file of the latest source from the OpenSSH website. If you are not running OpenBSD, you need the Portable OpenSSH. For me, it took about 16 megabytes of space to download, unzip, `configure` and `make` OpenSSH.

WHAT IS PORTABLE OPENSSH?

OpenSSH was originally developed for OpenBSD. The OpenBSD version of OpenSSH is smaller, and easier to maintain by the OpenBSD community. The OpenSSH portable version is designed to be taken care of by the OpenSSH Portability Team, which takes the OpenBSD version and adds the code required to give OpenSSH functionality on other platforms. This is a large effort because OpenSSH interacts with user authentication and login, which is handled very differently on different platforms.

OpenSSH is built just like many other source-based software packages are; it requires a fairly straightforward set of commands: unpack the files, then run `configure`, `make`, and `make install`.

```
stahnke@rack:~> gunzip openssh*tar.gz
stahnke@rack:~> tar xvf openssh*.tar
stahnke@rack:~> cd openssh-*
stahnke@rack:~> ./configure
```

For a list of configuration options, try `./configure --help`.

- `--prefix`: This sets up the base directory for the OpenSSH tree. Normally, programs built for source wind up in `/usr/local` or `/opt`. However, strictly from a personal preference, I consider `/usr/local` to usually contain items unique to this system and not found on other systems. OpenSSH is now on all systems I manage, and my comfort level with software has increased. I have been choosing `/usr` as the prefix directory in my latest builds. `/usr` is also the location often used for binary installation of OpenSSH.

- `--sysconfigdir`: This is where your configuration files will reside for OpenSSH. I like to use `/etc/ssh`.

- `--mandir`: This is the directory in which the `man` pages for your OpenSSH software will be stored. The default is `/usr/local/man`, but `/usr/man` can be used also.

- `--infodir`: This is the directory where info pages are stored. By default this is `/usr/local/share/info`.

- `--libexecdir`: This is where `sftp-server` and `ssh-keysign` will be stored. The default is `/usr/local/libexec`.

- `--with-pam`: Pluggable Authentication Module (PAM) allows for all sorts of authentication options. Most Linux systems, FreeBSD, NetBSD, and several traditional UNIX systems now make use of PAM.

- `--with-tcp-wrappers`: To enable TCP wrappers, I needed this option on my `configure`. TCP wrappers allow some control of what IP addresses I allow to connect.

While other options exist in the configuration, these are the options I normally use when rolling my own OpenSSH. If you have made the investment in Kerberos you might want to enable it with

```
--with-kerberos5=[Kerberos Path]
```

■Tip Options you choose can create dependencies on additional libraries. Enabling PAM, for example, may require PAM development libraries that should be provided by your operating system vendor.

For example, my configuration command follows:

```
stahnke@rack:~> ./configure    --prefix=/usr \
--sysconfdir=/etc/ssh \
--mandir=/usr/share/man \
--infodir=/usr/share/info \
--libexecdir=/usr/lib/ssh \
--with-pam \
--with-tcp-wrappers 2>&1 | tee outputfile
```

In this example, I used tee to direct the output to a file called outputfile because it is sometimes difficult to scroll back and find configuration options. Also, if I need to rebuild OpenSSH in the future, I will have the options I used for my configure execution saved.

```
stahnke@rack:~> tail -34 outputfile
OpenSSH has been configured with the following options:
                    User binaries: /usr/local/bin
                  System binaries: /usr/local/sbin
              Configuration files: /usr/local/etc
                Askpass program: /usr/local/lib/ssh/ssh-askpass
                    Manual pages: /usr/local/man/manX
                        PID file: /var/run
  Privilege separation chroot path: /var/empty
            sshd default user PATH: /usr/bin:/bin:/usr/sbin:/sbin:/usr/local/bin
                  Manpage format: doc
                     PAM support: yes
                KerberosV support: no
                Smartcard support: no
                    S/KEY support: no
              TCP Wrappers support: yes
              MD5 password support: no
      IP address in $DISPLAY hack: no
            Translate v4 in v6 hack: yes
                  BSD Auth support: no
              Random number source: OpenSSL internal ONLY
```

```
         Host: i686-pc-linux-gnu
     Compiler: gcc
Compiler flags: -g -O2 -Wall -Wpointer-arith -Wno-uninitialized
Preprocessor flags: -I/usr/local/ssl/include
  Linker flags: -L/usr/local/ssl/lib
     Libraries: -lwrap -lpam -ldl -lresolv -lcrypto -lutil -lz -lnsl -lcrypt
```

```
PAM is enabled. You may need to install a PAM control file
for sshd, otherwise password authentication may fail.
Example PAM control files can be found in the contrib/
subdirectory
stahnke@rack:~> make
stahnke@rack:~> make tests
stahnke@rack:~> su
root@rack:  # make install
```

Upon the completion of make, I needed to find the startup script so my newly installed OpenSSH could be started, and of course made to start on reboot. In the OpenSSH source tree under the contrib directory are many sample startup files for popular UNIX/Linux distributions, as well as some generic ones to get you started making your own if need be.

If the system you are working on has never had OpenSSH installed on it before, you will need to create a user and group called ssh. The UID/GID of the ssh user can be arbitrary. Binary installations of OpenSSH (e.g., rpms, pkg) will do this automatically. The ssh user and group allow sshd to operate in privilege separation mode, which is a very nice security feature in OpenSSH. This means that sshd will not run as root for each connection. If the user stahnke logs in, the sshd process he connects with will be owned by stahnke.

Starting SSH

Once installed and configured, it is time to start the OpenSSH server. You can do this in two fashions, manually and automatically. Both operations are introduced in this section.

Manually Starting and Stopping OpenSSH

After finding or modifying a startup script to suit your needs, copy the script to the proper startup location for your system. Daemon initialization can vary greatly depending on operating system. Listing 2-1 covers Fedora and SuSE Linux for example purposes.

Listing 2-1. *Copying* sshd *Startup Files to Their Proper Location for Fedora/SuSE Linux and Starting* sshd

```
root@rack:~# cp ~stahnke/openssh/openssh-x.xp1/opensshd.init /etc/init.d/sshd
root@rack:~#  chmod 700 /etc/init.d/sshd
root@rack:~# /etc/init.d/sshd start
starting /usr/local/sbin/sshd... done.
```

Similarly, to stop OpenSSH (make sure you can still get on your system another way), just replace the word start with stop. Restarting the OpenSSH server can be done with the word restart.

Of course, BSD variants will require using the rc scripts to start and stop sshd.

Automatically Starting and Stopping OpenSSH

The next time my system boots, I want to ensure that sshd starts and is ready for me to connect. The following method worked great on my Fedora and SuSE systems to get OpenSSH started.

```
stahnke@rack:~> chkconfig sshd on
```

Of course, getting a system setup to start services at boot time can vary widely on different platforms. Your system may vary.

OpenSSH is now running. You can telnet to port 22, as shown earlier, if you want to see what version you are running, but now would be a great time to start using the client tools.

Checking Your Work

Congratulations! OpenSSH is now running and waiting for you to make a secure connection. Let us verify everything went as planned.

```
stahnke@rack:~> ssh localhost
The authenticity of host 'localhost (127.0.0.1)' can't be established.
RSA key fingerprint is 0c:ae:42:c5:0a:3b:37:c7:c2:84:af:eb:dd:92:39:a0.
Are you sure you want to continue connecting (yes/no)? [yes]
stahnke@localhost's password: [my password]
Last login: Thu Aug 26 00:24:49 2004 from console
stahnke@rack:~>
```

To establish an SSH connection with the current user assumed to be username, start by using the ssh client program. If this is the first time you have used the ssh client to connect to localhost, you will see something about an RSA or DSA fingerprint (public key), and it will ask you if you want to connect. Is 127.0.0.1 the host you think it is? ssh does not already have a public record of this host in its cache. If you trust this is indeed the host you are looking for (of course, with 127.0.0.1 it really should be), type **yes**. If you wish to check the fingerprint as shown in the earlier example, do so.

Now if the fingerprint changes for localhost, ssh will not allow you to connect until you trust it again. After validating the host key, you should get a password prompt. Entering your correct password will gain your account access to the machine, just as a telnet connection does. I now encourage you to try the same procedure using the network DNS name/IP address of your machine, and not 127.0.0.1. You again will need to accept/validate your machine's public key.

Troubleshooting Your SSH Installation

Did you not get what you expected from your attempt at an SSH connection? If not, it is OK. Sometimes having a task not execute perfectly the first time can enable lots of hands-on learning.

First, review what has been covered.

- Did a `configure` complete successfully?

  If OpenSSH did not complete a `configure` properly, try removing an option or two and see if that helps. `configure` may be asking for paths to a few libraries if you specified additional options such as Kerberos or IPV6. Sometimes installation of development libraries is required, if they are not already installed. C header libraries, OpenSSL libraries, and zlib libraries are required. Some additional `configure` options, such as PAM, Kerberos, and others, will create dependency on their libraries also.

- Did the build succeed?

  If specific errors are reported while running `make`, it could be you are missing some libraries, but normally the `configure` script does an excellent job of finding and reporting errors with library locations if they exist. After heeding the errors, either by configuring with fewer options, changing a library path, upgrading libraries, etc., run `make` again.

- Is the syntax correct on the `sshd_config`?

  The `sshd_config` file controls the configuration of the OpenSSH server, `sshd`. The file is formally introduced in Chapter 4, but for now, running `sshd -t` will validate syntax of the configuration file, and report errors if any exist.

- Did OpenSSH start?

  To check, you can execute the following:

  ```
  stahnke@rack:~> ps -ef | grep sshd | grep -v grep
  ```

  BSD systems will require `ps aux`, or something similar. If you see nothing returned, try starting `sshd` manually once again. Did you reboot and not set up `sshd` for automatic start? If so, you will have to `telnet` in or get on the console to set up automatic starting of `sshd`.

  If you are having trouble getting `sshd` to start automatically, perhaps adding a line to `/etc/rc.local` will alleviate your pain. If `sshd` is having trouble starting, could it be that something else has claimed TCP port 22 on this machine?

- Are you able to connect to `sshd` on the `localhost`?

  You can `telnet` to port 22 as illustrated earlier to see if the port is open. Remember to `telnet` to the `localhost` and to the resolvable name of the machine to verify there is not a firewall blocking traffic on port 22.

  Additionally, port scanning tools such as Nmap (`http://www.insecure.org`) can be used to determine if port 22 is open on the target machine.

  A common problem after starting `sshd` occurs when a firewall is in place on the machine. If you run a firewall, the port you run `sshd` on, TCP 22 by default, will need to be opened.

- Has the host key changed?

  If a host key has changed on a remote host, ssh clients could deny you from connecting to the remote host, as shown in Listing 2-2. The warning message that occurs is shown in this listing. To fix the problem, you can remove the line number in the /home/username/.ssh/known_hosts file, (manually or with ssh-keygen -R).

Listing 2-2. *Attempting an* ssh *Connection to a Machine with a Different Host Key Presented Than What Is Cached*

```
stahnke@rack:~> ssh 192.168.1.104
@@@@@@@@@@@@@@@@@@@@@@@@@@@@@@@@@@@@@@@@@@@@@@@@@@@@@@@@@@@@@
@    WARNING: REMOTE HOST IDENTIFICATION HAS CHANGED!    @
@@@@@@@@@@@@@@@@@@@@@@@@@@@@@@@@@@@@@@@@@@@@@@@@@@@@@@@@@@@@@
IT IS POSSIBLE THAT SOMEONE IS DOING SOMETHING NASTY!
Someone could be eavesdropping on you right now (man-in-the-middle attack)!
It is also possible that the RSA host key has just been changed.
The fingerprint for the RSA key sent by the remote host is
11:40:54:80:d5:4a:46:25:f6:f1:13:7a:ed:90:c6:6e.
Please contact your system administrator.
Add correct host key in /home/stahnke/.ssh/known_hosts to get rid of this message.
Offending key in /home/stahnke/.ssh/known_hosts:6
RSA host key for 192.168.1.104 has changed and you have requested strict checking.
Host key verification failed.
stahnke@rack:~>
```

Turning Off Telnet

If you are comfortable with the way sshd is performing on your system(s), you can turn off the Telnet daemon. Please keep in mind that you may have applications and users very accustomed to using telnet, so be sure to communicate your change.

The Telnet daemon usually runs from inetd (xinetd in Linux) and can be turned off by adding a # in front of the telnetd line(s) and sending a hangup to inetd.

To verify the Telnet daemon is indeed turned off, try a simple telnet to your machine.

```
stahnke@rack:~>  telnet localhost
Trying 127.0.0.1...
telnet: connect to address 127.0.0.1: Connection refused
```

What About FTP?

FTP is used to transfer files, but, of course, it has the insecurity of clear-text usernames, passwords, and data. With OpenSSH, you replace the need for FTP with two different commands that both are invoked over port 22, the same as the sshd server. sftp is a way to transfer files securely with a very similar syntax to ftp; a simple example is shown in Listing 2-3. There is very little different about it from a command-line prospective, other than you need to specify your remote username on the remote system when invoking sftp. Additionally, there is no binary vs. ASCII mode in sftp at the time of this writing, though there is some discussion of adding it.

Listing 2-3. *A Simple* sftp *Session Where* foo *and* bar *Are Retrieved*

```
stahnke@rack:~> sftp stahnke@192.168.1.102
Connecting to 192.168.1.102...
stahnke@192.168.1.102's password:
sftp> ls -l
-rw-r--r--    1 stahnke   stahnke       19 Aug 28 13:37 foo
-rw-r--r--    1 stahnke   stahnke       87 Aug 28 13:37 bar
drwxr-xr-x    2 stahnke   stahnke     4096 Aug 28 13:35 public_html
-rw-r--r--    1 stahnke   stahnke    10240 Aug 28 13:37 vmlinuz.tar
sftp> get foo
Fetching /home/stahnke/foo to foo
/home/stahnke/foo                        100%   19     0.0KB/s   00:00
sftp> get bar
Fetching /home/stahnke/bar to bar
/home/stahnke/bar                        100%   87     0.1KB/s   00:00
sftp> quit
stahnke@rack:~>
```

As you can see, an sftp session looks very similar to a traditional ftp session. sftp can also be scripted in Perl, shell, and other languages. Scripting data transfers is covered in Chapter 9.

scp

Another alternative to ftp and rcp is scp, which works in almost the exact same fashion as rcp. In fact, it was originally based on the same code; however, it encrypts the data moving across the network. If the files foo and bar have been edited and need to be put back to their original location, scp can accomplish this. Also, the file foobar will be retrieved from the remote system as shown in Listing 2-4.

Listing 2-4. *An Example of File Transfers Using* scp

```
stahnke@rack:~> scp foo stahnke@192.168.1.102:
stahnke@192.168.1.102's password:
foo                                      100%  850    0.8KB/s   00:00
stahnke@rack:~> scp bar stahnke@192.168.1.102:remote_bar
stahnke@192.168.1.102's password:
bar                                      100%  731    0.7KB/s   00:00
stahnke@rack:~> scp stahnke@192.168.1.102:foobar .
stahnke@192.168.1.102's password:
foobar                                   100% 1581    1.5KB/s   00:00
stahnke@rack:~>
```

The format of the command is scp source destination. The remote host is always referenced with user@hostname:/path/to/file. If just a : is used, such as in the first transfer, scp treats this as a relative path to the remote user's home directory. scp has become an invaluable tool for me as a system administrator. It too fits well in scripts and provides a quick mechanism to grab updates without having to invoke a slightly more cumbersome sftp session. scp will be used heavily in Chapter 9 when automation and scripting via SSH is covered in depth.

Client Tools for Windows

If you are connecting from a Microsoft Windows workstation, you will need some additional tools. While Windows provides a Telnet client from the command line, an SSH client is not included. A heavily favored tool because of price and performance is PuTTY (http://www.chiark. greenend.org.uk/~sgtatham/putty/download.html), maintained by Simon Tatham, Owen Dunn, Ben Harris, and Jacob Nevins.

After downloading putty.exe and verifying its signature, launch it, and optionally configure PuTTY as shown in Figures 2-2 and 2-3. From there, enter the hostname of the machine you want to connect to, and make sure the SSH radio button is checked. Next, you might be prompted to accept the connection type yes to establish the remote host as a known host.

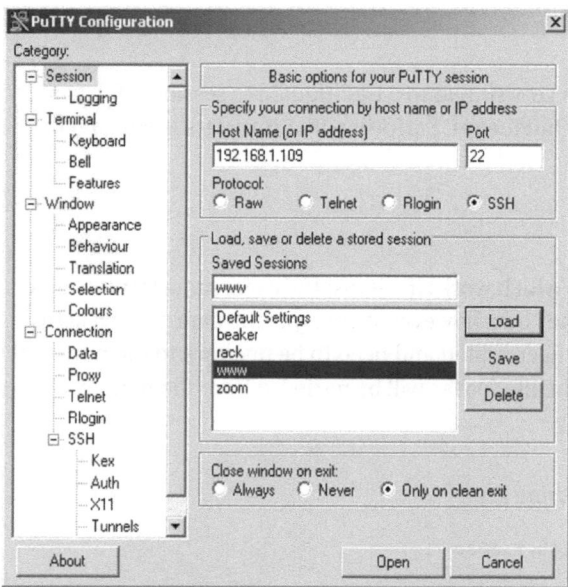

Figure 2-2. *PuTTY allows for many configuration options. To get started, just enter the name of the remote machine and click Open.*

Figure 2-3. *PuTTY provides a terminal session.*

To utilize SCP/SFTP from Windows, other means are necessary as well. The PuTTY software download page provides a command-line-only SCP/SFTP interface as shown in Figure 2-4. While this works just fine, I prefer a drag-and-drop approach to file transfer from Windows. For this, I recommend WinSCP, freely available from http://winscp.net. WinSCP is very easy to configure and gives you SCP/SFTP abilities from Windows. Figure 2-5 shows a WinSCP connected to a remote machine via sftp.

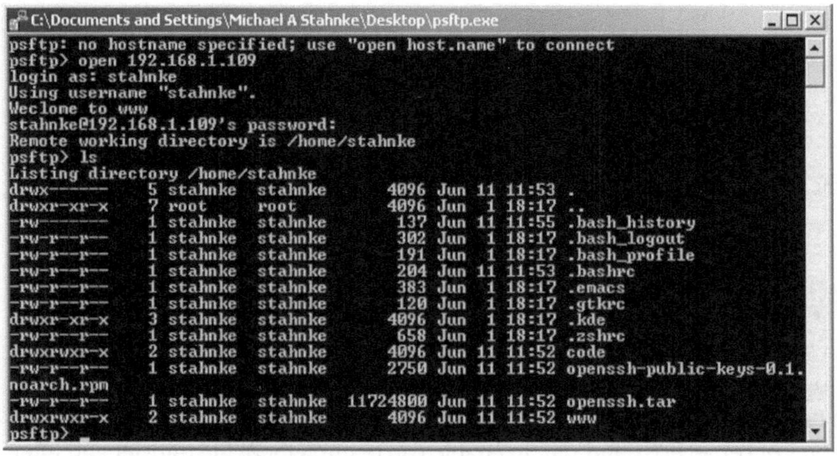

Figure 2-4. *Command-line SCP/SFTP interface as provided from PSFTP*

While there is a whole slew of other tools for terminal connections and data transfer available, I have found the freely available PuTTY and WinSCP meet my criteria for work 99% of the time.

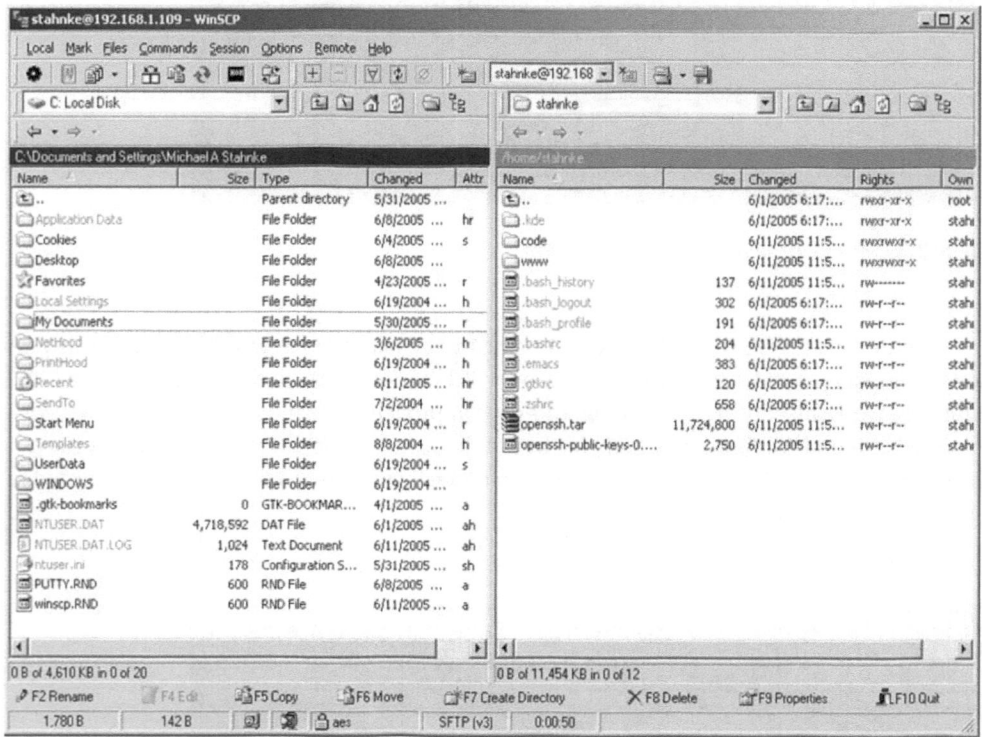

Figure 2-5. *WinSCP connected to a remote machine. To transfer files, simply drag and drop.*

Summary

In this chapter, we started with some background on SSH and its advantages over clear-text protocols, due to encryptions and asymmetric (public and private) host key exchange. You learned that, to be more secure, you install or build OpenSSH and utilize its connectivity to replace the features of telnet, ftp, and rcp. To enable you to implement file transfer and inter-action from Microsoft Windows machines, I also surveyed a few open source client options.

Now that you have a basic understanding of SSH, with OpenSSH up and running on at least one host, a new world of security options, tunneling, and administration configuration comes into play. In the next chapters, you will see in more detail why you should be concerned with security and policy recommendations, learn about Secure Shell architecture, and discover how to get more out of OpenSSH.

PART 2

∎ ∎ ∎

Configuring OpenSSH

CHAPTER 3

■ ■ ■

The File Structure of OpenSSH

Now that you understand the importance of secure connectivity protocols, and have learned how to install our chosen tool, OpenSSH, the time has come to begin configuring the software. Much of OpenSSH's configuration is done through a variety of files on both the client and server level. This chapter will introduce you to these files and provide a synopsis of their purposes. I will return to some of these topics throughout the book, beginning in the next two chapters, as they are devoted to an in-depth discussion of the `sshd_config` and `ssh_config` files, which control the server and client settings.

In addition to the myriad files OpenSSH uses exclusively, several files normally used during a login come into play when utilizing OpenSSH—this is due to the fact that SSH is a protocol that allows shell access to users. The details of the file layout, order of sourcing (using the contents of file), and roles each of the files play are important from a usability and functionality standpoint, and also from a security standpoint. A configuration mistake that lowers the overall security of system can be easy to make if the file structure and configuration is not understood and reviewed. Developing an understanding of the file layout will help prevent misconfiguration and enhance your overall level of comfort using OpenSSH. By the end of the chapter, you will have a clear understanding of the files utilized with OpenSSH, as well as their purposes.

OpenSSH provides files that can be loosely grouped into two sections: files for the clients and files for the daemon. This discussion will attempt to focus agnostically on any UNIX/Linux-type operating system.

Server Configuration Files

From a server perspective, many configuration settings are available, including options for allowing the root account to log in remotely and options for setting what level of logging is enabled, what encryption ciphers should be used, what port the service should be listening on, and more.

The configuration files for OpenSSH serve different purposes, but ultimately control how `sshd` operates. To simplify discussion of OpenSSH server settings, the default names for all files will be used in this chapter and throughout the book, even though several of the names can be changed by an administrator. The paths for many of the files can change depending on how you ran `configure` during your installation. The default location from the OpenSSH source

package is /usr/local. Also noted is the conventional path to the file if used in a binary installation, such as an rpm or pkg file, which is normally /usr/bin. In the file listing that follows,
executable files are denoted with an * after their name, much like an ls -F. In my example installation, the files are created on a Linux host. Some paths can vary on other operating systems.

ssh_host_key

Source-compiled path: /usr/local/etc
Vendor-provided path: /etc/ssh
Each host generates one or more unique keys to identify itself. For using SSH protocol 1, this
is the private key using the RSA algorithm. The importance of this file is covered in Chapter 6.
Right now, just remember to protect that file. If compromised, an attacker can pretend to be
the compromised host, which will appear to be legitimate on your network. This file can also
be used to decrypt OpenSSH session traffic arriving at the server. If this file is corrupt or removed,
authentication will fail if your configuration insists on strict host key checking. This file is normally
not edited, and should be kept at 600 permissions, with root as the owner.
    When using SSH protocol 2, the private key file names are ssh_host_rsa_key and
ssh_host_dsa_key. Using protocol 2 is a recommended best practice when working with
OpenSSH, so that the protocol 1 host key pair will not be used if protocol 1 is specifically
disabled.

ssh_host_key.pub

Source-compiled path: /usr/local/etc
Vendor-provided path: /etc/ssh
In asymmetric encryption algorithms, every private key has a public key that completes the
key pair. The asymmetric encryption algorithms used by OpenSSH are no exception. The
public key is the "fingerprint" of the server that is cached on a local client to provide a level of
assurance that the server is the one you are looking for. This particular file is the SSH protocol
1 public key. This file is normally kept with 644 permissions, and owned by root. Public/private
keys will be discussed in greater detail in Chapter 6.

ssh_random_seed

Source-compiled path: /usr/local/etc
Vendor-provided path: /etc/ssh
Encryption algorithms depend upon a source of *entropy* (randomness) in order to generate cryp-
tographic keys that are not easily guessable by an attacker. The UNIX-specific ssh_random_seed
file provides this entropy, and is used only if /dev/random or /dev/urandom devices do not exist.
If this file exists on your systems, it should be readable only by root.

WHAT IS ENTROPY AND WHY IS IT NEEDED FOR OPENSSH?

Entropy is the measurement of randomness in a given data set. In the case of SSH, high degrees of entropy are required to generate keys for users and the OpenSSH servers because these keys should not be guessable. If a private key is guessable, then an attacker can compromise an account and/or system.

The /dev/random and /dev/urandom devices provide very good sources of entropy on most modern UNIX-type systems—however, earlier versions of HP-UX, Solaris, AIX, and others did not have these devices. Luckily, the OpenSSH developers provide other mechanisms to generate random data sets in the form of ssh-rand-helper and ssh_random_seed. OpenSSL also normally provides the methods for generating random numbers.

Normal English sentences have a low entropy level because several letters are much more common than others. "s" is more common than "j," for example. This is a main reason why keys are stronger than passwords. English has about 1 bit of entropy per character, whereas a good random number generator can provide more than 8 bits of entropy per character.

sshd

Source-compiled path: /usr/local/sbin
Vendor-provided path: /usr/sbin
sshd is the OpenSSH server daemon file. This is the binary that receives traffic from your client software. It normally runs as a stand-alone service, not out of inetd like Telnet or FTP.

sshd_config

Source-compiled path: /usr/local/etc
Vendor-provided path: /etc/ssh
The sshd_config file controls almost every aspect of the SSH daemon, and accordingly is the most modified file of the group. Logging, protocol options, ciphers, authentication, and network settings are all configured from this file. The sshd daemon will not start without a sshd_config file (or without being directed to use another file in its place). Starting the daemon with a blank file will cause the defaults to be enabled, which can cause undesired results in some instances. Chapter 4 focuses specifically on this file. The sshd_config file should be owned by root at permissions of 600. Allowing users to see the server configuration can enable them to think of security exploits or workarounds that will lead to a less secure environment (though many of the settings are detectable via the protocol using an SSH client).

banner

Path: system administrator preference
A banner is a message that is displayed to users who attempt to access your system via SSH before a password prompt is received. Often, legal notices or informational messages are displayed with this optional file. A banner file can be at location, and can be named anything. Its location is set in the sshd_config file.

sshd.pid

Source-compiled path: /var/run, /etc, /usr/local/etc
Vendor-provided path: /var/run
The sshd.pid file records the process ID (pid) of the main OpenSSH daemon, which is the one listening for new connections. Sometimes these are stored in /etc, and sometimes they are stored in /var/run, depending on your system type. You should consult your operating system documentation to see where pid files are commonly stored. The configure script provided with OpenSSH will attempt to place the pid files in the appropriate location for a particular operating system.

nologin

Source-compiled path: /etc
Vendor-provided path: /etc
The nologin file is intended to be used during maintenance windows, when a system should be unavailable to its remote users. If this file exists, it will cause the OpenSSH daemon to allow access only by root; other users will see the contents of the file, and then their shell connection will be dropped. If the file exists, it should be world-readable.

Users can still have open and forward ports when /etc/nologin exists. See Chapter 7 for more information about port forwarding.

ssh_known_hosts

Source-compiled path: /usr/local/etc
Vendor-provided path: /etc/ssh
Because OpenSSH authenticates the server, it caches public keys of known hosts in a file; however, by default, this is done on a per-user basis. To eliminate the need for users to cache remote public keys, ssh_known_hosts can be used for caching instead. It is considered best practice to have a record of the public keys for hosts on your networks, and to know the cause if they are changing. If the master file at the server is empty or incorrect, users will approve the public key into their local cache. If the master file is incorrect, and the user has not already approved the public key, a key mismatch error will occur.

hosts.equiv

Source-compiled path: /etc
Vendor-provided path: /etc
Much like rlogin, the hosts.equiv file allows authentication to be based solely on IP address or domain name. Users on those hosts are permitted to log in without a password, provided they have the same username on both systems. Since replacing legacy protocols as more knowledge is gained about OpenSSH is a goal of this book, using hosts.equiv files is highly discouraged. Because of security concerns, recent versions of OpenSSH no longer support rhosts authentication.

shosts.equiv

Source-compiled path: /usr/local/etc
Vendor-provided path: /etc
This file is the same as rhosts.equiv, but it is used only by OpenSSH and not rsh. This type of host-based authentication uses the public key of the remote host as a method of authentication. This is more difficult to spoof than traditional host-based authentication using only IP address or hostname. Setting up host-based authentication using shosts.equiv files is covered in Chapter 6.

ssh-rand-helper*

Source-compiled path: /usr/local/libexec
Vendor-provided path: /usr/lib/ssh
ssh-rand-helper is a small executable utility that provides random numbers if OpenSSL is not configured to provide them, or if the system lacks a real /dev/random or /dev/urandom device. It works by hashing commands found in /etc/ssh/ssh_prng_cmds, which seeds random number generators. The program is not normally used by the end user, though.

ssh-keyscan*

Source-compiled path: /usr/local/bin
Vendor-provided path: /usr/bin
ssh-keyscan is an executable utility designed to build a known_hosts file at the per-user level, or the ssh_known_hosts file for system-wide caching of public keys. This utility will be covered more in Chapter 8, when security-related best practices for OpenSSH are discussed.

ssh-keygen*

Source-compiled path: /usr/local/bin
Vendor-provided path: /usr/bin
The executable utility ssh-keygen generates, manages, and converts authentication keys for OpenSSH. ssh-keygen can create RSA keys for use by SSH protocol version 1, and RSA or DSA keys for use by SSH protocol version 2. It can also be used to create resource records for publishing public host keys in DNS. ssh-keygen is covered in Chapter 6, while publishing host keys in DNS is covered in Chapter 8.

sftp-server*

Source-compiled path: /usr/local/lib/ssh
Vendor-provided path: /usr/libexec/openssh
sftp-server is an executable subsystem called from sshd. sftp is a secure file-transfer application with very similar capabilities to FTP. All communication is encrypted over SFTP. sftp-server is requested by the sftp client and used over SSH as the transport mechanism, so it uses TCP port 22 by default. Some scripts that use ftp can be set up to use sftp in a very short time.

Server Summary

Obviously, OpenSSH is a fairly complex environment—but at this point, you have already covered the files for the server portion of OpenSSH. Using OpenSSH only gets easier with practice. Many of these files will become just as familiar as /etc/passwd and /etc/hosts are to you over time. Also, keep in mind that some files such as /etc/profile were not mentioned, but are still used if a user is starting a shell. Although these files are critical to user environments, they are not unique to OpenSSH and thus were not discussed.

Client Configuration Files

The OpenSSH client configuration is just as important as the corresponding server configuration. sshd provides certain parameters to the client, and the client is then able to decide how to work within those parameters. For example, if sshd is configured to support four different ciphers for encryption, then the client can pick which one to use. As client files are discussed, think about the user base of your environment. What requirements will they have? Will they want to modify default settings?

Many clients exist that implement the SSH protocol, but in this section, the focus is on the command-line client tools provided with the standard OpenSSH package. The command line usually offers advanced features over other client tools, such as the ability to script transactions.

Client files also have some executable files, again denoted with an *. Most client files are found in the home directory for a user, represented by $HOME. Inside each user's home directory, OpenSSH sets up a hidden directory to store OpenSSH settings. This is the .ssh directory. This directory should not be readable or writable by the world or other users. I usually enforce permissions of 700 for my systems, but 750 is usually adequate. Some files that are actually used by the server but controlled by the user are also described in this section. The paths of the files can vary, but the user-controlled files in $HOME will not vary if the installation is source-compiled, or if a vendor provided installation.

Your UNIX user base will quickly realize they can configure the client to their liking, much like .profile overrides a system-wide /etc/profile—which means that the user's settings are taken before system-wide settings are applied to the ssh client. It is a good idea to try and understand what your users are doing, and if you find many of your users overriding the same options, perhaps you should make those changes globally.

ssh_config

Source-compiled path: /usr/local/etc
Vendor-provided path: /etc/ssh
Administrators will configure system defaults for the OpenSSH client software in this file. Client configurations can affect the overall security of an OpenSSH implementation. Client configuration, including overriding default settings and preferences, is covered in Chapter 5.

.rhosts

Path: $HOME
The .rhosts file provides someone the ability to log in without having to manually authenticate. Using this file is highly discouraged, and its use can be disabled via the server configuration file sshd_config.

This file is used by sshd, but is under user control in the user's home directory.

.shosts

Path: $HOME

The .shosts file is used with the OpenSSH service. It provides host-based authentication without requiring user-based interactive authentication. This option can also be overridden via sshd_config. This file is used by sshd, but is under user control in the user's home directory.

.Xauthority

Path: $HOME

OpenSSH has the ability to tunnel X11 sessions to prevent clear-text data transmissions. The .Xauthority file is created or updated upon login if X11Forwarding is enabled for a given session. The .Xauthority file is created by the server, but is owned and controlled by the user.

identity, id_dsa, id_rsa

Path: $HOME

If a user decides to use public key authentication (discussed in Chapter 6), the private key file is by default named id_dsa or id_rsa for protocol 2, depending on the type of key chosen. Having the private key and its passphrase is the equivalent of knowing a user's password, so protect this credential with strict permissions (600). Private keys can and should be protected via a passphrase. The counterparts to these files are pub files, which are the public key equivalents. These are distributed to remote systems to allow authentication. Public keys do not require such strict permissions either. identity is the name of the user-created SSH protocol 1 private key.

WHAT IS A PASSPHRASE?

Passwords are typically about eight characters in length, and can contain alphanumeric and a limited set of special characters. Passphrases on the other hand, are meant to be longer (thus more difficult to guess), but make sense (thus easier to remember). Passphrases also are normally entered less often than passwords. A passphrase is used to unlock a private key in OpenSSH and in other digital credential technologies such as digital certificates (X.509). An example of password would be

Beatles4

Even though this password uses uppercase, lowercase, and a number, a modern password-cracking tool can guess it without too much difficulty.

A passphrase on the other hand, could be

Here's another clue for you all/the walrus was Paul.

This passphrase does not use a number, but because it is longer, a cracking program would have a much more difficult time with it. Additionally, apostrophes, commas, and spaces are allowed, whereas in many password program utilities, they are not.

Passphrases need to be of a decent length to adequately protect the private key. Using punctuation and capitalization in unconventional character places will also greatly increase the difficulty of cracking the passphrase.

config

Path: $HOME/.ssh

This is the main configuration file for the OpenSSH client software, from the user perspective. Inside this file, the preferences for attempted authentication methods, connection timeout values, forwarding control, and other settings are controlled. The options for this file are covered in Chapter 5.

known_hosts

Path: $HOME/.ssh

known_hosts is the user's list of hosts whose public keys were accepted by the user. After a host is accepted, the user no longer must type yes to accept the remote system's public key. If the system-wide ssh_known_hosts file is fully populated, this file will not be needed. The user-controlled known_hosts file is utilized before the system-wide file.

authorized_keys

Path: $HOME/.ssh

The authorized_keys file lists all the public keys for those users who are authorized to assume the user's identity without a password (using public key authentication). Of course, if the file is world-writable, people can add themselves. Therefore, it's strongly suggested to make this file read- and write-accessible only by the owner. By default, with StrictModes enabled, the server will not allow public key authentication if this file is world-readable or writable.

authorized_keys is placed on the remote systems for a client, and is actually used by sshd. This file, however, is under the control of user.

environment

Source-compiled path: $HOME/.ssh

The environment file is responsible for setting environmental values at login. Whether or not this feature is available is determined by sshd_config. If this file is missing or blank, /etc/environment is used. The environment file is used by sshd on the remote system and is under user control.

rc

Source-compiled path: $HOME/.ssh

The rc file lists commands or scripts that are run automatically upon successful login. This is useful if using something like AFS as a file system. The rc file is executed by the server, but is under user control.

agent.<ppid>

Path: /tmp

agent.<ppid> is the UNIX domain socket file used to contain the connection to the authentication agent. The authentication agent is software that will store your digital credentials as a form of non-interactive authentication. These socket files should only be readable and writable by the owner. Incorrect ownership or permissions could allow an attacker to use someone else's authentication as their own. The sockets should be automatically removed when the agent exits.

ssh-keysign*

Source-compiled path: /usr/local/bin
Vendor-provided path: /usr/bin
The executable utility ssh-keysign is used by ssh when enabled in ssh_config via the EnableSSHKeySign option. It is used to access the local host keys and generate the digital signature required during host-based authentication with SSH protocol version 2. It is not intended to be invoked by the user directly. This utility allows ssh to not have permissions of SetUID root, but runs as SetUID root itself.

ssh-add*

Source-compiled path: /usr/local/bin
Vendor-provided path: /usr/bin
The ssh-add executable utility adds, deletes, lists, and locks authentication credentials to the authentication agent software. Digital credentials are supported by OpenSSH, which has the opportunity to be a universal access mechanism for many platforms—this tool helps you see that potential. ssh-add will be covered in more depth throughout the rest of the book, beginning in Chapter 6.

ssh*

Source-compiled path: /usr/local/bin
Vendor-provided path: /usr/bin
This is the core OpenSSH client binary. Chapter 5 is devoted to ssh and the global ssh_config and user-specific config files. This utility replaces the legacy telnet and rsh/rlogin clients.

If using host-based authentication via SSH protocol 1, the ssh binary must be SetUID root. This is not a recommended practice, and is not required for SSH protocol 2 because of the ssh-keysign program.

ssh-agent*

Source-compiled path: /usr/local/bin
Vendor-provided path: /usr/bin
The executable ssh-agent sets up a shell environment that holds private keys to use for public key authentication (RSA or DSA). ssh-agent can be started in the beginning of an X-session, login session, or shell. All other X11 windows or programs are aware of the ssh-agent program, and thus will use ssh-agent to allow public key authentication to occur. This will allow users with multiple windows to authenticate to multiple systems without having to retype passwords or passphrases, while not compromising security. ssh-agent and ssh-add are covered in Chapter 6 and used throughout the book.

scp*, sftp*

Source-compiled path: /usr/local/bin
Vendor-provided path: /usr/bin
The executables scp and sftp provide a secure way to transfer files. scp replaces rcp with nearly identical syntax. sftp does the same for FTP, although the underlying protocol is entirely different.

Both of these client programs use the ssh client as the transport mechanism, which allows the use of public key authentication. This type of authentication lends itself to automating data transfers via scripting, which is covered in Chapter 9.

Client Summary

The files used by the OpenSSH client and the users control the behavior of the command-line ssh client, along with scp and sftp. Keep in mind that some files controlled by the user are used by sshd on remote hosts.

The order or precedence for client configuration is also important. Command-line options will override user-specific configurations, which override system-wide configurations. The order of precedence is covered in more detail in Chapter 5, but it is a good idea to keep this in mind when beginning to work with OpenSSH.

Conclusion

Understanding the file structure, layout, and purpose will allow you as an SSH administrator to troubleshoot problems more efficiently, and to become a power user of SSH. Oftentimes, a complete configuration of OpenSSH involves setting up the server, client, and several user-controlled files to create a finely tuned experience for productive users.

OpenSSH provides a highly configurable mechanism to deliver secure communication. As discussed in this chapter, configuring OpenSSH becomes the challenge to supporting an OpenSSH environment. In everyday practice as an OpenSSH administrator, I work with the ssh_config and sshd_config files most often. The next two chapters will take a look at sshd_config and ssh_config in great detail.

CHAPTER 4

■ ■ ■

The OpenSSH Server

Chapter 3's coverage of the OpenSSH file structure sets the stage for this chapter, in which you will learn about the server configuration options and directives within the OpenSSH main configuration file, sshd_config. This chapter also offers some troubleshooting hints and general management tips. More advanced management tips, including architecture and key management, are covered in Chapter 8.

The next chapter will discuss the OpenSSH client and its configuration in detail. The goal for these two chapters is to provide you with the knowledge to make your OpenSSH implementation as secure and usable as possible. The discussion of the server will begin by providing information that will enable you to quickly identify mistakes in configuration files, and then move into instructions for running a daemon in debug mode. Following the debugging discussion, I cover the order of precedence for the server configuration files and directives, with a detailed at look at the directives in the sshd_config file.

OpenSSH Server Testing

When the OpenSSH daemon becomes the lifeblood of your administration infrastructure, careful change control is essential for optimal operation. Making a mistake in a configuration file can be the difference between having the newest, coolest script known to UNIX and having to drive out to that remote data center to reconfigure your OpenSSH server.

Checking the Syntax of sshd_config

By default, the OpenSSH server, or sshd, resides on TCP port 22. But when testing a new configuration on a server where connectivity services must remain available, it is best practice to place the sshd daemon on a different port to test functionality. Before using a new sshd_config file, whether it be on port 22 or in testing, it is a good idea to run sshd -t, which validates the syntax of the server configuration file. Keep in mind that the permissions on sshd_config should only allow for root to read from and write to this file, so running sshd -t against a properly secured configuration file requires root authority. In the following example, the sshd_config_new file has the invalid string Version. This was designed to be a comment, but because it was not prefaced with the # character, sshd sees it as an unknown directive. Running sshd -t locates the error and provides the line number where the problem occurs.

```
rack:/ # head -4 /etc/ssh/sshd_config_new
Version 2
# This is the sshd server system-wide configuration file.  See
# sshd_config(5) for more information.
rack:/ # /usr/sbin/sshd -t -f /etc/ssh/sshd_config_new
/etc/ssh/sshd_config_new: line 2: Bad configuration option: Version
/etc/ssh/sshd_config_new: terminating, 1 bad configuration options
rack:/ #
```

As with many UNIX commands, no output from running sshd -t means everything is fine.

Changing the Default Configuration File and Port

By default, sshd will use TCP port 22. However, if an alternative configuration file for your server is desired, and attempting changes on the production OpenSSH server already found on port 22 could create issues, you can run a separate instance on an alternative port. In the following example, the file sshd_config_new has been created, and it contains some different server options and needs to be tested.

```
rack:/ # /usr/sbin/sshd -f /etc/ssh/sshd_config_new -p 99
```

This tells sshd to start utilizing /etc/ssh/sshd_config_new as the server configuration file and to listen on port 99. While any port can be used, make sure you choose a port not already in use on your system. To establish a connection to the newly created port 99 server, use the ssh client software with the -p option, which specifies the remote port to connect to.

```
rack:/ # /usr/bin/ssh -p 99 127.0.0.1
```

Running the OpenSSH Server in Debug Mode

The -d option of sshd is another tool that will help you troubleshoot your OpenSSH configuration if you suspect something is not behaving as desired. The debug mode of sshd logs output to stderr instead of to the default AUTH facility of syslogd.

```
rack:/ # /usr/sbin/sshd -d -p 99 -f /etc/ssh/sshd_config_new
debug1: sshd version OpenSSH_3.9p1
debug1: private host key: #0 type 0 RSA1
debug1: read PEM private key done: type RSA
debug1: private host key: #1 type 1 RSA
debug1: read PEM private key done: type DSA
debug1: private host key: #2 type 2 DSA
debug1: rexec_argv[0]='/usr/sbin/sshd'
debug1: rexec_argv[1]='-d'
debug1: rexec_argv[2]='-p'
debug1: rexec_argv[3]='99'
debug1: rexec_argv[4]='-f'
debug1: rexec_argv[5]='/etc/ssh/sshd_config_new'
debug1: Bind to port 99 on ::.
Server listening on :: port 99.
```

```
debug1: Bind to port 99 on 0.0.0.0.
Bind to port 99 on 0.0.0.0 failed: Address already in use.
Generating 768 bit RSA key.
RSA key generation complete
```

As you can see, the output from debug mode is sent to the terminal. This will continue as long as this debug session of sshd is running. To stop it, press Ctrl-C from the controlling window or use the kill command. Of course, the debugging information can also be redirected to a file for further analysis. If a user logs in to a daemon running in debug mode, he or she is also presented with some additional information.

```
stahnke@rack: ~> /usr/bin/ssh -p 99 localhost
stahnke@localhost's password:
Environment:
  USER=stahnke
  LOGNAME=stahnke
  HOME=/home/stahnke
  PATH=bin:/usr/bin:/usr/local/bin
  MAIL=/var/mail/stahnke
  SHELL=/bin/bash
  SSH_CLIENT=::ffff:127.0.0.1 55894 99
  SSH_CONNECTION=::ffff:127.0.0.1 55894 ::ffff:127.0.0.1 99
  SSH_TTY=/dev/pts/4
  TERM=xterm
stahnke@rack: ~>
```

Additionally, information can be gathered by increasing the verbosity of debugging simply by using -dd or -ddd, and recent versions of OpenSSH may also need -e to force the debug messages to appear on stderr. Level three is the highest debug level for OpenSSH servers.

Reloading Configuration Files

Sometimes the need arises to change a directive on a running sshd server. After verifying the configuration file syntax and testing the new configuration as necessary, edit the main configuration file with your changes. Then to reload an SSH configuration, you can simply run HUP or kill -1 on the PID. Sending a -1 or HUP signal does not drop any connections currently utilizing the sshd server. If the server cannot restart for any reason, possibly due the configuration file having a syntax error, then the server will silently die.

Managing the OpenSSH Server

The contents of the OpenSSH server file, sshd_config, are set for the entire system. The server tells the client what authentication methods are offered, what encryption types to use, and so on. The client then has the choice of selecting from those offered settings when connections are established. When selecting the options that compose the sshd_config file, administrators must take extra care to ensure usability while at the same time striving for a configuration that mitigates risks their organization has deemed too great to accept.

As with any configuration file, keep in mind the defaults are not always suitable to your needs. Version changes, upgrades, or just forgetting what the defaults are can lead to undesirable behavior in your OpenSSH environment. I normally make a copy of the sshd_config file that includes heavy commenting to have as a reference for auditors, compliance managers, and technical reviews. When it comes to installing them onto machines, I often utilize the power of grep to strip the comments, leaving a bare-bones configuration file for my machines.

Also keep in mind that maintaining backup copies of configuration files, whether via manual backups or version control, or just keeping MD5 hashes around to ensure integrity is always considered best practice. Just because OpenSSH is a secure connectivity suite is no reason to side-step good system administration techniques for managing and protecting the appropriate configuration files.

Proper planning and architecture are essential when building a configuration for sshd. The settings chosen for the OpenSSH server will directly impact how users connect and which client options (as discussed in Chapter 5) will be usable for them. Security practices are established for the OpenSSH environment within the sshd_config file. If poor security is implemented in the server configuration, clients can, and most likely will, take advantage of it.

For example, allowing empty passwords seems like a bad idea, but if you accidentally enable that possibility, the benefits of having encrypted communication to protect authentication credentials have been trumped by the lazy user who decides passwords are more of a hindrance than a protective measure for him or her. The lazy user still has an encrypted session, without a password, but any user can, and probably will, try to authenticate without a password. Network sniffing is not required in this case, because poor security practices were accidentally in place. Of course, the operating system also would need to allow passwords for this to be real risk, but this is nonetheless demonstrative of the type of care required when selecting several directives for the server provided with OpenSSH.

Every administrator has encountered a user who thinks the rules apply to everyone except for him or her. Your job in planning your OpenSSH implementation is to make sure even the most innovative of users cannot bypass the intended security of your environment. Luckily, with OpenSSH, this is easy to do. The sshd_config file cannot be overridden by the client, therefore if the system administrator controls the sshd_config file, the user has no technical way of preventing the settings from affecting him or her. Of course, the user can still make a case to management about how the rules provided by the system administration team are ridiculous and prevent his or her productivity.

Several questions come into play when deciding what the right choice is for your particular application of OpenSSH. Keep these in mind as you study configuration options, and they will be addressed with best practices toward the end of the chapter in a sample configuration file.

- Do you have environments that require a stricter level of security than others—that is, DMZs, extranets, government contract networks, and so on?

- Are you intending to allow any user on a given system ssh access?

- Do you plan to make use of port forwarding? (Port forwarding is covered in Chapter 7.)

- Does your environment rely on the X-Windows System?

OpenSSH sshd_config

The OpenSSH sshd_config file is found in the configuration directory for OpenSSH along with your host keys and master client configuration file. Most installations place sshd_config in /etc/ssh; however, if you installed from source and did not specify another configuration directory, then the files will be found in /usr/local/etc. The sshd_config file is read at sshd startup time and not read again unless specifically told to by a command-issuing HUP signal, as was discussed earlier.

The sshd_config file should be readable and writable only by the root user. Allowing users to read this file may allow them to search for bypasses and exploits on particular settings. The server configuration file is fairly straightforward to manage. A # indicates a comment, which continues until the end of a line. Keywords are case insensitive, but arguments are not. For example, PermitRootLogin no can be expressed as permitrootlogin no. Also, many features of the OpenSSH server configuration are not used on a regular basis. Some settings are specific to working within certain system configurations, such as the existence of smart cards or Kerberos implementations. Other settings involve only SSH protocol 1, and thus will have little need to be included if protocol 1 is specifically disabled. The sshd_config file provided with the source or from your distribution of OpenSSH is probably a very good starting point from which to build a configuration file. Normally, the configuration files have a number of comments that explain the reasoning behind several of the settings. In the discussion that follows, each directive will appear in alphabetical order. Following the presentation of the directives, I will show you some scenarios in order to help you decide what type of configuration will benefit your environment the most.

AcceptEnv

By default, environment variables provided from the client (using the SendEnv directive) are not parsed. By enabling AcceptEnv, a client can send over environment variables upon connection. This can be convenient for setting $PATH and other variables, but can also lead to a user bypassing some security settings. Each instance of AcceptEnv uses the variable the OpenSSH server should allow as an argument. Multiple variables can be separated by a space or put on separate AcceptEnv lines. Variables can also be expressed with simple regular expressions.

Because this directive requires settings in the client configuration also, a complete example is provided in Chapter 5 in the section "SendEnv."

```
AcceptEnv       PATH
AcceptEnv       DB_HOME
```

AllowGroups

The AllowGroups directive pertains to UNIX/Linux groups normally found in the /etc/group file (or similarly provided entities inside of LDAP/NIS, etc.). The token can grant specific groups usage of the OpenSSH server. Simple regular expressions, such as * and ? characters, can be used to express multiple groups. The argument requires the group to be used by name, not by GID. Multiple groups can be used with spaces between each name. For example, to allow everyone in the users, user, and wheel group access to the OpenSSH server, the following line could be placed into the sshd_config. The *admin allows anyone in the linuxadmin, dbadmin, and ldapadmin groups to use the sshd server.

```
AllowGroups user* wheel *admin
```

AllowTCPForwarding

`AllowTCPForwarding` tells the `sshd` server whether or not it should allow tunneled connections of other TCP protocols over SSH. Tunneling is discussed in detail in Chapter 7, but at this point, keep in mind that tunneling is sometimes a security risk. Malicious protocols or applications can be tunneled, and an administrator will not always be able to detect its behavior, only its existence.

Disabling the forwarding will prevent users from forwarding TCP connections over OpenSSH. Some security organizations prefer to disable forwarding because it is difficult to see what types of connections are established and whether they are persistent.

Many times tunnels are used when crossing firewalls between a low-risk area and a higher-risk network. If a tunnel is used, a user (malicious or otherwise) could use the tunnel to connect to systems in the lower risk area. This behavior is normally not desired because high-risk systems do not initiate communication with low-risk machines.

The `AllowTcpForwarding` directive takes a `yes`/`no` argument:

```
AllowTCPForwarding no
```

AllowUsers

Much like the `AllowGroups` directive, `AllowUsers` specifies, by name, users permitted to connect to the OpenSSH server. Multiple names are delimited using a space. The default is to allow all local users access to `sshd`. Simple regular expressions are allowed. Additionally, a pattern can consist of `user@host`. The user and host are then each checked, which can allow users from controlled machines. This is a nice feature in a large network where the dba account, or something similar, might be different people coming from different machines. This allows you to make that distinction to grant only the proper users access.

```
AllowUsers stahnke  *admin dba@trustedhost
```

AuthorizedKeysFile

The `AuthorizedKeysFile` directive tells the OpenSSH server the location of file containing the public key strings for users to authenticate against. The default location is `$HOME/.ssh/authorized_keys`. The file `authorized_keys2` is also checked to allow for backward compatibility. On legacy systems, sometimes symbolic links are made between `authorized_keys` and `authorized_keys2`, which can help in ensuring authentication via public keys will take place as desired. This directive takes a path relative to the user's home directory as an argument, as the following example shows:

```
AuthorizedKeysFile .ssh/authorized_keys
```

Key authentication is covered in Chapter 6.

Banner

Many organizations require some legal verbiage such as the following before accessing a network or networked device:

```
Warning: Unauthorized access to this system is strictly prohibited.
Use of this system is limited to authorized individuals only.
All activities are monitored.
```

The Banner directive specifies a path to the file that should be displayed before login occurs. Many times it will contain notices about monitoring activity, and usage permitted per security policy, etc. No banner is enabled by default. The Banner directive does not apply to protocol 1. Following is an example of this directive:

```
Banner /etc/issue
```

ChallengeResponseAuthentication

The ChallengeResponseAuthentication directive allows for authentication using one-time passwords that use S/Key algorithms originally invented at Bell Labs. This was designed to make eavesdropping on network transmissions useless, as the authentication credentials expire after a single use. OpenSSH supports S/Key authentication, but eavesdropping on network connections is not a significant concern because OpenSSH encrypts all traffic sent across the network. The possible arguments to this directive are yes and no.

Ciphers

The Ciphers directive specifies which cipher to use for encryption using protocol 2. Multiple ciphers can be specified and separated via commas. The default value for the Ciphers directive is aes128-cbc,3des-cbc,blowfish-cbc,cast128-cbc,arcfour,aes192-cbc,aes256-cbc,aes128-ctr, aes192-ctr,aes256-ctr.

For most practical purposes, the default Ciphers arguments are acceptable. AES is a very fast and strong cipher, which is used by default. The vast array of cipher options is chosen to be compatible with many different types of clients and programming libraries.

Selecting the encryption methods can become a debate with an encryption specialist due to performance gains of certain algorithms and whether or not some encryption methods and strengths can be exported and used internationally. Please remember that in certain parts of the world, lower levels of encryption are required such as 128-bit instead of 256-bit. It is recommended that encryption experts be consulted before implementing international encryption schemes. Take some time to determine what circumstances apply to your organization.

ClientAliveCountMax

The ClientAliveCountMax directive sets the number of attempts the OpenSSH server should make contacting the client before issuing a disconnect. This is dependent on ClientAliveInterval being set. Three attempts is the default value for this directive. In the following example, ten attempts is specified. Multiplying ClientAliveCountMax by ClientAliveInterval will tell you how long a session can be idle before it is terminated. If the result is zero, the session will stay connected indefinitely.

```
ClientAliveCountMax 10
```

With the ClientAliveCountMax and ClientAliveInterval selected, a connection can be nonresponsive for 100 seconds before it is dropped.

ClientAliveInterval

Using protocol 2, the OpenSSH server can send a request for response from the client. If a response is received, the connection continues. If no response is received, sshd will send a request for response ClientAliveCountMax number of times before dropping the connection. By default, the server does not request responses from the client, which is a setting of 0.

Some firewalls drop connections if they are detected as idle. The ClientAliveInterval directive can prevent that because messages and acknowledgements will be sent between the client and the OpenSSH server.

Following is an example of this directive:

```
ClientAliveInterval 10
```

Compression

The Compression directive directs OpenSSH as to whether or not compression is enabled. The arguments are yes (the default, as shown in the syntax example) and no. Enabling this feature entails a small CPU overhead, but it also can be overcome by transferring less data.

```
Compression yes
```

DenyGroups

The DenyGroups directive will deny UNIX groups based on name. If a user is member of a group on this list, the user is not permitted to use sshd. By default, all group members are allowed to log in. This directive recognizes simple regular expressions, and multiple arguments are separated by spaces:

```
Denygroups wheel lp bin ?adguy
```

DenyUsers

DenyUsers will ban specific users based on name. If you have multiple users with the same UID (not a best practice), all of their names need to be specified to eliminate that user. Simple regular expressions are parsed. Multiple arguments are separated by spaces. By default, all users are allowed to use sshd. If a user@host pattern is specified, then user and host are evaluated separately. This can prevent certain users coming from untrusted machines.

If you are using AllowUsers and DenyUsers simultaneously, a wildcard on DenyUsers as shown in the following example will override anything you have on AllowUsers. It is not possible to say DenyUsers *, but AllowUsers root.

```
DenyUsers stahke@badhost.com badguy hack*
```

GatewayPorts

When using forwarding, normally the forwarded connection is only bound to the localhost, because it binds to the loopback address. If gateway ports are specified, remote machines can use a forwarded port on the local system because the forwarded connections bind to all addresses on the machine. This can sometimes defeat the point of tunneling, or it can allow for sophisticated setups, such as remote machines connecting to bastion hosts through firewalls for tunneled connections. The GatewayPorts directive is disabled by default (set to no as the example shows); you can enable it by setting it to yes. Most often, the default is adequate unless a specific application of the technology is in mind. More information on tunnels is provided in Chapter 7.

```
GatewayPorts no
```

GSSAPIAuthentication

The GSSAPI is a relatively new application programming interface (API) that allows for programs to use common mechanisms for authentication. Thus far, most GSSAPI work has been done in conjunction with Active Directory. GSSAPI usage for UNIX systems currently consists of Kerberos implementations. The GSSAPIAuthentication directive is disabled by default and only works with protocol 2.

GSSAPICleanupCredentials

If using GSSAPI, it is a best practice to destroy user credentials that are cached when the user's session ends; otherwise a malicious user could reuse your authentication credentials to pose as another identity. This is done by default. The GSSAPICleanupCredentials directive takes yes/no arguments and applies only to protocol 2.

HostbasedAuthentication

The HostbasedAuthentication directive tells OpenSSH whether or not host-based authentication is permitted via a yes/no argument, as shown in the example that follows. This directive applies only to protocol 2. Because the intention is to derive the maximum security out of OpenSSH, host-based authentication is not recommended unless evaluated thoroughly and the risk accepted. More discussion on host-based authentication occurs in Chapter 6.

```
HostbasedAuthentication no
```

HostKey

The HostKey directive requires a path to the private host key as an argument. By default, the file /etc/ssh/ssh_host_key is used for protocol 1. The files /etc/ssh/ssh_host_rsa_key and /etc/ssh/ssh_host_dsa_key are used for protocol 2. Protection of the host key files is paramount, and OpenSSH will refuse to use host keys that are accessible to the group or world. Multiple host keys are permitted. Protocol 1 uses rsa1 keys. DSA and RSA key algorithms are used in the version 2 implementation of OpenSSH:

```
HostKey /etc/ssh/ssh_host_rsa_key
HostKey /etc/ssh/ssh_host_dsa_key
```

IgnoreRhosts

The `IgnoreRhosts` directive allows an administrator to enhance security by ignoring the legacy `.rhost` file from users. This is a best practice, in case `rsh`/`rlogin` are enabled or could accidentally become enabled.

System wide, `/etc/hosts.equiv` and/or `/etc/ssh/shosts.equiv` are still permitted for use. Once again, it is best practice to shy away from host-based authentication. Secure host-based authentication is covered in Chapter 6.

This directive takes a `yes`/`no` argument and by default is set to `yes`:

```
IgnoreRhosts yes
```

IgnoreUserKnownHosts

The `IgnoreUserKnownHosts` directive is designed to protect against users setting up host-based authentication with hosts other than those set up by the administrator. For host-based authentication to work, a cache of the remote host's public key must exist. If the user's cache is ignored, the system administrator must set up the cache. The default is `no`. For security purposes, it is often best to change this argument to `yes`.

```
IgnoreUserKnownHosts yes
```

KerberosAuthentication

If the `KerberosAuthentication` directive is set to `yes`, sshd `PasswordAuthentication` will take place though the Kerberos Key Distribution Center (KDC). For this to be enabled, Kerberos must be in place. The default is `no`.

KerberosGetAFSToken

When using Kerberos with the Andrew File System (AFS), OpenSSH can access the AFS home directory before authentication completes. The `KereberosGetAFSToken` will enable public key authentication even with the public key stored on a remotely mounted directory. By default, this is set `no`.

KerberosOrLocalPasswd

If Kerberos authentication fails, then other authentication mechanisms will be allowed, such as password authentication, public key authentication, or host-based authentication if the `KereberosOrLocalPasswd` directive is set to `yes`. The default is `yes`.

KerberosTicketCleanup

Much like the `GSSAPICleanupCredentials` directive, the `KerberosTicketCleanup` directive specifies whether or not the authentication ticket stored in cache should be deleted upon session termination. This defaults to `yes`.

KeyRegenerationInterval

In SSH protocol 1, the host key changes at a certain intervals, specified in seconds. By default, 3600 seconds is the interval for the KeyRegenerationInterval directive. The key is not stored on disk; it resides in memory, so it is less likely to be compromised. If the value is 0, the key is not regenerated.

ListenAddress

sshd can be configured to listen to all addresses of a system, or tied to specific addresses and ports using the ListenAddress directive, which requires the argument of an IP address. This directive supports IPv4 and IPv6. The default is for sshd to listen on all addresses. Multiple ListenAddress lines are permitted. For example, these configurations could be used on my workstation (192.168.1.101):

```
# Does not bind to 127.0.0.1
ListenAddress 192.168.1.101
#Only port 22
 ListenAddress 192.168.1.101:22
#Requires DNS or /etc/hosts
ListenAddress rack:22
# All addresses at port specified by the Ports Directive
ListenAddress *
```

Machine names and IP addresses can be used interchangeably. By default, all local addresses listen on the sshd port.

LoginGraceTime

sshd can be configured to drop connection attempts if a successful login has not occurred with the LoginGraceTime parameters. By default, the grace time is 120 seconds, as in the following example. If set to zero, authentication attempts have an unlimited amount of time.

```
LoginGraceTime 120
```

LogLevel

The sshd process is capable of logging at different verbosity levels. Listed from the lowest verbosity to most, the possible arguments for LogLevel are QUIET, FATAL, ERROR, INFO, VERBOSE, DEBUG, DEBUG1, DEBUG2, and DEBUG3. Normally running at the VERBOSE level, as shown in the following syntax line, will provide good amounts of information for the security conscious administrator. DEBUG and DEBUG1 levels are equivalent.

```
LogLevel Verbose
```

MACs

MACs are a type of hash used to verify data including the utilization of a secret key. MACs, or Message Authentication Code algorithms, are verified and computed using the same secret key to prevent nonintended recipients from verifying the message integrity. MACs can be specified inside the sshd_config file. The MACs directive applies only to SSH protocol 2. Different options are available. By default, the MACs directive is set to hmac-md5,hmac-sha1,hmac-ripemd160, hmac-sha1-96,hmac-md5-96.

MaxAuthTries

The MaxAuthTries token is designed to combat a brute-force password attack, or the user who cannot remember his or her password. The number MaxAuthTries takes as an argument will tell sshd how many attempts a connection is allowed to authenticate; after failing MaxAuthTries times, the failed attempts are logged. By default, a user gets six attempts. Oftentimes six attempts is higher than local security policy recommends, so you may want to set this directive as follows:

MaxAuthTries 5

MaxStartups

The MaxStartups directive specifies how many unauthenticated sessions (users attempting to log in via passwords, keys, etc.) sshd will allow at once. By default, it is set to 10, as shown in the syntax line. Other attempts to authenticate will not be honored until one of the previous sessions authenticates, closes, or times out.

MaxStartups 10

PasswordAuthentication

By default, OpenSSH allows password authentication to occur. Sometimes, especially for very secure systems, PasswordAuthentication is set too, because normally public key authentication is thought to be much more secure than traditional password-based authentication. If setting this to directive to no, ensure some other form of authentication such as public key authentication is enabled.

PasswordAuthentication yes

PermitEmptyPasswords

By default, the OpenSSH server does not allow empty passwords. If the PermitEmptyPasswords directive is set to yes, the operating system must also be configured to allow for empty passwords. If you are using empty passwords, you are foregoing some basic security principles, such as integrity and perhaps confidentially, because you might not know who is working with data or what they have done to it. Usage of empty passwords is discouraged:

PermitEmptyPasswords no

PermitRootLogin

The PermitRootLogin directive offers special behavior for the root account outside of AllowUsers and DenyUsers. Root's login can be controlled using four possible arguments:

1. `yes`: This allows root to log in via any form of allowable authentication, including passwords. In most operating systems, the root account does not lock after a number of unsuccessful authentication attempts. This can leave your system open to brute-force password attacks against the root account.

2. `no`: Many administrators feel that `no` is the best argument for `PermitRootLogin`. Allowing root to log in using most services is generally a bad idea. For auditing purposes, normally a user should log in using a standard account and then run `su` or `sudo` to invoke root-level access.

3. `without-password`: The `without-password` argument allows root to log in, but using methods that do not use passwords. Public key authentication, for example, is still permitted. This allows for scripting and access to the root account. Keys of appropriate length are extremely difficult to crack, thus still securing the root account. Allowing root to log in using keys via SSH still does not mean direct root access should be available in the form of other services.

4. `Forced-commands-only`: This implies public key authentication with the `command=` option in root's public key. Keys are covered in more detail in Chapter 6. Using this directive can restrict the root account to only running specific commands such as scripts or reporting mechanisms.

PermitUserEnvironment

`PermitUserEnvironment` tells `sshd` whether or not it should allow a user to specify a user environment within `$HOME/.ssh/environment` or through the `environment=` option inside of an `authorized_keys` file.

Passing environment variables can sometimes be a security risk or cause problems, if usernames differ between systems or environments/shells differ greatly between systems. Additionally, sometimes environment variables contain sensitive information such as which sockets to connect to for `ssh-agent` authentication. Therefore, although the `PermitUserEnvironment` directive takes arguments of yes/no, this directive defaults to no, as you see in this syntax line:

```
PermitUserEnvironment no
```

PidFile

The `PidFile` directive takes a path to a file that will contain the process identifier (PID) of the `sshd` daemon. By default, on most systems, this is `/var/run/sshd.pid`. The PID file can be used in scripts to see if `sshd` is running or to kill `sshd` by issuing `kill `cat /var/run/sshd.pid``.

```
PidFile /var/run/sshd.pid
```

Port

By default, `sshd` listens on TCP port 22. However, it is possible to configure the server to listen on multiple ports by using the `Port` directive. This can be useful if only certain points are permitted through a firewall, or if different `sshd` server configurations are running on different ports (perhaps one for the administrators and one for the end users).

For example, if sshd listening on port 22 and 99 is desired, the following options may be set:

```
Port 22
Port 99
```

Be careful when using multiple port statements in conjunction with the ListenAddress directive. If you specify ports inside of ListenAddress, they can conflict and take precedence over the port statement. Using a -p on the command line when starting sshd will also allow for port specifications for that instance of the daemon.

PrintLastLog

Setting PrintLastLog to yes will cause the user's last login time to be displayed on the screen at the time of login. This is enabled by default, as in the syntax line that follows, because it can empower the user to check for security. A user might be alerted if he or she sees that the last time he or she supposedly logged in was 3 a.m. last Saturday (if this is not the user's normal behavior).

```
PrintLastLog yes
```

PrintMotd

If the PrintMotd directive is set to yes as shown in the syntax line, sshd will print /etc/motd (Message of the Day) when an interactive login occurs. The default is to print /etc/motd. Sometimes the contents of /etc/motd are displayed via other configuration files, so displaying it twice could be redundant.

```
PrintMotd yes
```

Protocol

The Protocol directive allows you to specify which version of the SSH protocol to use. While by default protocol 1 and 2 are supported, using only protocol 2, as shown in the syntax example, is strongly recommended. Protocol 1 has several known exploits that are believed to be fixed now, but most material and documentation recommends against its usage. It also has some flaws that are inherent to the protocol, and not fixable.

Specifying 2,1 is the same as 1,2 for this directive. Protocol 2 is the primary focus of this book and most modern OpenSSH documentation. Protocol 1 exists for backward compatibility and is still sometimes seen for communication with embedded systems and network appliances.

```
Protocol 2
```

PubkeyAuthentication

The PubkeyAuthentication directive, which takes a yes/no value, tells the OpenSSH whether or not public key authentication should be used. The default is yes, as shown in the following example, and should be left as such. Properly managed keys are more secure and convenient than passwords. This option is only applicable to protocol 2.

```
PubkeyAuthentication yes
```

RhostsRSAAuthentication

The RhostsRSAAuthentication directive, which applies to protocol 1 only, specifies whether .rhosts or /etc/hosts.equiv (associated with the Berkeley r-utilities) authentication is allowed. This setting defaults to no, as shown in the syntax line example, and normally should be left at this setting. Setting RhostsRSAAuthentication to yes could open the systems to potentially weak authentication methods if rlogin/rsh becomes enabled, because they use the same files for authentication.

   If you are using host-based authentication, using protocol 2 is a best practice. Host-based authentication utilizing protocol 2 is discussed in Chapter 6.

```
RhostsRSAAuthentication no
```

RSAAuthentication

If the RSAAuthentication directive is enabled (set to yes), RSA authentication is allowed via protocol 1. RSAAuthentication is set to yes by default, but if protocol 1 is not enabled, this option will have no bearing on the OpenSSH configuration.

ServerKeyBits

ServerKeyBits defines the key length for the protocol 1 host key. By default, the bit length is 768, with a 512-bit minimum. If protocol 1 is disabled, this setting can be left alone. If protocol 1 is enabled, using 1024-bit or stronger keys is encouraged.

StrictModes

The StrictModes directive determines whether sshd should check permissions on the user's files and home directory before allowing a public key authenticated login. This check is designed to nullify authorized_keys files that are left open for group/world members to insert their public keys into. Leaving StrictModes in place is a best practice, as without it, users can assume another user's identity and bypass several security mechanisms. StrictModes by default is yes:

```
StrictModes yes
```

Subsystem

By default, no subsystems, applications relying on the SSH protocol for transport, are utilized from the source version OpenSSH. To implement sftp (Secure File Transfer Protocol) inside of sshd, you must specify the subsystem name and subsystem path. Mine is in /usr/local/libexec, but this will be wherever your libexec directory is configured on your system. The Subsystem directive applies to protocol 2 only. Most binary distributions of OpenSSH have the sftp-server enabled:

```
Subsystem       sftp    /usr/libexec/sftp-server
```

SyslogFacility

Logging is important for connectivity daemons to see who is using services, monitoring machine utilization, change control, and troubleshooting. The SyslogFacility directive takes syslog's facilities as arguments. By default, sshd logs to the AUTH facility, as shown in the syntax example. In some Linux systems, this is set to AUTHPRIV, which puts the authentication information in a log only readable to the root user. Argument possibilities are DAEMON, USER, AUTH, and LOCAL1–LOCAL7.

SyslogFacility AUTH

■ **Tip** When changing the facility, be sure to check on what else is using that facility, as having sshd information in the boot.log file does not often make sense.

TCPKeepAlive

If TCPKeepAlive is enabled (the default), sshd will send keep-alive requests to the clients. If they are being sent, a network glitch will cause the session to terminate. If they are not being sent, the session might terminate on the client side, but the server will still have resources allocated to the client process. That scenario can cause unnecessary resource constraints on the system running sshd. When set to yes, as in the following example, the server will properly terminate an abruptly ended session from the client side, such as a client-side crash or network disconnection:

TCPKeepAlive yes

UseDNS

If the UseDNS directive is enabled (the default), sshd will attempt to resolve the host name for the remote IP address, and then ensure that hostname maps back to the IP address that is attempting the connection. This is a security feature to prevent rogue clients from connecting on a network, because oftentimes DHCP address spaces do not have reverse records in DNS. This type of setting restricts the client usage of sshd to those with a reverse record. Of course, this setting assumes DNS is working accurately and reverse records are found for all relevant IP addresses.

UseDNS yes

UseLogin

UseLogin is another yes/no directive that defaults to no, as shown in the syntax example. /bin/login or /usr/bin/login is the normal way in which most legacy connectivity services allow users to access system. sshd provides its own mechanism, which is more sophisticated and can allow X11 forwarding over the SSH protocol. The default value of no should be used in most cases. If other legacy applications are being used, perhaps through graphical user interfaces, sometimes `UseLogin` is required. If SSH is being used to execute commands remotely, even with `UseLogin` set to yes, login is not used.

`UseLogin no`

UsePAM

The `UsePAM` directive, which takes `yes`/`no` values, determines whether PAM (Pluggable Authentication Module) authentication should be used. If your system requires PAM, OpenSSH should be configured with the `--use-pam` option and the `UsePAM` directive set to `yes`, as shown in the syntax line. I normally build with PAM support and enable it in my configuration files for Linux systems. Other systems that do not use PAM should set the `UsePAM` directive to `no`. Binary packages of OpenSSH from UNIX/Linux vendors normally have PAM configured to match the requirements of the specific system.

`UsePAM yes`

UsePrivilegeSeparation

Privilege separation is a nice feature that lets each child process of `sshd` run as the user invoking it rather than root. This practice should protect against attacks trying to gain root access via the OpenSSH server because the attempts can be made only against a standard user process. The default to the `UsePrivilegeSeparation` directive is `yes`, and should be enabled:

`UsePrivilegeSeparation yes`

X11DisplayOffset

When forwarding X11 connections, `sshd` sets the display variable to something like `localhost:10.0`. If you run more than ten X11 servers on the machine running `sshd`, increment the `X11DisplayOffset` variable as needed. More information about X11 forwarding is in Chapter 7.

`X11DisplayOffset 10`

X11Forwarding

X11 forwarding is one of the great benefits of OpenSSH if X-Windows applications must be used. When set to `yes`, as in the syntax example, `X11Forwarding` will establish a tunnel for X11 traffic over an SSH connection. This will encrypt X11 traffic and automatically set your `$DISPLAY` variable. By default, `X11Forwarding` is not enabled. If your organization does not rely on X11 technology, it is best to leave it that way. If `UseLogin` is enabled, this directive will automatically be disabled. X11 forwarding is discussed in detail in Chapter 7.

`X11Forwarding yes`

■**Caution** As with other environment variables, a user can reset his or her $DISPLAY variable. If set to a valid address such as rack:0.1, then encryption has been defeated. Many users automatically set their $DISPLAY variable in their .profile. Additionally, a user could set their $DISPLAY to another user's tunnel and .Xauthority file, and display X11 applications on an X server that is not their workstation.

X11UseLocalhost

Setting the X11UseLocalhost directive to yes will allow remote connections to use the forwarded X11 connection because it binds to the wildcard address. Some older X11 clients require a name other than localhost. This should normally be left at the default (enabled).

```
X11UseLocalhost yes
```

XAuthLocation

The XAuthLocation directive takes a path as an argument to the xauth program. Normally, xauth is found at /usr/X11R6/bin/xauth, as shown in the following example, which is the default on many Linux systems. The xauth program is used by OpenSSH to authorize the X11 clients. Running configure will normally find the xauth program before compiling OpenSSH.

```
XAuthLocation /usr/X11R6/bin/xauth
```

Building the sshd_config File

As mentioned before, the provided sshd_config file, whether it is from the OpenSSH source or from your UNIX/Linux vendor, is normally a good place to start. From there, analyze your needs, and decide what directive arguments make the most sense for your environment.

Keep in mind this file can be changed, and sshd can be reread without dropping connections. My standard OpenSSH configuration file looks like this; however, it often changes to suit specific needs.

```
# sshd_config file
# VERSION 1.0
# Network Information
Port 22
#Disables protocol 1
Protocol 2

# Protocol 2 HostKeys
HostKey /etc/ssh/ssh_host_rsa_key
HostKey /etc/ssh/ssh_host_dsa_key

# Logging
# On Linux
SyslogFacility AUTHPRIV
```

```
# Other UNIX
#  SyslogFacility AUTH
#shows key fingerprints
LogLevel VERBOSE
# Users/groups
AllowUsers *
#Deny Users badguy
AllowGroups *
#DenyGroups badgroup

# Authentication:
LoginGraceTime 120
MaxAuthTries 5
PermitEmptyPasswords no
PasswordAuthentication yes
#public keys allowed for root login
PermitRootLogin without-password
# Users must have good permissions on .ssh and authorized_keys
StrictModes yes
# protocol 1
RSAAuthentication no
#recommended authentication method
PubkeyAuthentication yes
AuthorizedKeysFile      .ssh/authorized_keys
ChallengeResponseAuthentication no
# Do not have Kerberos environment
KerberosAuthentication no
#GSSAPI not needed
GSSAPIAuthentication no
#Configured --with-pam
UsePAM yes
UseLogin no

# Host-based Authentication
#protocol 1
RhostsRSAAuthentication no
#protocol 2
HostbasedAuthentication no
#must be set by system Admin
IgnoreUserKnownHosts yes
# Squash Rhosts

IgnoreRhosts yes

# FORWARDING
# I like to know what is being forwarded
AllowTcpForwarding no
```

```
GatewayPorts no
X11Forwarding yes
X11DisplayOffset 10
X11UseLocalhost yes
# Environment
PrintMotd yes
PrintLastLog yes
Banner /etc/issue
AcceptEnv PATH

# System Settings
UsePrivilegeSeparation yes
PermitUserEnvironment no
Compression yes
PidFile /var/run/sshd.pid
#set to no if no reverse records
UseDNS yes
Subsystem       sftp    /usr/libexec/openssh/sftp-server
MACs hmac-md5,hmac-sha1,hmac-ripemd160,hmac-sha1-96,hmac-md5-96
# Leave ciphers at default values, will not mention

# Client Connection
TCPKeepAlive yes
ClientAliveInterval 5
ClientAliveCountMax 3
MaxStartups 10
```

The configuration file I normally use tries to provide security and usability at a decent trade-off. For example, I allow X11 forwarding because I know users like to use X11 applications for backups/restores and modeling applications; however, I do not allow TCP forwarding because I would like to know about the tunnels being requested, and I can set those up for a user.

To make this file readable for coworkers and auditors, I try to break the directives into sections. Most directives are explicitly specified. I leave Kerberos and GSSAPI directives alone after specifying that I am not using them. Ciphers I also leave alone, because some clients prefer different ciphers over others.

Different scenarios could cause this file to be heavily modified. For example, if host-based authentication is allowed, several directives in this file must change. Allowing protocol 1 connections also would cause me to include more protocol 1–specific directives. Normally, I do not include protocol 1 directives because they create confusion. The client configuration, however, does need to have protocol directives in it if the possibility of connecting to a protocol 1 client exists.

■**Note** The server configuration, in this state, will allow for nearly every client to connect to the sshd processes without issue. For OpenSSH to accept clients from Microsoft Windows GUIs such as PuTTY or WinSCP, no additional configuration is necessary. If a client is specifically for protocol 1 only, however, the connection will not work.

Ensure Security of sshd_config

After creating, testing, and editing the sshd_config file, remember once again to check the ownership and permissions of the file. It is also a good idea to have a digest (SHA-1 or MD5) of the file, so you can quickly tell whether the file has been tampered with in any way. The following examples must be done as root:

```
rack: / # ls -l /etc/ssh/sshd_config
-rw-------  1 root root 1817 Mar 01 14:52 sshd_config
rack: / # md5sum /etc/ssh/sshd_config
b8f83d7c556fd5b37898f350e1c65ebc  /etc/ssh/sshd_config
```

After recording the MD5 sum, its best to move that MD5 sum digest to a safe remote location. Additionally, a pristine sshd_config file should be kept somewhere not in production for verification purposes. I normally run processes that check against that MD5 sum and ensure the file is correct. If it is not, I follow up with administration staff to see why it is not. Normally, a change was made for application migration or debugging. I then overwrite the configuration file with my good one.

Managing the OpenSSH server can seem difficult at first, but in time it will become quite simplified. With the OpenSSH server, you can reload configuration files without dropping connections, so simple changes can be made without impacting end users. The ability to run in debug mode and validate syntax of configuration changes is also a feature of sshd that administrators should be sure to take advantage of. Testing changes in directives is the most daunting task, but hopefully going forward you will have a good foundation of what those entail.

Summary

Building the server configuration file takes time and testing to best fit your environment. After creating a server configuration that is workable, it is time to build the client configuration. Chapter 5 covers the command-line ssh client in the same level of detail presented here about the server. The client settings need to be carefully examined to ensure that users are not circumventing your security design. In the later chapters that discuss forwarding and key-based authentication, any deviation from the server configuration file presented in this chapter is shown. Chapter 6 will get you started with key-based authentication that hopefully will enable you to have new authentication practices to securely and efficiently manage your systems and OpenSSH services. Chapter 7 covers forwarding and tunneling, including X11 forwarding.

sshd from OpenSSH provides a practical and secure alternative to the legacy protocol connectivity daemons such as rshd and telnetd, and should ultimately lead to their elimination on your network. This transition will not occur in a single night, but with proper planning and utilizing the best possible directives in your configuration files, you can make the implementation a success.

Hopefully, your OpenSSH server configuration can be added with no compromises for backward compatibility and applications that still rely on .rhost files. If you are running into issues with older batch jobs, scripts, and applications, check out Chapter 9, which covers scripting with ssh.

CHAPTER 5

■ ■ ■

The OpenSSH Client

In Chapter 3, I discussed OpenSSH's file layout and structure. Chapter 4 built upon this knowledge, covering server configuration, including the all-important sshd_config file. Utilizing the knowledge gained in those chapters, it is now time for a formal introduction to the OpenSSH client.

The goals of this chapter are to familiarize you with the OpenSSH client commands and the configuration files they read from, and to help you construct client configuration files (ssh_config) for both the system-wide settings' default client and also your personal account(s).

OpenSSH Client Order of Precedence

The SSH client consists of three main commands: ssh, scp, and sftp. Each of these programs inherits settings from the command line, the user's specific settings, and system-wide settings, in that order. This can be a bit confusing at first glance, but in reality it is no different from command aliases in .profile.

If in /etc/profile you alias df to df -h because you like to see output displayed in gigabytes/megabytes rather than 1K blocks,[1] anyone on the system who enters df actually invokes df -h. However, if a user, perhaps comfortable with traditional df, aliases df to df -k in his or her .profile, then when he or she types df, df -k is actually invoked. On top of that, the user can execute df --sync from the command line, which will actually run df -k --sync.

When using the OpenSSH client programs, the user is also allowed to override the system-wide default settings. OpenSSH will set the value for a directive only once. After it has been set, it will not be changed, even if another file has a different value. Options set via command-line options take precedence over a user's local ssh configuration stored in $HOME/.ssh/config, which supersedes the system-wide ssh_config file controlled by the system administrator.

The order of precedence for the OpenSSH client program configuration is as follows:

1. Command-line options

2. Local configurations inside $HOME/.ssh/config

3. System-wide configuration file

Keep in mind that in this configuration, ultimately users have control of the way their client performs and behaves. The precedence is set in a first-match hierarchy. If an option is set on the command line, options in the local file or system-wide file will not be taken into account.

---

1. df on Linux systems provides output in 1K blocks unless the environment variable POSIXLY_CORRECT exists. If it does, Linux reverts to traditional 512-byte blocks.

The Client Commands

The three main commands from a client perspective of OpenSSH are ssh, scp, and sftp. These commands are quite similar in function and syntax to telnet/rsh, rcp, and ftp, respectively; however, the security of host-based authentication, user-based authentication, and encryption make these alternatives very promising.

■**Note** For users accustomed to rlogin, a feature of OpenSSH called slogin is available. slogin is normally a symbolic link to the ssh binary. This can sometimes ease conversions for legacy scripts to allow administrators to use ssh when converting from rsh and slogin when converting from rlogin. This can aid in readability of scripts as well as comprehension for users.

---

ssh

ssh, or the client packaged with OpenSSH, is used as a connectivity tool for remote interactive sessions similar to telnet, only more secure. The same command, ssh, also replaces the functionality of rsh. When invoked from the command line, the ssh command supports several options. While oftentimes ssh is executed with no or few options, executing more complex tasks can require that you specify quite a few command-line options. In this section, the discussion will begin with the most common options for ssh, followed by escape sequences, and then conclude with an introduction to the less commonly used options for completeness' sake. Keep in mind that the scp and sftp utilities use ssh to provide the transport mechanism for them. Therefore, the command-line options used with ssh are similar to those used with scp and sftp, but not identical. Later in the chapter, I cover the scp and sftp options in detail as well.

Common Usage

The ssh client is used in a variety of ways. I introduce you to each of those methods in this section.

Interactive Session

To initiate an interactive session, simply invoke the ssh command to connect to the remote host. This will create a terminal emulation session similar to a telnet session. Environment variables are defined, and the look and feel is virtually indistinguishable from a typical telnet session. A typical ssh session might look something like this:

```
stahnke@rack:~> ssh stahnke@www
Password:
stahnke@www:~> ls
BannerBott.psd  bigfile        file             TRcorner.psd
Banner.psd      BlockRTop.psd  HeaderBottom.psd
stahnke@rack: ~> set
BASH=/bin/bash
BASH_ARGC=()
BASH_ARGV=()
BASH_LINENO=()
BASH_SOURCE=()
```

```
BASH_VERSINFO=([0]="3" [1]="00" [2]="14" [3]="1" [4]="release"
[5]="i386-redhat-linux-gnu")
BASH_VERSION='3.00.14(1)-release'
COLORS=/etc/DIR_COLORS.xterm
COLUMNS=80

...
```

Note Specifying the username is optional if you are logging to a remote system with the same username from the localhost. Alternatively, a -l with a remote username can be specified if the user@host syntax is not desired.

Remote Commands

To replace the functionality of rsh, append your argument as the remote command, which is the last argument of the ssh connection statement. The previous ssh connection command string looked like this:

```
stahnke@rack:~> ssh stahnke@www
```

To execute commands remotely, the noninteractive remote command is appended to the end of this statement. For example, the following demonstrates how to execute the uptime command on server www without starting an interactive session and entering uptime:

```
stahnke@rack:~> ssh stahnke@www uptime
Password:
 11:15pm  up 111 days  9:52,  4 users,  load average: 0.62, 0.12, 0.00
stahnke@rack: ~> echo $?
0
```

To verify the command executed properly, I queried for the command's return code, which was zero because the command completed successfully. Keep in the mind the return code is for the ssh connection, not the remote program or command. If the ssh session is unable to execute the remote command, an error code of 127 is returned. These error codes can be used to verify success during scripting of SSH connectivity. For instance, the following command fails:

```
stahnke@www: ~> ssh rack test.sh
Password:
bash: test.sh: command not found
stahnke@www: ~> echo $?
127
```

When I try to execute test.sh, which resides in /home/stahnke/bin, the command fails and the return code is as expected.

Notice on the successful ssh command with uptime the path was not included, and it still ran fine. If the script was in /home/stahnke/bin, however, the task would fail. This is because environment variables are configured in a very basic way when ssh is used remotely. Not all files sourced upon interactive login are read. To see what the $PATH variable contains on a remote command, you can execute this:

```
stahnke@www: ~> ssh root@rack echo \$PATH
Password:
/usr/bin:/bin:/usr/sbin:/sbin:/usr/local/bin:/usr/sbin:/sbin:
/usr/local/sbin
```

This shows the path for remote commands. The \ character instructs the local shell not to process the $ and pass it to the remote shell. The default $PATH for remote command execution is set when the configure script is run before you compile OpenSSH. If you installed OpenSSH as a binary package, $PATH has been set for you by your vendor. The results on your systems may vary.

Interactive commands cannot be used in this fashion. For example, if a user tries to remotely launch a shell, such as bash, the session still requires input. This means that commands can be run by typing them as you normally would in bash, but no environment variables or aliases are defined. Additionally, no prompt is set, so shell navigation is difficult.

```
stahnke@rack: ~> ssh www bash
Password:
uptime
 13:18pm up 111 days,  9:58,  1 user,  load average: 0.10, 0.04, 0.01
which ssh
/usr/bin/ssh
exit
stahnke@rack: ~>
```

If interactive sessions are desired, simply use ssh to get to the system and begin working from there.

```
stahnke@rack: ~> ssh www
Password:
stahnke@www ~> vi myfile.pl
...
stahnke@www ~> exit
```

ssh Acting As a Transport Mechanism

ssh supports secure connectivity between hosts. Sometimes this connectivity can be used to accomplish tasks over the network that seemed rather difficult before. For example, if I need to copy an ISO image on my local system and copy it to a remote location, I can execute the following:

```
stahnke@www:~> dd if=/dev/cdrom |ssh rack dd of=my_cd.iso
```

This will use the dd command to dump the contents of /dev/cdrom to the ssh pipe and then execute dd on the remote host rack to create the ISO file. Of course, this could take quite a bit of time depending on network speed, but this illustrates the ability of ssh to understand pipes also. Chapter 9 has additional discussion of using pipes with ssh for network file transfers.

Escape Sequences

ssh possesses the ability to escape from an interactive session, much like an ! will provide in many FTP clients. When connected to remote hosts, if you wish to execute a command from the localhost, beginning the line with ~ (or whatever you have defined as the EscapeChar in your ssh_config) will invoke escape sequence processing.

Note In this material, the client configuration will be referred to as the ssh_config file. In a typical OpenSSH setup, ssh_config is the system-wide configuration file and $HOME/.ssh/config is the user client setup. The same options are allowed in either, but for simplicity's sake, the configuration file will be referred to as ssh_config.

Assuming the default tilde (~) is the chosen escape character, the escape sequences that can be used via the ssh client are as follows:

~.: This sequence will cause your current SSH session to disconnect. Normally, I prefer exit, or Ctrl+D, because I can get a visual confirmation of what is happening in my session.

~^Z: As with most UNIX processes, this causes the current ssh session to move into the background. To resume the session, use the fg command.

~#: This character sequence will show the forwarded connection that is currently in use. Forwarding is covered in Chapter 7, but here is an example:

```
stahnke@rack: ~> ssh -L12345:localhost:80 www
Password:
stahnke@www ~> ~#
The following connections are open:
  #2 client-session (t4 r0 i0/0 o0/0 fd 6/7 cfd -1)
stahnke@www ~>
```

~&: Under normal circumstances, when an ssh session is terminated, all programs spawned in that session are closed, such as forwarded connections or X-Windows programs. However, with the ~& escape sequence, the session can terminate without closing previously established X-Windows applications and forwarded connections. This is useful if you are tunneling X-Windows over SSH and have a few windows open. When you close the terminal windows that spawned your X-Windows ungracefully, memory and processing issues can occur. This command-line option will ensure a graceful termination of those connections.

~?: The escape sequences OpenSSH offers are not always easy to remember. Luckily, using this option will display all supported escape sequences on the system you are connected to.

~C: The ~C option allows a user already connected via SSH to open an ssh> prompt. From this prompt, forwarded connections can be created or cancelled. This is a nice feature if you are already connected to a remote system and do not want to reconnect to establish a forwarded connection. Here is an example. Entering help at the ssh> prompt will print out the syntax to forward a connection or cancel it.

```
stahnke@rack: ~> ~C
ssh> help
Commands:
```

```
              -Lport:host:hostport    Request local forward
              -Rport:host:hostport    Request remote forward
              -KRhostport             Cancel remote forward
stahnke@rack: ~> ~C
ssh> -L12345:localhost:80
Forwarding port.
```

~R: The SSH protocol provides encrypted communication; however, if you think your session is being tampered with or just want to use a new key, this sequence, assuming the client and server support it, will cause the currently connected session to have the symmetric encryption keys renegotiated. This is only supported in SSH protocol version 2.

ssh Command-line Options

The rest of the available ssh command-line options are provided here for reference. While the man pages offer a fairly straightforward description of many options, this discussion is aimed at showing you the important options for interactive command capability along the lines of both telnet and rsh. Many options for the ssh command can be specified on the command line or in an ssh_config file, and I point out, where appropriate, which options fall into this category.

-1

This command-line option requires ssh to use protocol 1. This is useful for backward compatibility, perhaps to legacy embedded devices. Inside the ssh_config file a line declared as follows will cause the same behavior:

```
Protocol 1
```

-2

This option forces the ssh client to use only SSH protocol version 2. For security practices, protocol 2 is recommended as the primary means of communication. The OpenSSH server (sshd) can be forced to use protocol 2, therefore implying all connections are protocol 2. However, if the option is open, using the -2 command-line option can only increase your security level. This option can also be set inside the ssh_config file like so:

```
Protocol 2
```

-4

-4 will require the ssh client to use IPv4 addresses only. This option can be set in the ssh_config file as shown here:

```
AddressFamily inet
```

-6

-6 requires the ssh client to use IPv6 addresses only. This option can be set in the ssh_config file like so:

```
AddressFamily inet6
```

-A

The -A option specifically allows agent forwarding. This can be specified in the ssh_config file with the line that follows. Authentication agents deal with public key authentication and are explained more thoroughly in Chapter 6.

```
ForwardAgent yes
```

-a

The -a options specifically bars agent forwarding from occurring, even if allowed in your ssh_config file. This can be useful during scripting or troubleshooting, as agents add one more layer of debugging and complexity to an SSH connection. See Chapter 6 for details. This option can be declared in the ssh_config file as follows:

```
ForwardAgent no
```

-b bind_address

Binding addresses are defined to specify the network interface to connect to remotely. This is useful in environments with many IP addresses, such as web server environments or clustered systems.

-C

To compress all data moving to and from your session, use the -C option. Some argue that compression causes too much overhead and slows down the overall speed of SSH. Yet others argue that transferring less data can make up for the overhead incurred by compression. Compression is disabled by default; leaving it off will probably make the speed closer to that of rsh, unless you are using slow connections such as those through modems. Keep in mind that enabling compression for the daemon via the sshd_config file only means that compression is allowed, not enabled. This option can be set on the client side in the ssh_config like so:

```
Compression yes
```

-c cipher-name

To select which cipher (encryption methods) should be used in your SSH connectivity session, use the -c option on the command line. Several ciphers are available for use, but 3DES (triple-des) is used by default. Blowfish is another cipher option that is very secure and speedy. DES is also supported but should not be used unless legacy integration prevents the use of a stronger cipher. Ciphers are selectable in the ssh_config file using the Ciphers directive. Multiple choices for ciphers can be selected for protocol 2.

-D port

When using SOCKS, which is commonly employed to allow connectivity across firewalls, the -D option allows dynamic application-level port forwarding. This occurs by creating a socket listening to the port locally and forwarding connections to that port over SSH. The protocol of the connection is used to determine on which port, remotely, the connection should be established. SOCKS version 4 and SOCKS version 5 protocols are allowed. Dynamic port allocation causes the SSH client to act as a SOCKS server. Only root can forward privileged ports (< 1024). Chapter 7 covers forwarding in more detail.

-e character

The -e option will override the default ~ character and set the specified character as the escape character. The escape sequences described earlier will then be initiated with the specified character. Setting the character to none disables escape sequences.

-F config_file

If a different configuration for this particular session is desired, using the -F option to specify another configuration file is a way to establish different parameters for the session. When the -F option is used, the system-wide configuration file for the client is ignored. As an example, for some scripts different configuration options are often set to handle errors more appropriately. In those scripts, the -F option is used to source a configuration file other than the default at $HOME/.ssh/config.

-f

If you want to run ssh commands in the background, but also want to require a passphrase or password to do so, the -f option will enable this task. This option implies a -n also. As an example, if an X11 server is listening on my workstation, I could run

```
stahnke@rack: ~>  ssh -X -f www xterm
```

This will cause an xterm from my host www to be displayed on the local desktop. My command-line session will connect to www in the background. My X connection is also encrypted using this method, thus adding a nice layer of security for X-Windows applications. X11 forwarding is covered in Chapter 7.

-g

When forwarding connections, normally only the localhost can connect to the forwarded host. If a scenario occurs where the remote host needs to connect to the forwarded connection, you need to use the -g option (which is covered in more detail in Chapter 7). This option can be set in the ssh_config file like so:

```
GatewayPorts no
```

-I smartcard_device

If smart-card devices are in use, the -I option will allow you to point the ssh client to the device that reads the smart card for a user's RSA private key.

-i identity_file

The identity file contains the private key for RSA or DSA key pairs. By default, this file is named $HOME/.ssh/identity when using SSH protocol version 1, or $HOME/.ssh/id_rsa and $HOME/.ssh/id_dsa when using SSH protocol version 2. These identities can be specified in the ssh_config file using the IdentityFile directive as follows:

```
IdentityFile ~/.ssh/identity
IdentityFile ~/.ssh/id_rsa
IdentityFile ~/.ssh/id_dsa
```

-k

If using GSSAPI, -k will disable credential forwarding.

-L port:host:hostport

When forwarding a connection, the -L option specifies the local (client-side) system is to connect a local port to a remote port over a secured connection. This is covered in Chapter 7 in greater detail. Local forwarding can also be set up in the ssh_config file using the LocalForward directive.

As an example, the remote server www is running a telnet server, but I do not want to use telnet in its normal unencrypted state. To encrypt that connection, I can execute the following:

```
stahnke@rack: ~> ssh -L12345:localhost:23 www
password:
stahnke@www: ~>
```

In another window, I can then telnet to port 12345 on the localhost (from rack) and end up talking to the telnet server on www, all the while encrypting the traffic.

```
stahnke@rack: ~> telnet localhost 12345
Trying 127.0.0.1...
Connected to localhost (127.0.0.1).
Escape character is '^]'.
login: stahnke
Password:
stahnke@www: ~>
```

-l login_name

This specifies the name of the connecting user. The -l user and user@host functionality are identical. The option is also configurable using the user directive in ssh_config, and in the user's individual $HOME/.ssh/config file, on a per-remote-host basis. During the discussion of ssh_config later in this chapter, I provide examples of accounts having different remote usernames.

-M

This enables master mode for the client when connection sharing is enabled. An example of this behavior is provided later in the chapter when ssh_config is discussed in detail.

-m mac_spec

This specifies the MAC (Message Authentication Code) algorithms to be used. This option only applies to protocol 2.

-N

When forwarding connections, the -N option can be used so that no remote command is needed. This option is only available when using SSH protocol 2.

```
stahnke@rack: ~/.ssh> ssh -f -N -L 12345:localhost:23 www
password:
stahnke@rack: ~/.ssh> telnet localhost 12345
```

```
Trying 127.0.0.1...
Connected to localhost (127.0.0.1).
Escape character is '^]'.
login: stahnke
Password:
stahnke@www: ~> hostname
www
```

This example forwards my connection to localhost port 12345 to the telnet services on www, all while encrypted. Only one terminal window is required to perform this task when using the -N option.

-n

This command-line option tells ssh to redirect input from the /dev/null device, thus not allowing stdin to be used. To run ssh in the background, -n is commonly used. This is similar to the -f option, although the -n option will not work properly if password or passphrase input is required.

-o option

Any option allowed in the ssh_config file can be specified on the command line using the -o option. This is useful for options that do not have a dedicated command-line option such as BatchMode. The following example failed because batch mode is enabled and public key authentication is not set up. Multiple -o options are permitted.

```
stahnke@rack: ~> ssh -o "BatchMode yes" www
Permission denied (publickey,password).
```

-p port

This specifies which port on the remote host the ssh client should connect to. This option can be set up in the ssh_config file per host by using the Port directive like so:

```
Port 22
```

-q

The -q option enables quiet mode, which suppresses error messages. In the newer versions of OpenSSH, it also will suppress the login banner if one is present. This option is useful in scripts. It can also cause problems because no diagnostic messages will be received if authentication fails for any reason. If you are concerned with suppressing banners only, creating a $HOME/ .hushlogin file on the remote server will also suppress banners without suppressing SSH diagnostic messages.

-R port:host:hostport

When forwarding ports remotely, the -R option is used. Forwarding ports remotely entails specifying a port on the remote system to be forwarded to a port on the local system. To forward the telnet server on www using port 54321 on rack, I can execute the following from www:

```
stahnke@www: ~> ssh -f -N -R54321:www:23 rack
password:
```

Remote forwarding can also be specified in the ssh_config file. IPv6 syntax is available by using the / character instead of :. Here is an example configuration in the ssh_config file:

```
RemoteForward 54321 rack:23
```

-s

The -s option can be used to invoke a subsystem (program requiring SSH for transport) once connected to the remote server. This option only applies to protocol 2. The subsystem should be specified as the command on the remote host. This option normally is not used unless new subsystems have been created by system administrators/programmers.

-T

The -T option will disable allocation of pseudo-tty.

-t

Forcing a tty allocation can be accomplished using the -t command-line option. Under normal circumstances, the sshd server does not allocate a tty when executing remote commands. Certain commands require a tty to work, and the -t option will allow for this.

From a previous example, when an attempt to execute bash remotely occurs, no environment variables are set. When used with the -t option, ssh will allocate a tty and thus set up the environment. Normally, it would be easier to just use ssh to get to the host and not run a remote command, though.

```
stahnke@rack: ~> ssh www bash
echo $SSH_TTY

exit
stahnke@rack: ~> ssh -t www bash
stahnke@www: ~> echo $SSH_TTY
/dev/pts/0
stahnke@www: ~>
```

-V

When you are curious about which version of OpenSSH is installed, ssh -V will display it.

```
stahnke@rack: ~> ssh -V
OpenSSH_3.9p1, OpenSSL 0.9.7a Feb 19 2003
```

-v

The -v option can be used up to three times for maximum verbosity. This allows for debugging to occur on the client side. If you are having trouble with authentication or configuration issues, verbosity can normally pinpoint what is not behaving as desired.

-X

To specifically allow X11 forwarding, use the -X option. This can override the system-wide client configuration file, but the remote server must allow X11 forwarding. X11 forwarding can also be controlled in the ssh_config file.

```
ForwardX11 yes
```

-x

The lowercase -x disables X11 forwarding. Sometimes during troubleshooting, disabling X11 forwarding can eliminate a layer of complexity. X11 forwarding options can be controlled in the ssh_config file using the X11Foward directive.

```
ForwardX11 no
```

-Y

Using the -Y option will allow trusted X11 forwarding. If enabled, the ssh client has access to the X11 display. ForwardX11Trusted was created in OpenSSH 3.8. The option causes the ssh client to create an untrusted X cookie so that attempts to attack the forwarded X11 connection are thereby not successful in reaching the X client on the remote system.

scp

scp is used to copy files from one system to another. When managing an environment consisting of at least two servers, scp becomes invaluable to send updates, gather logs, distribute media, and so on. Once a system administrator becomes familiar with scp, that administrator will wonder how he or she ever got along without it.

scp Examples

The following section shows common usages of the powerful and secure remote copy utility scp. This command can be used to copy single files, entire directory structures, or even files on the same system.

Using Regular Expressions with scp

scp understands regular expressions, so if you have a group of files to move such as /var/log/messages.[1-4], you could do that with a simple command.

```
stahnke@rack: ~> scp root@www:"/var/log/messages.[1-4]" ./log
Password:
messages.1                        100% 1074KB   1.1MB/s   00:00
messages.2                        100% 1040KB   1.1MB/s   00:00
messages.3                        100% 1800KB   1.2MB/s   00:00
messages.4                        100% 1753KB   1.1MB/s   00:00
```

In this example, I specify that on the remote host www, the root user should access files /var/log/messages.[1-4] and copy them to my local system, placing them in the ~/.log directory. The path is quoted because it contains a regular expression. Quotes tell scp to have the remote system expand the regular expression and not the local shell. This can be important when file layouts are not the same.

File Transfer and Rename

Renaming files is also possible via scp.

```
stahnke@rack: ~> scp root@www:/var/log/messages \
~/logs/www_messages
```

Now the file that was messages on www is ~/logs/www_messages locally on the workstation rack.

Implied Path

Normally, the syntax for scp is user@host:path. However, if no path is specified (the : is still required), the user's home directory is assumed to be the path. In this example, a file named file is in root's home directory on rack.

```
stahnke@www: ~> scp root@rack:file .
Password:
file                              100%    82      0.1KB/s    00:00
```

Recursive Copy

Recursively copying files is a common task when transferring files. Under normal circumstances, when copying files, the files are placed in the path specified. If you recursively copy a directory, the directory will be created at the remote path specified. For example, locally a /root/crons directory exists. Remotely, where a backup is required, a crons directory does not exist. To accomplish directory creation, use the -r option.

```
root@www: ~> scp -r crons root@rack:
Password:
build_update.sh                               100%  269      0.3KB/s    00:00
make_apt.sh
```

After the secure recursive copy, the crons directory is created remotely.

```
root@rack: ~> ls -d crons
crons
```

Local Copy

Because I use scp extensively in my work as a system administrator, I sometimes use scp to copy files locally on the same system. cp in every situation will accomplish copying files on a single server, but because I get so used to using scp, I do so in this situation.

```
root@rack: ~> scp ldap.pl /home/stahnke
```

Implied User

When transferring files with a remote server, if the same login name is used on both systems, that login name is not required. For example, I am stahnke on both of my systems, rack and www. Therefore, I can use scp to copy the files with an implied username.

```
stahnke@www: ~> scp file rack:
Password:
file                                      100%   82     0.1KB/s    00:00
```

Pushing and Pulling Files Using scp

scp can push or pull files. If I want to copy the files from rack to www, I would just reverse the order of my two arguments after scp. If no path is specified after the :, the home directory for the remote user is assumed.

```
stahnke@rack: ~> scp foo stahnke@www:
Password:
foo                                    100%   730      0.7KB/s   00:00
```

Recursive copy also can be quite useful when moving data. For example, to deploy some code from my workstation rack, I use scp to transfer it to www.

```
stahnke@rack: ~> scp -r /code/php/* root@www:/var/www
```

Permissions

As with any file transfer utility, if the user does not have rights to the remote location, the file transfer will fail. This means that a nonprivileged user cannot write files to /etc nor to root's home directory.

```
stahnke@www: ~> scp Banner.psd stahnke@rack:/etc
Password:
scp: /etc/Banner.psd: Permission denied
```

scp Options

The scp options are very similar to those used with the ssh command. Many of them perform identical functions and simply instruct ssh how to carry out the operations. Only a handful of options are new to scp, but all are covered here for completeness. scp reads its configuration from the same ssh_config or $HOME/.ssh/config files that ssh sources.

-1

scp is completely compatible with SSH protocols 1 and 2. To force scp to use protocol 1, a -1 command-line option should be used.

-2

Using a -2 option will force scp to use protocol 2. This can also be forced in the ssh_config file using the Protocol directive.

-4

To enable IPv4 addresses only, use -4. The AddressFamily directive in the ssh_config file can also set this option.

-6

Inside the ssh_config file or on the command line, IPv6 is supported. Using a -6 will force a single command to IPv6. The option AddressFamily inet6 will enable it in the client configuration file.

-B

When using scp in scripts or loops, *batch mode* can be enabled. Batch mode simply means you cannot use interactive authentication methods. If a password or passphrase is required, authentication will fail. If the connection fails, it simply returns, rather than waiting indefinitely for user interaction. This becomes more prevalent in Chapter 9 when I cover scripting.

-C

The -C option will enable compression during scp transactions. Using -C on big files is sometimes useful because less data will transferred. Compression on low-bandwidth networks, especially modem connections, often creates better performance.

-c cipher

The -c option allows the symmetric encryption cipher to be specified on the command line. The cipher chosen is passed to the ssh client as the connection occurs.

-F ssh_config

If special options are required, scp can read in a separate configuration file using the -F option.

-i identity_file

The -i option will instruct scp as to which private key should be used for authentication.

-l limit

Bandwidth utilization can be limited for scp using the -l option. This is useful when moving files to areas with limited bandwidth to avoid completely saturating the pipe. At many companies, overseas servers or remote areas have limited bandwidth. Throttling the bandwidth can show some of the real power of ssh and can save media shipping headaches.

-o ssh_option

Using the -o option with scp provides the same functionality as with ssh. If any option that is specifiable inside the ssh_config file does not have a command-line option, using an -o with the directive and argument in quotes will enable that particular configuration.

-P port

The capital -P option is used to specify the port for connection on the remote servers. Notice that this is option uses a capital "P," unlike the option used with the ssh client, because -p is used as the preserve option, which was inherited from rcp.

-p

The -p option will preserve access times, modification times, and modes on the remote host as they were on the original file.

-q

The -q option enables quiet mode. Normally, scp has a meter running on the screen when files are being transferred that approximates the time remaining and how much of the file has been transferred successfully. Quiet mode will suppress this.

```
stahnke@www: ~> scp bigfile stahnke@rack:
Password:
bigfile                         17%    11MB    2.3MB/s    00:22 ETA
```

-r

As discussed earlier, the -r option will recursively copy directories from a local directory to a remote target.

-S program

The -S option, which is rarely used, specifies the path of the ssh executable if for some reason the path has changed. Other programs can be specified instead of ssh, but they must understand the same options as ssh. Sometimes wrappers for ssh might perform this task.

-v

The -v option, as with ssh, enables verbosity. This can be used with up to three levels of debug messages.

sftp

sftp can be used in ways very similar to FTP, though under the hood FTP and sftp are very different. Keep in mind that sftp does not mean Secure FTP; at least it is not a secured enhancement of the FTP protocol. Because of this, traditional FTP clients on both UNIX and Windows systems will not work with sftp. sftp is a different file transfer mechanism altogether, originally developed at SSH Communications Security for SSH protocol version 2. The sftp client speaks to the sftp-server subsystem inside of the SSH connection. This means that commands sent via ssh are passed to the sftp-server subsystem.

End users enjoy the simplicity and comfort of sftp. They can use many commands inside of an sftp session that they are used to from a traditional ftp client session. Once a user familiar with FTP is introduced to sftp, normally the transition is quite simple. sftp, however, transfers files as found on the file system. Normally, in FTP the ASCII mode will convert DOS files to UNIX and visa versa; when using sftp, the file is transferred exactly without any conversion.

Caution If you are using the SSH Communications Security SSH implementation with OpenSSH in your environment, sftp is the best way to transfer files, as scp from an OpenSSH client to an SSH Communications server will fail due to incompatibilities unless portions of OpenSSH are still installed. sftp will work from any combination of client and server software. The SSH Tectia product uses sftp as the protocol for both scp and sftp connections, whereas OpenSSH uses SCP1 (rcp over SSH) for SCP and sftp for SFTP transfers.

---

sftp Examples

Examining the options of sftp is a little trickier than those of scp because not only are command-line options present for sftp, but once the sftp client is invoked, it takes its own set of commands. Luckily, many traditional FTP commands work as expected in the sftp client.

To connect with a remote host, you can start with sftp remote_user@remote_host. From there, ls, get, put, and quit all work inside the sftp client.

Simple Interactive sftp Session

Using sftp under most circumstances is a matter of logging in, traversing the file system layout, and transferring the files needed.

```
stahnke@rack: ~> sftp stahnke@www
Password:
sftp> ls
      .
      ..
foo
vmlinuz
code
sftp> get foo
Fetching /home/stahnke/foo to foo
/home/stahnke/foo                         100%    0     4.0KB/s   00:00 ETA
sftp>
```

Batching sftp Commands

sftp can also be run in a batch mode quite simply. The -b option specifies a batch file. If a file is created with the intended commands, it will run without requiring interaction from the user. Listing 5-1 shows the contents of an sftp batch file, whereas Listing 5-2 uses the batch file to automate the file transfer.

Listing 5-1. *A Batch File That Will Be Read During an* sftp *Session*

```
stahnke@rack: ~> cat batch_file
cd /var/log
get messages
cd /home/stahnke
put .bashrc
```

Listing 5-2. *Using a Batch File During an* sftp *Operation*

```
stahnke@rack:~> sftp -b batch_file stahnke@localhost
Password:
sftp> cd code/php
sftp> get index.php
Fetching /home/stahnke/code/php/index.php to index.php
sftp> cd /home/stahnke
sftp> put .bashrc
```

```
Uploading .bashrc to /home/stahnke/.bashrc
sftp>
stahnke@rack:~>
```

As demonstrated, the sftp session connected and executed all commands placed in the file specified, batch_file. Batching sftp commands is obviously designed for scheduled jobs and scripts. Sometimes using sftp over scp has advantages in scripts because only one connection needs to be established, which is especially nice on slower systems and networks; however, most scripts seem to use scp for its simplicity.

sftp Command-line Options

The sftp command-line options are similar to those from ssh and scp. The -b option is the most notable option change when moving from scp to sftp. Keep in mind that sftp uses SSH protocol 2 by default.

-1

The -1 option will allow sftp to fall back to protocol 1.

-B buffer_size

A buffer size can be specified when using sftp. Small buffer sizes use less memory, but will require more back-and-forth network communication between the end points. By default, the buffer is set to 32768 bytes.

-b batchfile

The ability to batch commands with sftp is a nice feature. When using a batch file, stdin is not read. To make an sftp session unattended, public key or host-based authentication should be used, and is covered in Chapter 6. Normally, a batch file contains commands, one per line, that should be executed upon connection to the sftp-server. Under normal circumstances, if commands fail, sftp will abort the session. This behavior can be changed if a - is used in front of the command.

Normally, a batch sftp session would abort if I was unable to get a file. Listing 5-3 shows the batch file that will be used. Listing 5-4 demonstrates the failure that occurs when an error is encountered.

Listing 5-3. *An* sftp *Batch File*

```
stahnke@rack: ~> cat batch
put foo
get file_that_does_not_exists
chmod 700 foo
quit
```

Listing 5-4. *An* sftp *Batch Session That Fails Because a File Transfer Could Not Occur*

```
stahnke@rack: ~> sftp -b batch stahnke@www:
Password:
Changing to: /home/stahnke/
sftp> put foo
Uploading foo to /home/stahnke/foo
sftp> get file_that_does_not_exists
Couldn't stat remote file: No such file or directory
File "/home/stahnke/file_that_does_not_exists" not found.
stahnke@rack: ~>
```

If the - character is added at the beginning of a line in an sftp batch file, the batch script will continue, even if an error occurs. Listing 5-5 demonstrates this.

```
stahnke@rack: ~> cat batch
put foo
-get file_that_does_not_exists
chmod 700 foo
quit
```

Listing 5-5. *An* sftp *Batch Transfer That Will Not Abort Upon Error*

```
stahnke@rack: ~> sftp -b batch stahnke@www:
Password:
Changing to: /home/stahnke/
sftp> put foo
Uploading foo to /home/stahnke/foo
sftp> -get file_that_does_not_exists
Couldn't stat remote file: No such file or directory
File "/home/stahnke/file_that_does_not_exists" not found.
sftp> chmod 700 foo
Changing mode on /home/stahnke/foo
sftp> quit
```

-C

The -C option will enable compression for sftp. This is done by passing the -C option to the ssh transport.

-F ssh_config

The -F option, as with ssh and scp, allows a specific client configuration file to be used instead of the defaults found for the system and user.

-o ssh_option

sftp can also use the -o option to specify any client option that sftp does not have an option for. For example, to suppress having to have the public key of the remote host already cached, the StrictHostKeyChecking option can be utilized.

```
stahnke@rack: ~> sftp -o "StictHostKeyChecking no" stahnke@www
```

-P sftp_server_path

For debugging purposes, sometimes it can be a good idea to connect to the local sftp-server. This can be done using the -P option. When using the -P option, the connection is made from the client to server without passing through SSH. If the connection here works, something between the sftp client and ssh passing the commands to the sftp-server is probably causing the issue. Usually, it is best to run in verbose mode then to see what is occurring.

```
stahnke@rack: ~> sftp -P /usr/local/libexec/sftp-server root@localhost
Attaching to /usr/local/libexec/sftp-server...
sftp> ls
sftp-server   ssh-keysign
sftp>
```

-R num_requests

Under normal circumstances, 16 sftp requests are allowed to be outstanding at once. Increasing this number will use more memory, but could improve your transfer time.

-S program

If sftp is unable to find the ssh binary on the system, it can be specified with the -S option.

-s subsystem

If the remote host does not have the sftp-server subsystem enabled, it can be specified with the -s option. This also can be a benefit when protocol 1 is being used.

-v

The -v option enables verbosity. Up to three levels of verbosity are available to sftp.

Interactive Commands

After the sftp client has established a connection to the remote ssh server, a new set of commands is used. These commands mimic the behavior of a traditional ftp client. If a command has a space character in it, the string must be enclosed with quotation marks. Many commands that can be executed on the remote host are also available to the local system by putting an l before the command.

bye

When the sftp session is complete, bye is used to exit. quit or exit will also work.

cd path

To change directories on the remote system while connected via sftp, use the cd command. Here is an example:

```
cd /usr/local/bin
```

chgrp GID path

Use the chgrp option to change the group ownership of a remote file by specifying a GID and a path. GID is the numeric GID assigned to the group. Here is an example:

chgrp 500

chmod mode path

To change permissions on a remote file, use chmod. Octal arguments are expected. The following shows an example of this option:

chmod 755 /usr/local/bin/file

chown own path

As with chgrp, chown requires a numeric value as the owner argument. Here is an example:

chown 0 /usr/local/bin/file

exit

exit will terminate an sftp session. This is equivalent to quit or bye.

get [flags] remote-path [local-path]

To receive files from the remote server, use get. get can include a -P option to preserve the file permissions and access time from the remote host. Additionally, a local path can be specified to place the file in the proper location. If no local location is specified, the file is transferred into the current local directory. mget also is available for compatibility with ftp clients. Following is an example:

```
sftp> get -P ldap.pl /home/stahnke/code
Fetching /home/stahnke/ldap.pl to /home/stahnke/code
/home/stahnke/ldap.pl             100% 1215     1.2KB/s   00:00
sftp>
```

help

help or ? both output help messages inside the sftp client.

lcd path

To traverse directories on the local system, use lcd.

lls [ls-options [path]]

To list files on the local side of the connection, use lls. lls can use most arguments of a traditional ls command; however, not all of them might work.

lmkdir path

To create a local directory while inside an sftp session, use lmkdir, as in the following example:

lmkdir /usr/local/foo

ln source link

Symbolic links can be created by using ln in the form of ln source link as follows:

ln /usr/local/foo /usr/local/link

lpwd

To find out where on the local system you are, use lpwd, which prints the local working directory.

ls [flags] [path]

As with the lls command, ls can use most traditional ls options. ls displays the directory listing on the remote host in the current working directory or at the specified path.

lumask umask

To change the local umask, use lumask. The argument for the umask must be in octal notation.

lumask 027

mkdir path

mkdir will create a directory on the remote host at the specified path.

progress

To disable or enable the progress reporting meter, using the progress command.

put [flags] local-path [remote-path]

put uploads a file to the remote server from the localhost. The -P option can be used to preserve access time and file permissions. If no remote path is specified, sftp defaults to the working directory on the remote target. mput is also available to be compatible with ftp commands. Here is an example:

put /usr/local/file

pwd

To determine your present directory location on the remote system, use pwd.

quit

quit will terminate the sftp connection. This is equivalent to exit and bye.

rename oldpath newpath

To change the names of files, use the rename command, as in this example:

rename /usr/local/file /usr/local/testing

rm path

rm will delete remote files at the path specified. Here is an example:

```
rm /usr/local/testing
```

rmdir path

rmdir will remove a remote directory at the path specified, as shown in this example:

```
rmdir /usr/local
```

symlink source link

symlink and ln are equivalent. symlink allows for symbolic link creation using the format symlink source link, as demonstrated here:

```
symlink /usr/local/file /usr/local/link
```

version

The version command displays which version of the SFTP protocol is in use. Here is an example:

```
sftp> version
SFTP protocol version 3
```

! command

Sometimes during an interactive sftp session, shell commands need to be executed. To escape from the sftp> prompt into a shell, use the ! character followed by the command that should be executed in the local shell. Here is an example:

```
sftp> ! locate ssh_config
/var/www/.ssh/ssh_config
/var/cache/man/cat5/ssh_config.5.bz2
/etc/ssh/ssh_config
/usr/share/man/man5/ssh_config.5.gz
sftp>
```

!

When escaping to a local shell, sometimes many commands are required. An ! without any arguments will return you to your normal shell. When you exit that shell, you will be returned to the sftp> prompt.

?

Entering a ? at the sftp> prompt will display the help dialog box.

ssh_config

The ssh_config file is the default configuration file of the OpenSSH client, ssh. Remembering that the order of precedence is command-line, user-specific, and then system-wide authority for ssh_config, I encourage you to make a copy of your system-wide client configuration file, oftentimes found at /etc/ssh/ssh_config, into your $HOME/.ssh directory to experiment with. Of course, the path to your system-wide configuration file depends on the --sysconfigdir argument to configure if you compiled from source. Most binary installations will use /etc/ssh. /etc/ssh/ssh_config should be group-/world-readable and owned by root. Your personal configuration file should be owned by you, and you should restrict access as you see fit. Additionally, user-specific files are called config, not ssh_config. A personal configuration for the stahnke account is stored at /home/stahnke/.ssh/config.

In the next few sections, the focus of discussion will be the ssh_config file, its options and impact to the ssh environment. From there, a few scenarios are discussed that will allow you to come up with a client configuration that will be flexible and secure. Remember, with clients one size does not fit all. I use three different client configuration files on a daily basis. I have one for my interactive user account, one for my cron jobs, and one for scripts I write and expect other people will be running. While most of the keywords and arguments in the client configuration files are the same, there are some differences to improve security for my personal account and to improve usability for cron and other users.

During the discussion of the options, remember to make a note of what seems important to you; also remember that any option you set now you can change later if you find more value from it.

Debugging OpenSSH ssh_config

The ssh_config file does not have a syntax-checking mechanism analogous to the sshd -t option. From my experience, however, it appears that an invalid entry can be in ssh_config and not cause issues for the OpenSSH client utilities. To debug OpenSSH connections, as with many traditional UNIX commands, use the -v options. Up to three levels of debugging are provided via -v, -vv, and -vvv. Debugging statements are then directed to stderr.

Some editors (vim, emacs, etc.) provide syntax highlighting for ssh_config and sshd_config files. When a keyword matches the known template for an ssh_config file, it is highlighted and the arguments are also highlighted when recognized. This can assist in building a correct client configuration file. Keep in mind, however, that newer options from OpenSSH (both server and client) are sometimes not in the editor templates, and then are not highlighted, but are syntactically correct.

ssh_config keywords

Applying what you have learned throughout this chapter thus far, take some time to create a client configuration that you feel will work in your environment. You can start with what the system provided, or what is discussed throughout the rest of this chapter, and work from there. One nice feature about ssh_config is that the system-wide file is only a starting point, as all users get one to edit on their own if they so chose. Placing the system-wide client configuration file in the /etc/skel directory (or equivalent) will give each new user a starting point to optimize his or her own SSH experience.

`ssh_config` supports a vast array of keywords. Many times taking the defaults will leave you with a relatively secure system, but as you tweak your configuration files, you will see the usability level increase. Some keywords change or are removed when new versions of OpenSSH are released. This discussion is based on OpenSSH 3.9p1, but most should be applicable to other versions as well. Much of this discussion is credited to the OpenSSH man pages, with bits of my own experience supplemented to describe the options. Also note that during the discussion the keywords and directives are equivalent.

AddressFamily

The `ssh` client can be told which version of IP should be used. The following are the three options normally used:

```
# Allow IPv4 and IPv6
AddressFamily any
# Allow IPv4 only
AddressFamily inet
# Allow IPv6 only
AddressFamily inet6
```

BatchMode

Batch mode, when enabled, will automatically skip authentication that requires a passphrase or password to be entered. This is very useful when running scripts. The possible arguments are yes or no, and the default is `no`. In batch mode, an authentication failure simply returns an error code. With batch mode set to `no`, a password prompt will wait for user input. There is no command-line directive for this option, so oftentimes an `-o "BatchMode yes"` is required. The option is set like so:

```
BatchMode no
```

BindAddress

The `BindAddress` keyword allows you to specify which address your client uses for outbound traffic. This can be useful if the remote host uses TCP wrappers, `sshd` configurations, or some other mechanism to determine what IP addresses are allowed to make connections. This directive is not required on systems with only one address. The option also is not used if `UsePrivilegedPort` is enabled. A example inside the `ssh_config` file would be as follows:

```
# Allow all addresses
BindAddress *
```

ChallengeResponseAuthentication

This directive specifies whether your client should attempt challenge response authentication. By default, this is enabled (set to yes):

```
ChallengeResponseAuthentication yes
```

CheckHostIP

To verify the DNS entry of a remote host, ssh will check the IP address in the already cached known_hosts file. If a host key has changed due to a DNS compromise or DNS reassignment, ssh will detect this and issue a warning. This is enabled by default, as shown in the following line of code:

```
CheckHostIP yes
```

Listing 5-6 shows the message ssh delivers when IP addresses do not match their already cached public host keys.

Listing 5-6. ssh *Provides a Warning When* CheckHostIP *Is Enabled*

```
[root@rack ~]# ssh www
@@@@@@@@@@@@@@@@@@@@@@@@@@@@@@@@@@@@@@@@@@@@@@@@@@@@@@@@@@@
@       WARNING: POSSIBLE DNS SPOOFING DETECTED!        @
@@@@@@@@@@@@@@@@@@@@@@@@@@@@@@@@@@@@@@@@@@@@@@@@@@@@@@@@@@@
The RSA host key for www has changed,
and the key for the according IP address 192.168.1.102
is unknown. This could either mean that
DNS SPOOFING is happening or the IP address for the host
and its host key have changed at the same time.
```

ssh will issue a warning if the host key it has cached does not match the IP address it should belong to. To set this up, I changed my /etc/hosts file and gave www the IP address assignment of another host on my network.

Cipher

The Cipher keyword lets the client choose which cipher should be used for protocol 1 from the ciphers offered by sshd. The options are blowfish, 3des, and des. des should not be used unless it is the only option that will work, as it is a weak cipher. By default, 3des is used.

Ciphers

The ssh client can select which ciphers to use for protocol 2 connections as well. Multiple ciphers can be specified and should be delimited with a comma. Normally, the defaults for this directive are sufficient. The default is aes-128-cbc,3des-cbc,blowfish-cbc,cast128-cbc,arcfour,aes192-cbc, aes256-cbc. These are attempted in the order listed. In this case, the 256-bit AES cipher would be the last try at establishing which cipher should be used between the client and server.

ClearAllForwardings

When forwarding connections, sometimes it becomes necessary to clear forwardings. If a forwarding is causing collisions, ClearAllForwardings can be set to yes, so that collisions do not occur. This option is automatically set to yes by scp and sftp, but defaults to no when connecting via ssh. Normally, the defaults will be appropriate.

Compression

To allow the client to attempt compression, set `Compression yes`. By default it is `no`, as shown in the following code line. The server must allow for compression for it to be utilized.

```
Compression no
```

CompressionLevel

If using compression via protocol 1, the compression level can be specified in ranges from 1 to 9. 1 is a speedy compression, and 9 uses maximum compression. By default, 6 is used, which represents a compromise between high compression and high speed.

ConnectionAttempts

This directive specifies how many attempts the client will make to connect before exiting, at one per second. An integer must be used as the argument. The default is 1.

```
ConnectionAttempts 1
```

ConnectTimeout

Normally, if a remote system is down and an attempt to `ssh` to that remote host is made, `ssh` will hang until the default TCP timeout value is reached. This behavior can have negative impacts on scripts that do not ensure the remote host is available before connecting with `ssh`. If `ConnectTimeout` is set, as shown in the following line of code, a simple error message is returned. The `ConnectTimeout` option is only used when a host is unpingable (see Listing 5-7). I normally set the `ConnectTimeout` value to be around four seconds.

```
ConnectTimeout 4
```

Listing 5-7. *Attempting a Connection to a Down System with* `ConnectTimeout` *Set*

```
stahnke@rack: ~> ssh downmachine
ssh: connect to host down port 22: No route to host
```

ControlMaster

The `ControlMaster` feature, one of the newer features in OpenSSH, allows multiple connections to a remote host to use the same network connection. This can be useful in scripting, when several remote commands need to be executed on a remote system. The majority of the overhead when using SSH connections comes from establishing the connection. In the case of a `ControlMaster`, the additional commands use an already established connection, causing much faster execution of remote commands.

This directive takes yes, no, and ask arguments. If set to yes, the `ControlPath` argument is used as the path to a socket that can be used for authentication once the initial authentication succeeds. By default, this keyword is set to no. If set to ask, the `ssh` client will listen for control connections and ask the user using `$SSH_ASKPASS` (prompting for a passphrase) to confirm the connection.

ControlPath

The `ControlPath` option specifies the socket that should be used for connection sharing enabled by `ControlMaster`. Listing 5-8 shows the setup required to use a `ControlPath` and `ControlMaster` ssh client.

Listing 5-8. *User-specific Configuration to Use* `ControlPath` *and* `ControlMaster`

```
stahnke@rack: ~/.ssh> cat config
Host www
ControlMaster yes
ControlPath ~/.ssh/cpath

Host www-cp
ControlMaster no
ControlPath ~/.ssh/cpath
```

The local client config file has two hosts defined, www and www-cp. They are the same remote host, but one sets up a `ControlPath`, while the other one (www-cp) uses it. In the following example, I connect to www first and establish a socket (`ControlPath`). The second window uses the `ControlPath` and automatically allows my connections. This example uses interactive sessions, but passing commands over an already established ssh connection is oftentimes used when scripting.

```
# Terminal Window 1
stahnke@rack: ~/.ssh> ssh www
Weclome to www
Enter passphrase for key '/home/stahnke/.ssh/id_dsa':
stahnke@www: ~>
# Terminal Window 2
stahnke@rack: ~> ls -l .ssh/cpath
srw-------  1 stahnke stahnke 0 Mar 31 21:15 .ssh/cpath
stahnke@rack: ~> ssh www-cp
stahnke@www: ~>
```

As you can see, the second connection uses the `~/.ssh/cpath` on rack to connect to a remote host via a socket. This causes speedier connections; however, if the first connection is terminated, subsequent connections are also disconnected.

DynamicForward

You can use `DynamicForward` to specify a port on the client system to be forwarded via the secure connection. The application protocol is then analyzed to determine which port the traffic should connect to on the remote server. This uses SOCKS version 4 and SOCKS version 5, which let ssh act as a SOCKS server. The argument is a port number. Only root can forward ports below 1024.

EnableSSHKeysign

During host-based authentication, the helper program ssh-keysign is used to check localhost keys via a digital signature. Users do not normally use ssh-keysign; it is called internally from ssh. This directive takes yes or no arguments, as in the following example, and defaults to no:

```
EnableSSHKeysign yes
```

EscapeChar

This directive allows you to set the escape character for the ssh client. The default is ~. As an argument, this directive takes a single character, or none to disable the escape character. If it is explicitly set, this directive looks like this:

```
EscapeChar ~
```

ForwardAgent

ForwardAgent tells ssh whether or not it should allow agent forwarding. Agent forwarding can be used during public key authentication. This directive takes arguments of yes and no. By default, it is disabled.

Agent forwarding, as shown in the following code line, is one of the settings that is normally changed in client configurations depending on the type of environment you are working with. In hostile or nontrusted environments, it should be left off. In a more secure environment, it can become quite a time saver. Further discussion of agents takes place in Chapter 6.

```
AgentForwarding yes
```

ForwardX11

By default, X11 traffic is not encrypted and uses fairly weak authentication. SSH can tunnel that traffic to encrypt it and require SSH authentication. The ForwardX11 directive tells the ssh client whether or not it should attempt to forward an X11 connection.

The server must also enable this for X11 forwarding to work. By default this is disabled. X11 forwarding can open a system to some insecurities if a malicious user is able to access the X11 display because of insufficient file permissions.

Forwarding X11 is another option that is often toggled depending on whether or not a network is trusted. If enabled, as in the following code example, X11 connections are auto-forwarded and no longer in plain text. Note that if the sshd server does not allow X11 to forward connections over ssh, the client option is nullified.

```
ForwardX11 yes
```

ForwardX11Trusted

If ForwardX11Trusted is enabled (set to yes), clients can access the original X11 display. If no, as in the following line of code, remote X11 clients are not trusted and therefore are prevented from working with data owned by trusted X11 clients. By default this option is disabled, as not all X11 clients are compatible in this mode.

```
ForwardX11Trusted no
```

GatewayPorts

Normally, when forwarding a TCP connection, it is bound to the localhost (see the following code example). If having other hosts connecting to the forwarded connection is desired, set GatewayPorts to yes. More detail on this option is provided in Chapter 7.

```
GatewayPorts no
```

GlobalKnownHostsFile

This directive accepts the path to the system-wide file containing the public host keys as an argument. As the following example shows, the default is /etc/ssh/ssh_known_hosts (or ssh_known_hosts wherever your configuration directory is).

```
GlobalKnownHostsFile /etc/ssh/ssh_known_hosts
```

GSSAPIAuthentication

This keyword instructs ssh whether or not to attempt GSSAPI authentication using SSH protocol 2. By default, this is set to no, as you see in the following line of code. If you have taken the time to invest in Kerberos 5 authentication, you may wish to enable GSSAPI options.

```
GSSAPIAuthentication no
```

GSSAPIDelegateCredentials

If using GSSAPI authentication, you can forward the credentials to the server. By default this is disabled. GSSAPI options apply to protocol 2 only.

Host

The client configuration file can be changed significantly for each remote host you plan on connecting to. Once a Host is specified, the keywords and argument following it apply to that host, until the next Host keyword. Hosts can be expressed using simple regular expressions such as * and ? as well.

```
stahnke@rack: ~/.ssh> cat config
Host www
ControlMaster yes
ControlPath ~/.ssh/cpath

Host www-cp
Hostname www
ControlMaster no
ControlPath ~/.ssh/cpath

Host zoom
ControlMaster no
ForwardAgent no
ForwardX11 no
Port 22

Host *
HostbasedAuthentication no
ConnectTimeout 4
StrictHostKeyChecking yes
```

This user client configuration file uses the Host keyword several times. Each host has some specific configuration information. Global settings are set (as they should be) at the bottom of the configuration file.

HostbasedAuthentication

If you wish to enable host-based authentication, set this directive to yes. By default, it is disabled, as you see in the following line of code. This option applies to host-based authentication via SSH protocol 2 only. This type of host-based authentication uses cached public keys rather than IP addresses as in a traditional rhosts environment. Most often, host-based authentication of any type is discouraged because of potential security problems, but if host-based authentication is desired, this is the safest method. Chapter 6 discusses some parameters on which to evaluate the usage of host-based authentication.

```
HostbasedAuthentication no
```

HostKeyAlgorithms

This keyword tells the client what host key algorithms should be attempted. This applies to protocol 2 only. By default, the value is ssh-rsa,ssh-dss.

HostKeyAlias

The HostKeyAlias keyword can be used to create an alias for a host. This will cache the remote public under the alias name. This is useful if different OpenSSH servers are listening on different ports of the same physical server, because normally the port number is not stored when caching public host keys. However, if the key has another name, due to having an alias, both keys can be cached and valid. The following is an example of how a client config could use the HostKeyAlias directive. This assumes that www and www2 are the same physical system, but with sshd listening on different ports.

```
Host www
Port 22
HostKeyAlias   www_22
Host www2
Port 222
HostKeyAlias www_222
```

HostName

Under a Host keyword, a HostName can be specified. This allows users to shorten fully qualified names or come up with their own nicknames for systems for the Host argument. HostName should be the real name of the host or IP address.

```
Host john
Hostname 192.168.1.109
```

This client configuration allows me to call 192.168.1.109 john. I can then run ssh john on the command line.

IdentityFile

The IdentityFile keyword takes a path as an argument. The file should contain private keys. For protocol 1, $HOME/.ssh/identity is the default; for protocol version 2, $HOME/.ssh/id_rsa and $HOME/.ssh/id_dsa are the defaults. Multiple identities are allowed, which is useful if multiple keys are required in your environment.

```
IdentityFile ~/.ssh/identity
IdentityFile ~/.ssh/id_rsa
IdentityFile ~/.ssh/id_dsa
```

IdentitiesOnly

Sometimes, using ssh-agent, identities can be added that are not of the format specified in the system-wide ssh_config file. To disallow this behavior, set IdentitiesOnly to yes, as shown in the following example. This means that only identities defined in the ssh_config file can be used. By default, any identity can be used, so it is set to no.

```
IdentitiesOnly yes
```

LocalForward

Using the LocalForward keyword inside of a client configuration file, automatically forwarded connections can be created whenever an SSH connection is established. The syntax for the arguments is host:port for IPv4 and host/port for IPv6. The host is the remote system and the port that you would like to forward. Multiple forwardings are permitted via the client configuration file. Port forwarding is discussed in Chapter 7.

LogLevel

Logging is of vital importance when using OpenSSH. When logging messages from the ssh client, the level can be specified. By default, INFO is used. The supported arguments in order from least amount of data to the most are QUIET, FATAL, ERROR, INFO, VERBOSE, DEBUG, DEBUG1, DEBUG2, and DEBUG3. I prefer VERBOSE when logging, as shown in the following example, because it offers public key fingerprint information and a nice amount of data if authentication troubleshooting needs to occur:

```
LogLevel VERBOSE
```

MACs

Message Authentication Code algorithms are used to verify checksums in conjunction with a secret key. These are used in protocol 2 for data integrity verification. Different algorithms are permitted and must be comma delimited. The default is hmac-md5,hmac-sha1, hmac-ripemd160,hmac-sha1-96,hmac-md5-96.

NoHostAuthenticationForLocalhost

When using a network shared home directory (NFS, AFS, Samba), public host keys are cached. However, the localhost public key will change depending on which system the user is currently connecting from. If this is set to yes, users will be allowed to ssh to the localhost without any warnings about host key changes. By default, host keys for the localhost are checked, as demonstrated in the following code:

```
NoHostAuthenticationForLocalhost no
```

NumberOfPasswordPrompts

This keyword requires an integer as an argument. It specifies how many password attempts should be made before the client gives up. By default, this is 3, as shown in the following example:

```
NumberOfPasswordsPrompts 3
```

PasswordAuthentication

This token instructs the ssh client to attempt or not to attempt password-based authentication via a yes/no argument. When using key-based authentication for automated jobs or system activity, it is often a good idea to set PasswordAuthentication to no. This is covered in more detail in Chapter 6.

```
PasswordAuthentication yes
```

Port

This keyword tells the client what port on the remote server should be used for the SSH connection. The default is 22, as shown in the following example:

```
Port 22
```

PreferredAuthentications

This keyword tells ssh the order of preference for authentication techniques. By default, this uses hostbased,publickey,keyboard-interactive,password. As you see in the example that follows, I often take out hostbased authentication because of my fondness for user-specified security. This option only applies to protocol 2.

```
PreferredAuthentications publickey,keyboard-interactive,password
```

Protocol

This argument tells the client which protocol should be used. The default is 2,1—meaning that protocol 2 will be attempted, and if it fails, protocol 1 will be used. Normally, I explicitly specify protocol 2 only, as in the following code line. Multiple arguments are comma separated.

```
Protocol 2
```

ProxyCommand

When using a proxy, the command string can be specified with a few expandable parameters. %h is used for hostname, and %p is used for port. The command can be any appropriate string for your proxy. Setting the command to none will disable this option.

PubkeyAuthentication

This keyword tells the ssh client whether or not public key authentication should be attempted. This protocol 2–only option defaults to yes, as shown here:

```
PubkeyAuthentication yes
```

RemoteForward

Remote forwarding of TCP traffic can be done via SSH. To specify a remote forward, use the RemoteForward keyword. The syntax is host:port for IPv4 and host/port for IPv6. Multiple remote forward connections are allowed. Forwarding is covered in more detail in Chapter 7.

RhostsRSAAuthentication

This protocol 1 keyword will allow rhost-based authentication with RSA host authentication if set to yes. By default, as shown in the following code line, this is set to no. It also requires ssh to have SetUID root permissions. For security reasons, both with host-based authentication and ssh protocol 1, the default is acceptable.

```
RhostsRSAAuthentication no
```

RSAAuthentication

If set to yes, as in the following example, RSA authentication will be attempted, provided the identity file exists. By default, this option is enabled. This option applies to protocol 1 only. RSAAuthentication takes yes/no arguments.

```
RSAAuthentication yes
```

SendEnv

The client can use SendEnv to send local environment variables to the remote server, provided that sshd is configured to allow it. This is only allowed using protocol 2. Environment variables may contain simple regular expressions using the * and ? characters.

```
stahnke@rack: ~/.ssh> export TEST_ENV="OpenSSH testing"
stahnke@rack: ~/.ssh> cat config
...
Host *
HostbasedAuthentication no
ConnectTimeout 4
StrictHostKeyChecking yes
SendEnv TEST_ENV
```

After setting the SendEnv parameter and ensuring that environment variable is permitted on the server (checking for AcceptEnv TEST_ENV in the sshd_config), a user can ssh to a remote host and pass along certain environment variables.

```
stahnke@www: ~> set | grep TEST
TEST_ENV='OpenSSH testing'
```

ServerAliveInterval

The `ssh` client can be configured to request data from the `sshd` server at given intervals using `ServerAliveInterval`. This is different from `TCPKeepAlive`, because the request is sent in the SSH tunnel, encrypted at the application level. `TCPKeepAlive` requests are standard TCP packets that can be spoofed.

The arguments are specified in seconds; after the specified amount of time, if the `ssh` client has received no data from the `sshd` process it is connected to, it will send a message that requires a response. This option only applies to protocol 2. By default the value is 0, which means that no keep-alive messages are sent. Here is an example of `ServerAliveInterval`:

```
ServerAliveInterval 5
```

ServerAliveCountMax

This keyword tells the `ssh` client how many server keep-alive requests it should send without response before giving up and terminating the connection. These keep-alives are sent through the `ssh` pipe and are therefore encrypted. By default the value is 3. Following is an example:

```
ServerAliveCountMax 10
```

The time without response before the `ssh` client gives up on the server is `ServerAliveCountMax` × `ServerAliveInterval`.

SmartcardDevice

Smart cards are devices (about the size of a credit card) that hold your personal identification information. When dealing with SSH, this means your private key; either RSA or DSA is stored on the smart card.

If you are using a smart-card reader, specify the path to the device. By default, smart-card usage is not enabled.

StrictHostKeyChecking

When a connection is made to a remote system with a host key that is not cached or does not match the key cached on disk, `ssh` will normally balk. If `StrictHostKeyChecking` is enabled, `ssh` will refuse to connect to any remote host for which there is not a correct public key cached. If set to `no`, `ssh` will make the connection and cache it automatically; however, a layer of security against the man-in-the-middle attack is lost with this setting. The default of `ask` requires `ssh` to ask whether a connection should proceed if there is no record of the remote host's public host key on disk. If a public host key changes in `ask` mode, the old key must be removed from the `known_hosts` file for a connection to be established.

`StrictHostKeyChecking` can cause many users to dislike SSH; however, its added security benefits are real. This allows the client to verify and reverify the server's identity each connection. This prevents IP spoofing from being a viable attack. Educating users about the importance of host key caching can assist with improving security.

If your network is mainly DHCP based, then setting `StrictHostKeyChecking` to `no` is probably the best option, as the host keys will constantly change.

For scripting and batch processing, sometimes setting StrictHostKeyChecking to no will allow the script to deal with more anomalies and complete successfully, if you are relatively sure the network is secured.

```
# StrictHostKeyChecking set to yes
stahnke@rack: ~/.ssh> > known_hosts
stahnke@rack: ~/.ssh> ssh www
No RSA host key is known for www and you have requested strict checking.
Host key verification failed.
```

After removing my public key cache, my connection to www is denied because no public key is present.

```
# StrictHostKeyChecking set to ask
stahnke@rack: ~/.ssh> ssh www
The authenticity of host 'www (192.168.1.109)' can't be established.
RSA key fingerprint is d9:2f:0d:72:a9:cb:5d:07:e6:23:23:e5:cb:ba:35:3f.
Are you sure you want to continue connecting (yes/no)? yes
Warning: Permanently added 'www,192.168.1.109' (RSA) to the list of known hosts.
```

When set to ask, StrictHostKeyChecking allows the connection to continue by having me enter yes.

```
# StrictHostKeyChecking set to no
stahnke@rack: ~/.ssh> > known_hosts
stahnke@rack: ~/.ssh> ssh www
Warning: Permanently added 'www,192.168.1.109' (RSA) to the list of known hosts.
```

The connection occurs without my intervention when StrictHostKeyChecking is disabled.

TCPKeepAlive

This directive tells the ssh client whether or not it should send TCP keep-alive messages to the server via a yes/no argument. By default, TCP keep-alive messages are sent. For most purposes ServerAliveInterval and ServerAliveCountMax work as well as TCPKeepAlive and are more secure since they cannot be tampered with because of the encrypted connection. Following is an example:

```
TCPKeepAlive no
```

UsePrivilegedPort

Normally ssh uses a high-numbered (> 1024) port for outbound connections. If UsePrivilegedPort is set to yes, it will use ports below 1024. The arguments for this keyword are yes and no. By default, it is set to no. If enabled, the ssh client must have permissions of SetUID root, and therefore should be avoided.

User

If you have different login names on remote systems, they can be specified per host under the Host keyword. Then the remote username is not required on the command line.

```
Host www
User stahnke
Host www-cp
User stahnke
Host zoom
User mastahnke
```

UserKnownHostsFile

If you store your known_hosts file in a location other than $HOME/.ssh/known_hosts, specify its path here.

VerifyHostKeyDNS

If SSHFP (SSH FingerPrint) records are stored in DNS, the ssh client can check to see whether the fingerprint returned from the server matches the one published via a resource record in DNS. If they do match, the key is automatically trusted. Otherwise, the public keys are handled as if this option was set to ask, thus making the user allow or deny the connection. By default, this keyword is set to no. This applies to version 2 only. Chapter 8 offers more discussion on this topic.

XAuthLocation

The argument to XAuthLocation is the full path to the xauth program. On Red Hat Linux systems, it is found normally in /usr/X11/bin/xauth. Your results may vary. If no xauth is present, this option is disabled.

ssh_config documented

In an enterprise environment, accountability is a must. Auditors, whether they are internal or third party, come to audit information technology spaces and discover your adherence and noncompliance toward policy.

In my past experience with auditors, I find I have far fewer meetings to attend if I can provide everything in a well-documented format with comments that make more sense to auditing and business personnel than to UNIX administrators like myself. It seems that without exception, the auditors are more concerned about processes and following procedure than with the actual security of the complete environment. A configuration file with policy numbers next to the line in the configuration file that shows compliance is oftentimes a good idea. For example, if your organization has a control that says "SSH Control 1) Only SSH Protocol 2 is allowed," then you might have a line in your ssh_config file that says Protocol 2 #Compliance to SSH Control 1. Note that the headings I use in the configuration file shown in Listing 5-9 are there to improve readability for auditors and technical administrators; they are not provided in the stock configuration files. Arguments can be made that some keywords belong under headings other than the ones I have chosen. While they hail from my system-wide configuration file, copying them directly to $HOME/.ssh/config will work, if permissions/ownership are correct.

Listing 5-9. *A Fully Documented System-wide* ssh_config *File*

```
# ssh_config system-wide configuration for OpenSSH clients
# This is the ssh client system-wide configuration file.  This
# file provides defaults for users that are compliant with SSH
# policy and ensure best practices are followed.  While this file
# is compliant, please keep in mind that users can change settings
# with user-specific overrides from the command line or their own
# config file in some cases.

# Configuration data is parsed as follows:
#  1. command-line options
#  2. user-specific file
#  3. system-wide file

# Site-wide defaults for various options
# Relying on defaults can be challenging because the defaults can
# change upon upgrades.  Specifying settings explicitly is
# recommended if you understand the settings.

# Version x.x
# Date:

Host *
#This means the configuration applies to any host.  In
# some cases options can be given that will allow different
# configurations depending on what host the user would like to
# connect to. Under normal circumstances, all machines are treated
# the same.

# Network Settings
#################
Port 22
# SSH by default runs on port 22.

AddressFamily inet
# This network relies on IPv4 only.

ConnectTimeout 4
# Because this network occasionally has machines offline, we set a
# timeout value so scripts do not hang.

CheckHostIP yes
# The DNS has been deemed quite reliable on this network.  This is
# recommended as another form of host validation.

TCPKeepAlive no
# We are using ServerAliveInterval and ServerAliveCountMax
```

```
ServerAliveInterval 10
ServerAliveCountMax 5

# Identifcation
##############
IdentitiesOnly yes
# We would like only specified identities to be allowed to be
# used.
IdentityFile ~/.ssh/identity
IdentityFile ~/.ssh/id_rsa
IdentityFile ~/.ssh/id_dsa
# The above files are defaults for user identification (keys).

# Authentication
###############
# Host-based Authentication
RhostsAuthentication no
RhostsRSAAuthentication no
HostbasedAuthentication no
# We do not allow Host-based authentication in general.

RSAAuthentication yes
PubkeyAuthentication yes
# We encourage the use of digital credentials.  They are more
# difficult to spoof and cause less support calls/password resets.

PasswordAuthentication yes
# Some users/applications need passwords.  Password policy
# (complexity, etc.) is enforced by the machines, not by OpenSSH.

NoHostAuthenticationForLocalhost no
# Home directories are not on NFS

# Forwarding
###########
ForwardAgent yes
# In the intranet, agent forwarding is allowed to ease use of
# patching, and system hopping via ssh. In a DMZ or untrusted
# network, we disable agent forwarding to prevent accessing the
# agent and crawling up the tunnel.  While we have no evidence of
# this being a simple task, or a policy, we have found it best
# practice.

ForwardX11 yes
ForwardX11Trusted yes
# We always enable X11 forwarding.  Invariably our users will
# want to use an X-Windows System from somewhere, and we would
```

```
# rather it be over an encrypted connection than the standard X11-
# type connections.

# System Settings
#################

Protocol 2
# Because of deficiencies in protocol 1, this network only
# utilizes protocol 2.

GlobalKnownHostsFile /etc/ssh/ssh_known_hosts
# This file contains the public key cache of remote machines for
# the local system.

BatchMode no
# This is a setting we change frequently on a per-user basis.
# While the system-wide setting is no, users often change it to
# yes from running scheduled tasks (cron) or application
# connections. This setting prevents the ssh client from asking
# for passwords or passphrases.

StrictHostKeyChecking ask
# Ask is the default for the system and for the interactive users.
# In a batch mode (cron), oftentimes this is changed to no.
# We educate users about what a host key change is and why
# OpenSSH will not connect to a host with a changed key if they
# have already cached it. This is done via emails and motd
# (message of the day on unix).

EscapeChar ~
# This character allows users to background their current
# session to run commands on the host they are connected from.

SendEnv PATH
# Permit users to send PATH due to odd configurations on some
# machines

# Control Master is only allowed and configured by the user.

LogLevel Verbose
# Verbose Logging provides nice amounts of logs.

# Encryption
############

Ciphers aes128-cbc,3des-cbc,blowfish-cbc,cast128-cbc,arcfour,aes192-cbc,aes256-cbc
# These ciphers are acceptable in the USA.  The legal department
# handles what encryption is allowed outside the USA.
```

```
# These only apply to protocol 2, because that is all that is
# allowed.
```

Reading that configuration file is challenging if it is on a production system. When I want to troubleshoot, reading through lines of explanation is costly and not fun. I shortened the configuration file for use inside of a production environment, as you can see in Listing 5-10. The values of the settings have not changed. Keeping the two documents in sync between commented and not commented versions can be difficult. I suggest editing the heavily commented one and grepping out the comments. Also, using a version control system of some sort can aid with the task. I do add a small header in this file to help the administrators who are less familiar with OpenSSH.

Listing 5-10. *Less Verbose* ssh_config *Client Configuration File*

```
#/etc/ssh/ssh_config

# This is the ssh client system-wide configuration file.  See
# ssh_config for more information.  This file provides defaults
# for users, and the values can be changed in per-user
# configuration files or on the command line.

# Configuration data is parsed as follows:
#  1. command-line options
#  2. user-specific file
#  3. system-wide file
# Configuration values only changed the first time they are set.
# Thus, host-specific definitions should be at the beginning of
# the configuration file, and defaults at the end.

#Version x.x
#Trusted Network (intranet)
Host *
Port 22
AddressFamily inet
ConnectTimeout 4
CheckHostIP yes
TCPKeepAlive no
ServerAliveInterval 10
ServerAliveCountMax 5
IdentitiesOnly yes
IdentityFile ~/.ssh/identity
IdentityFile ~/.ssh/id_rsa
IdentityFile ~/.ssh/id_dsa
RhostsAuthentication no
RhostsRSAAuthentication no
HostbasedAuthentication no
RSAAuthentication yes
PubkeyAuthentication yes
```

```
PasswordAuthentication yes
NoHostAuthenticationForLocalhost no
ForwardAgent yes
ForwardX11 yes
ForwardX11Trusted yes
Protocol 2
GlobalKnownHostsFile /etc/ssh/ssh_known_hosts
BatchMode no
StrictHostKeyChecking ask
EscapeChar ~
SendEnv PATH
LogLevel Verbose
Ciphers aes128-cbc,3des-cbc,blowfish-cbc,cast128-cbc,arcfour,aes192-cbc,aes256-cbc
```

ssh_config scenarios

Normally, system-wide client configurations are left fairly static. Once options are agreed upon and set, they are oftentimes left alone for years, unless new releases of OpenSSH provide new features for the client configuration that could potentially add value to your implementation. In many environments, the preceding client configuration files will allow maximum security without inhibiting usability too much. There are, however, scenarios in which enabling a bit more usability far outweighs the security needs.

ForwardAgent

Agent forwarding is discussed in more depth in the next chapter, but for now think of it as a backstage pass. If you have a backstage pass, once you get past the first guard, the guard in front of the makeup area will not ask to see your pass, because if you are back there, you already have provided authorization somewhere.

Agent forwarding allows you to move around to different hosts that forward authentication agents once you have authenticated the first time. Once you provide the passphrase to your digital credential, in this case an OpenSSH key, you can move to any system that accepts that key, if you add it to the agent.

I use this every day in my job. I start from the server where my private key is located. I then move to a system I am working on. Oftentimes I will find I need to grab a patch or configuration file update. I then will scp to our patch repository and retrieve the patch I need, without ever reauthenticating.

This is only useful when public key authentication using the same private key is enabled on multiple targets. Inside the client configuration file, setting the ForwardAgent keyword to yes as in the following example will enable this time-saving authentication mechanism:

```
ForwardAgent yes
```

StrictHostKeyChecking, BatchMode, and ConnectTimeout

To create an environment that can be run in an unattended manor, the system must be fault tolerant. Enabling BatchMode means that a script or job will not just sit forever waiting for a user-supplied password or passphrase if public key authentication fails. Additionally, if a host is unpingable, it will just move on.

Strict checking of host keys can also cause issues. If your job is waiting for you to specify yes to accept this key, it is not running. If your environment does not get many host key changes, leaving this at ask will probably be fine. If you are constantly getting new systems, new IP addresses, or new keys, setting this to no will greatly reduce the problems in your scripts. It will auto-cache the public keys of the remote hosts.

The more educated end users of ssh often figure out they can get around the pesky prompt for a yes or no by changing this option to no. Depending on your organization's system policy, that might be acceptable.

Keep in mind that tuning a batch client configuration file requires public key authentication as well. Poor network reliability has also caused me to invoke a batch-like configuration file before, where failures were very common and frustrating, perhaps in a wireless setting.

Systems sometimes are offline due to incidents or scheduled maintenance. It is also recommended you set a ConnectTimeout value that makes sense on your network(s). If a network connection is expected to route around the world, a value of 4 seconds could be too short. Adjust this value to meet your needs.

```
BatchMode yes
StrictHostKeyChecking no
ConnectTimeout 4
```

Host-based Authentication

Many fellow administrators and other information technology architects ask me about whether or not they should allow host-based authentication inside of OpenSSH. I highly discourage it in nearly every situation. It has been my experience that host-based authentication is enabled because someone wants to take a shortcut. At first glance, it might seem that this is the best way to create a drop-in replacement for rlogin/rsh, and it is probably the easiest, but user-based authentication has more auditing capabilities and can be controlled at a more granular level. Host-based authentication can be enabled to use host keys as the authentication credentials, rather than simply an IP address, and does provide an encrypted communication mechanism, so it is much more secure than traditional trust relationship authentication; however, host-based authentication still requires that Host A trust the authentication performed on Host B.

If the desire is to not be prompted for a password upon login, use user-based public key authentication. There is no limit for how many keys can be on a host, or even how many a single user can have.

Host-based authentication, if you wish to use it, requires a few changes be made to ssh_config and to sshd_config, along with caching of the host keys for the hosts involved. In Chapter 6, when I cover all types of authentication, I discuss and demonstrate host-based authentication.

Dealing with Users

Educating your user base about the options and security concerns available in the ssh_config file is a daunting task. On my systems that have large numbers of users, I provide users with a .ssh/config from /etc/skel that is populated in their home directory upon creation and allows them to change it as they see fit. Of course, certain settings can be completely overridden by ssh_config and sshd_config from the remote system, which root solely controls.

If your organization and users are new to ssh, perhaps providing a web page or tutorial can help them out. I wrote a few and posted them onto our internal support site. As users asked additional questions, I updated and added to them. Later, I even provided a zip file with some Windows client programs and a Word document about the organizational security policies surrounding SSH.

If your users primarily are dealing with Microsoft Windows workstations to connect to OpenSSH on various types of UNIX or Linux systems, you will want to take a look at Appendix A, which covers graphical Windows clients. Many options that can be set inside of an ssh_config file are configurable inside of a graphical client as well.

Dealing with Administrators

Having all of the UNIX administrators on the same page for SSH can be difficult. Some administrators prefer telnet and ftp, while others have hundreds of scripts and refuse to convert them.

Other challenges specifically with the client often lie in education about order of precedence. In one of the largest SSH implementations I was a part of, I commonly found the system-wide configuration client would be changed to enable batch usage. This causes issues with real interactive users. The root cause of these unexpected changes was because the administrator did not understand the order of precedence for client settings, and because he had root-level access, he just edited the system configuration rather than his individual file. Once he and the rest of the team learned about the .ssh directory and what type of settings and environments can be set up inside of it, the problem plaguing this particular system for weeks occurred no more.

Summary

In this chapter, I covered the ssh client on as many levels as possible. From the command-line options to the primary and user configuration files, you have been introduced to all command-line options. I demonstrated a few tricks involving common usage as well. The knowledge you have gained in this chapter and about the sshd server will provide an excellent foundation for learning about public key authentication and uncovering some very serious power for automating administrative tasks.

CHAPTER 6

■■■

Authentication

The discussion of OpenSSH thus far has covered its Telnet-like capabilities in conjunction with introducing the ability to securely transfer files utilizing this technology. For many end users, their introduction to SSH is complete. For power users and administrators, the discussion thus far of OpenSSH has left out a drop-in replacement for rsh. Traditional rsh allows users to connect to a remote host based on IP address. SSH supports per-user public key authentication, allowing maximum flexibility without compromising security, which provides a drop-in, secure replacement for rsh.

This chapter begins with an introduction to public key authentication, discussing both how it works and showing you how to configure it. From there, I cover host-based authentication and discuss OpenSSH's authentication methods. The chapter concludes with a quick how-to section to serve as a reference.

Note The discussion of authentication in this chapter will focus on SSH protocol version 2. Similar options are available using the now deprecated protocol 1, but the use of protocol 2 is encouraged.

Public Key Authentication

Keys are a fixed bit length of data stored in a file that controls the encryption or decryption of data and are used to authenticate a user or system. *Authentication* is the ability to prove the user is who he or she claims to be. SSH understands keys and accepts these digital credentials to allow remote access.

When public key authentication is configured, a user can use ssh to access a system from another with authentication taking place behind the scenes. To an end user or administrator, it appears very similar to rsh or rlogin. From a security perspective, keys are extremely difficult to forge and offer much higher security than traditional password- or IP address–based authentication. This type of behavior enables several administrative benefits, including the ability to script commands on multiple hosts, and eases the burden of password management.

What Is Public Key Authentication?

Public key cryptography, sometimes referred to as an *asymmetric encryption algorithm*, is comprised of two pieces, a public key and private key. When keys are created, the public and private keys are generated at the same time. In the case of SSH, the private key needs to be kept private with strict permissions (600). The public key can be distributed to any system or person who would like it. If your private key is ever compromised, you must regenerate a new key pair, revoke your old public key, and redistribute your public key. If your public key has become corrupt or misplaced, you can regenerate it, assuming your private key is still intact.

Asymmetric algorithms require both keys to perform any type of decryption.[1] For example, if I encode a message with Sally's public key, I know that only Sally (or anyone with her private key) can decode the message. Conversely, if she has a message for me, she can encrypt it using my public key, and then only I am able to decrypt it using my private key.

Public key operations take a considerable amount of time to perform when compared with symmetric or block ciphers such as 3DES and AES. With SSH, the public key authentication takes place to establish the session and provide the end point with the secret key for the block cipher. The session then is connected via block ciphers and allows the encryption to occur at a much faster rate. This initial session setup ensures confidentiality by making sure the transmission of the secret block cipher key is encrypted.

How Secure Is Public Key Authentication?

As you may recall from Chapter 2, after installing OpenSSH for the first time, when the connection attempt was made to the server, the ssh client told you the public key for this host was not known. After verifying the public key and accepting it by typing **yes**, the ssh client cached the public key of the remote host. This provided protection against man-in-the-middle attacks, because if a new server was put online that did not offer the same host keys, the ssh client would require user intervention to connect and accept the key change. Using user-based public keys takes this security to a new level, because the host is authenticated (via the host keys), and the user is authenticated via his or her private/public key. This provides a layer of security over passwords because password authentication is normally allowed from any host, while private keys are often stored only on well-secured hosts, and therefore are not normally allowed from any source node on a network.

A user of SSH can generate a key pair consisting of one private and one public key. The private key is meant to be kept private, which includes providing strict permissions so other users of the system cannot access the file, nor store it on an FTP server, nor exchange private keys with coworkers. The private key is just that, private. Compromising the private key allows an attacker or adversary to assume your identity and act as you. The public key, on the other hand, can be shared with anyone. The public key, if lost or tampered with, can be regenerated as long as the private key still exists. The public key file is what is placed on your remote systems to allow user authentication via keys. The private key provided by the client is then paired with the public key on the remote host. If they cryptographically match, the user is authenticated and thus granted access to the remote system. If they do not match, depending on your configuration,

---

1. In some cryptographic algorithms, such as those used with OpenSSH, the private key is all that is needed for encryption and decryption because the public key can be regenerated from the private key.

SSH may try other authentication methods such as password authentication, or it may just report a failed connection attempt.

Public key authentication has a distinct advantage over password authentication in that passwords are not randomly generated because they normally have some semblance to words. Additionally, passwords allow authentication for users from any source node.

Key-based authentication restricts the source nodes to the hosts with the private key stored or available to them. To compromise key-based authentication, either the private key must be compromised or cracked. Cracking a private key entails using ciphertext (encrypted communication packet captures) and applying mathematical algorithms to it until it unlocks. This is extremely time consuming and computationally intensive. Provided a key length of 1024 bits or greater is used, cracking private keys is not practical using today's computing technology.

Public Key Authentication vs. Password Authentication

Public keys offer some distinct advantages over password-based authentication, such as the ability to automate tasks easily through scripting of SSH commands, and assignment of multiple public keys to a single user is allowed. This can be advantageous in situations with accounts that are used by several people (application and root accounts). Assigning each individual a key means each login to the shared account is traceable to a user. Public keys, however, can be more difficult to manage and support from an end-user perspective.

Password authentication must be performed each time a login is desired to a remote host. Additionally, changing passwords is sometimes difficult in environments with large numbers of nodes. Passphrases only have to be changed on private keys, which is normally a much smaller number than for the total environment.

Oftentimes, even when using public key authentication, the need for passwords does not decrease significantly, as other services still require password for authentication, such as sudo, ftp, and many commercial applications. Getting rid of passwords completely is not always an option, but if you use keys whenever possible, the speed at which you perform your job can greatly increase.

Table 6-1 shows a comparison between passwords and public key authentication.

Table 6-1. *Passwords vs. Public Key Authentication*

Passwords	Public Key Authentication
Passwords are normally not random, and are oftentimes easily guessed strings.	Keys are designed and generated using algorithms involving random numbers.
Single accounts generally do not have multiple passwords.	Multiple keys per account are inherent to SSH.
Passwords are written down and oftentimes stored poorly.	Keys can be stored on USB drives or preferably smart cards for quick and secure authentication.
Users are normally more familiar with passwords.	Public key authentication requires user education.
Passwords are subject to brute-force attacks that normally complete in a quick manner.	Keys are also subject to brute-force attacks, but the effort and computing power is normally orders of magnitude greater than the effort required to break passwords.

Ensuring Public Key Authentication Is Available on the Server

This chapter focuses primarily on public key authentication. Before public key authentication can be used, it is imperative to ensure that public key authentication is an available authentication method. If the OpenSSH server, sshd, does not support public key authentication, using passwords or other mechanisms to authenticate is required. If you have root access on the remote server you wish to connect to, you can check to see whether public key authentication is available by checking for the keyword PubKeyAuthentication in the sshd_config file. By default, this setting is enabled. If you do not have root access to the remote system, running a client command in verbose mode will show what authentication methods the server provides. The first level of debug (-v) from the client will show what authentication methods are available from the remote SSH server. As an example, Listing 6-1 shows my server www offering publickey and password as authentication methods.

Listing 6-1. *Using the* -v *Option to Determine If the Remote Server Allows Public Authentication*

```
stahnke@rack: ~> ssh -v www
...
debug1: expecting SSH2_MSG_NEWKEYS
debug1: SSH2_MSG_NEWKEYS received
debug1: SSH2_MSG_SERVICE_REQUEST sent
debug1: SSH2_MSG_SERVICE_ACCEPT received
debug1: Authentications that can continue: publickey,password
debug1: Next authentication method: publickey
```

Ensuring the Client Allows Public Key Authentication

The OpenSSH client can control what authentication methods are attempted for each connection. By default, public key authentication is allowed; however, to be sure, look at the local config file found in $HOME/.ssh. You may recall from Chapter 5 that two keyword lines determine whether the client will allow public key authentication. These settings are from an OpenSSH client config file that ensures public key authentication is available (protocol 2):

```
PreferredAuthentications publickey,keyboard-interactive,password
PubkeyAuthentication yes
```

Because the PreferredAuthentications client option defaults to allowing public key authentication, if your client configuration does not have that line, public key authentication is available. If authentication methods are specified, ensure publickey is an option, specifically before password and keyboard-interactive, as publickey authentication requires less interaction. Additionally, to instruct the client whether or not it should try public key authentication at all, the PubkeyAuthentication keyword must be set to yes.

Setting Up Public Key Authentication

Setting up public key authentication involves generating a key pair for a user, installing the public key on remote host(s), and ensuring permissions and ownership of the key files are correct.

Generating Your Key Pair

In order to use public key authentication, you must generate a key pair, and then install your public key on the remote host(s) you wish to access. Generating a key pair involves using the OpenSSH utility ssh-keygen. The ssh-keygen command is normally found in the bin directory of the OpenSSH installation tree. Listing 6-2 shows how to generate a key pair for a user.

Listing 6-2. *Generating a 1024-bit RSA Key Pair for a User*

```
stahnke@rack:~> ssh-keygen -t rsa -b 1024
Generating public/private rsa key pair.
Enter file in which to save the key (/home/stahnke/.ssh/id_rsa):
Enter passphrase (empty for no passphrase): <a passphrase>
Enter same passphrase again: <a passphrase>
Your identification has been saved in /home/stahnke/.ssh/id_rsa.
Your public key has been saved in /home/stahnke/.ssh/id_rsa.pub.
The key fingerprint is:
a4:ae:ff:6d:4e:05:f1:5b:d9:1b:3f:44:ba:c2:96:84 stahnke@rack
stahnke@rack:~>
```

This command generates a key pair for the user stahnke. The -t switch defines what algorithm (type) to use for key generation, and the -b specifies the key length in bits. The command prompts for a passphrase.

The ssh-keygen command prompts for a passphrase, which is not displayed on the screen when input by the user. It is considered best practice to have a passphrase on private keys. The passphrase locks or encrypts the private key so that is not usable until it is unlocked via a passphrase. Once it is unlocked via a properly entered passphrase, it can be used for authentication. See the sidebar "Working with Passphrases" to learn more.

Once my key pair has been generated, the private key file is stored in /home/stahnke/.ssh/id_rsa. The public counterpart is at /home/stahnke/.ssh/id_rsa.pub. The output form ssh-keygen also provides the fingerprint of the key. The fingerprint is an md5 checksum of the public key that can be used for verification, especially in a system log to see which private key is used for authentication; I will demonstrate this in the section "Tracing Public Keys to Users" later in this chapter.

WORKING WITH PASSPHRASES

The passphrase is a phrase (at least four characters long) that is used to protect the private key file. The passphrase can contain spaces, punctuation, and any alphanumeric character. It is meant to be easy to remember by design, but with a length that makes cracking the passphrase extremely difficult. You should specify a passphrase so that your private key must be unlocked before using it; otherwise the root user and anyone else who can gain access to your private key file can assume your identity on remote hosts.

Unencrypted private keys, or those without passphrases, are subject to many methods of retrieval and compromise. System backups could allow access to a private key, or network sniffing of NFS, just to name a couple. Home directory security is also a fundamental security practice that will assist with OpenSSH key management in addition to the other benefits. Many arguments have been made for using private keys without passphrases; however, this is highly discouraged. For using keys in automated jobs, look into an ssh-agent tool such as Keychain, which is covered in Chapter 8.

Remember Your Passphrase

Unlike passwords on UNIX/Linux systems, passphrases cannot be reset. Therefore, if you forget your passphrase, a new key must be made. Root cannot reset a passphrase. This helps security in that root cannot assume your identity on other systems by using your private key, but it hinders usability because if you need a new key, many times it can take a significant amount of effort to redistribute your new public key. Remember, a passphrase need not be all that complex; length is more important than the number of special characters, numbers, and such. For instance, a great passphrase might be, "I downloaded OpenSSH from http:// www.openssh.com today." That would take a long time to crack, and is easy to remember.

BIT LENGTH OF KEYS

From a security point of view, a longer key length is stronger and very difficult to crack or forge. Keep in mind, however, that long key lengths take more time to generate and to operate with. Authentication with a 2048-bit key can take noticeably longer than with a 1024- or 768-bit key. Your organization may have standards on key length; in general, 1024 is thought to be strong enough for most usage. If your system is on a hostile network or Internet facing, you might consider 2048-bit keys. The maximum number of bits allowed is 32768. OpenSSH 4.2 and above have a default key length of 2048 bits.

Installing a Public Key on a Remote Host(s)

Now that I have a key pair created, I need to install the public key on the remote system, which is shown in Listing 6-3. To do so, I will use the scp mechanism to transfer the file over and run a command. Installation of the public key entails copying it to a remote system and added it to the .ssh/authorized_keys file.

Listing 6-3. *An RSA Public Key Is Securely Copied and Appended to* authorized_keys

```
stahnke@rack:~> scp /home/stahnke/.ssh/id_rsa.pub stahnke@www:.ssh/public_key
Password:
id_dsa.pub                                    100%  598      0.6KB/s   00:00
stahnke@rack:~> ssh stahnke@www "cat /home/stahnke/.ssh/public_key >>
/home/stahnke/.ssh/authorized_keys"
Password:
```

Installing the public key onto a remote server can also be done in one command using redirection. This command will cat the local id_rsa.pub and through ssh append it to the .ssh/authorized_keys on the remote hosts.

```
stahnke@rack: ~> ssh user@remote_host cat < $HOME/.ssh/id_rsa.pub   ">>" \
.ssh/authorized_keys
```

The authorized_keys File

To install your public key on a remote host, simply use scp to copy the public key file over to your remote systems and place the contents in a $HOME/.ssh/authorized_keys file. The authorized keys file consists of public keys, one per line.

There are a few things to keep in mind while doing this:

- The $HOME/.ssh directory should have the most restrictive permissions possible. Owner-controlled directories are best (700), but 750 permissions will still allow public key authentication to occur. Someone can assume your identity on a server very easily if he or she can place his or her public key into the authorized_keys file residing in your home directory. $HOME/.ssh/authorized_keys files are a target for attackers, so watch them carefully. It is a best practice to have some integrity verification system available for authorized_keys files. Some possible solutions are presented in Chapters 8 and 9 that will allow for checksum integrity verification of the authorized_keys files.

- You can simply use scp to copy id_dsa.pub as the authorized_keys file on the remote host if the authorized_keys file does not exist or if you want to overwrite it, as shown in this example:

```
stahnke@rack: ~> scp .ssh/id_rsa.pub stahnke@www:.ssh/authorized_keys
id_rsa.pub                              100%  614     0.6KB/s   00:00
```

- Multiple keys are allowed in authorized_keys, one per line. If you have different keys from different hosts, or you want to allow other users access to a particular account, you can grant them that access via a single authorized_keys file.

- In older implementations of OpenSSH, the authorized_keys file designed for protocol 2 was called authorized_keys2. This file is still consulted for backward compatibility, but it has been deprecated. Therefore, authorized_keys (without the 2) should be used to store public keys for users.

Connecting via Public Key Authentication

Now that a key pair has been generated and the public key installed on a remote host, a connection can be made to the host using public key authentication. In this example, the user attempts the connection to the remote system using public key authentication. This user is also prompted for a passphrase of the private key.

```
stahnke@rack:~> ssh www
Enter passphrase for key '/home/stahnke/.ssh/id_rsa': <passphrase>
```

Notice that the ssh client calls for the passphrase to unlock the private key. The primary benefit of public key authentication, from a user perspective, is that it requires less interaction. At this point, using public key authentication or password authentication seems equivalent, as far as requiring user input to perform the authentication. The assistance of SSH agents, covered in the section "ssh-agent," will demonstrate caching the passphrase to require its entry only once per session. After that, authentication will be noninteractive, which is ideal for scripting and quick command execution.

Troubleshooting Public Key Authentication

If you are having problems setting up public key authentication, I have a few troubleshooting tips for you that can help. There are mainly three common issues when dealing with public key authentication, which I outline next.

Invalid authorized_keys Entry

The authorized_keys file requires that the public key be on one line. Many times, I have seen issues occur because users or administrators copied and pasted a public key from a text editor that automatically inserted line breaks in the key. The authorized_keys will be invalid if this is done. While it may appear that the key spans multiple lines inside of an editor, it should be on one line. This is why using scp to distribute a public key file is among the best options. scp creates an exact copy of the file, including line spacing.

Password Expiry

If a user's password is expired on a remote host, public key authentication may fail; however, this is not immediately obvious when looking at the log generated by sshd. The best hint from the sshd reporting is it found the public key, but then the authentication fails. This is shown in Listing 6-4. On AIX and OpenBSD, an expired password will not cause failure. Systems implementing a newer version of PAM probably will fail.

Listing 6-4. *A Public Key Authentication Failure Because of an Expired Password*

```
root@www: # cat  /var/log/secure
...
Mar 15 12:39:06 www sshd[6237]: Found matching RSA key:
f9:e5:2d:29:e2:1b:79:1f:b7:82:14:8c:ec:cd:a1:b8
Mar 15 12:39:06 www sshd[6237]: Failed publickey for stahnke from
 ::ffff:192.168.1.101 port 48806 ssh2
```

File Ownership and Permissions

If the StrictModes keyword is set to yes in the server configuration on the remote system, the user's home directory, .ssh directory, and authorized_keys file must not be group- or world-writable. If they are, sshd will reject the public key authentication attempt and fall back to another method such as password authentication if it is available. If sshd is logging at INFO or higher, a syslog message will be generated by sshd. The following example shows a log entry when public key authentication fails due to poor permissions on the .ssh directory:

```
root@www # cat /var/log/secure
...
Mar 15 23:22:41 www sshd[3296]: Authentication refused: bad ownership or modes
 for directory /home/stahnke/.ssh
...
```

A Look at the Keys

Now that you have created a private and public key pair, take a moment to become a little more familiar with them. In my example, I chose RSA (named for its inventors Ron Rivest, Adi Shamir, and Len Adleman) over DSA (digital signature algorithm) as the type of keys to generate. The use of DSA versus RSA seems to be fairly split. In the past, RSA was a patented algorithm, so DSA seemed to be a better choice based on cost. DSA keys take longer to generate, but are faster to use during authentication. DSA relies heavily on the ability to generate random numbers. If a random number generation sequence can be predicted, DSA keys can be compromised; however, in modern implementations of DSA generation, this is extremely difficult to do. Now, because the patent for RSA has expired, thus negating the cost issue, I do not know of any reason to pick one key type over another; it is mostly personal preference.

If you take a look at your private key file, an example of which is shown in Listing 6-5, you will see that it is just some comments and ASCII text. While this is not particularly useful, it is nice if you are confused on what filenames are public and private. By default, the public key is the name of the private key with a .pub extension. In some more complex SSH implementations I have been a part of, however, the public keys were renamed to avoid having several public keys named id_rsa.pub in a key repository.

Listing 6-5. *The Contents of an RSA Private Key*

```
stahnke@rack:~> cat .ssh/id_rsa
-----BEGIN RSA PRIVATE KEY-----
MIICWgIBAAKBgQDK+CsBLLxUjkXM7ilNU3Dj08YUPcHVCJFGxDM3engnj07Y/3oo
xnQGIFDPx7kPUcLAiFvZZHLAHpYhA1ZktkrWAtRm4ZpLEKzROGwK9YXcnmAmtFGO
Ur+bD63SOhyDf3x8auObhN/oaOsZO/SGyUG2tQ5gA/GZWrjRFy7elx9R1QIBIwKB
gEWW6ixJ2iueflTj8OdPzu8Gx5HpScViBexghpatpYnn/ca9/gN3Pbj1IwVpDD/E
QsWrGC1qAsWG1GMXFk5qYsxrBsKRjE/TOZgboMI+25BcsSvQdzJsilt2gNgqlcua
JOxf7gWKkIHe1QUvm8AArS72VOzVj/nnevRnSfw6CuGLAkEA/oS6O5ljXRL/DZ4r
uZGZhR5+EOv9JL45B5H++Rp3AN3gCoBKuVJmPjuyhKQN12JSWdNR1DysNgsFv2V/
I3uXopJBAMwmn9LSVDR2gc3OU1nz3grnk4D/ZBwYge55XVzNJVJWqEiXwKISsgts
wtnKM5qQ8LduBhYmVEGHLSqG6nUD/bUCQHufjafrasbOtmWzOc8pdnPbnFKD/pzR
bCg/mRnoSG4ioAUZveT8IwhI4a4jzDVqRUGShtTNAzAxPU5V3qrVoWsCQQCL/Tpk
rXuRsFj93fADKuFmkCqhmS6Oig/z+3M4Uig4de+8v9SMZJdYSpQ9kfd/7lvrfqUW
gK7NbQkHN/E6S+ErAkBSpju2kqv+P6ycrzhTpST4OIr1hLOUT6OCddWXGWOx9B/R
7unKmlMLPq2MQhsm/XEsVyk4Sr/uoTarrA3G8GU9
-----END RSA PRIVATE KEY-----
```

The public key file looks very similar to the private file. Please note the main string of the public key file is all one line inside of a UNIX editor such as vi or emacs. If you try to copy and paste a key file from an editor that inserts return carriages, such as notepad.exe, the key will not be valid. Listing 6-6 shows a public key file.

Listing 6-6. *An RSA Public Key*

```
stahnke@rack:~> cat .ssh/id_rsa.pub
ssh-rsa AAAAB3NzaC1yc2EAAAABIwAAAIEAyvgrASy8VI5FzO4pTVNw49PGFD3B1QiRRsQz
N3p4J49O2P96NMZOBiBQz8e5D1HCwIhb2WRywB6WIQNWZLZK1gLUZuGaSxCsOdBsCvWF3J5gJ
rRRtFK/mw+tOtIcg398fGrjm4Tf6GjrGdPOhslBtrUOYAPxmVq4ORcu3pcfUdU= stahnke@rack
```

Public Key Restrictions

The public keys created for OpenSSH offer additional security and restrictions by using one or more keywords at the beginning of the public key specified in the authorized_keys file. Restrictions can limit source nodes, limit commands, or allow restrictions on agent forwarding.

The format for keyword restrictions requires that they be placed before the main text of the key. Multiple options are comma delimited, and white space is not permitted unless it is in double quotes. The keywords are not case sensitive.

■**Caution** While `authorized_keys` files can offer a good method of access control, these files are accessible to the account using them, therefore changes can be made by the user. Best practices for restrictions are set up inside the `sshd_config` file. The `authorized_keys` file restriction options are primarily designed to prevent key misuse.

Source Restriction: from

As an additional method of access control, in an `authorized_keys` file, a source host can be specified, which will only enable public key authentication from specific hostnames or IP addresses. In this case, I specified my primary workstation named `rack` as the host to use this public key. Simple regular expressions using an * or a ? are permitted, such as `from="*.mycompany.com"`. The `from` restriction can deny specified hosts using the ! operator. The following is an RSA public key with a source host's restriction placed on it. This key allows connection from my workstation named `rack`, but denies connections from `*.badguy.com`.

```
stahnke@rack:~> cat .ssh/id_rsa.pub
from="rack,!*.badguy.com" ssh-rsa
AAAAB3NzaC1yc2EAAAABIwAAAIEAyvgrASy8VI5FzO4pTVNw49PGFD3B1QiRRsQzN3
p4J49O2P96NMZOBiBQz8e5D1HCwIhb2WRywB6WIQNWZLZK1gLUZuGaSxCsOdBsCvWF3J5gJrR
RtFK/mw+tOtIcg398fGrjm4Tf6GjrGdPOhslBtrUOYAPxmVq4ORcu3pcfUdU= stahnke@rack
```

Placing host restrictions on public keys provides a further method of protection against fraudulent usage. If an attacker is able to compromise a key, he or she also must gain access to specific systems, or compromise DNS/routing, thus multiple targets must be compromised for malicious activities to occur via key-based authentication.

Command Restriction: command

Restricting the commands a key can perform is also permitted inside of an `authorized_keys` file. For example, if a user should have access only to the `uptime` command, his or her public key inside of an `authorized_keys` file would have a entry like the one in the following example, which shows a public key with a host and command restriction specified.

```
command="/usr/bin/uptime"  ssh-rsa AAAAB3NzaC1yc2EAAAABIwAAAIEAyvgrASy
8VI5FzO4pTVNw49PGFD3B1QiRRsQzN3p4J49O2P96NMZOBiBQz8e5D1HCwIhb2WRywB6WIQN
WZLZK1gLUZuGaSxCsOdBsCvWF3J5gJrRRtFK/mw+tOtIcg398fGrjm4Tf6GjrGdPOhslBtrUOYAPxmV
q4ORcu3pcfUdU= stahnke@rack
```

If this user tries to run another command, such as `cat /etc/passwd`, the authentication will occur, and the `uptime` command will be executed. `sshd` does not execute the arbitrary `cat /etc/passwd` command, instead the specified command runs.

```
stahnke@rack: ~> ssh  www "cat /etc/passwd"
 21:08:55 up 5 days, 22:53,  1 user,  load average: 0.50, 0.15, 0.00
```

Environment Restriction: environment

Setting up restriction environment variables can be done in the authorized_keys file. The values set using the environment keyword in the authorized_keys file overwrite the default values, but this feature is disabled by default inside of the sshd_config file. Because PermitUserEnvironment is not enabled by default inside sshd_config, it is normally better to use SendEnv in a client configuration file and AcceptEnv inside the sshd_config file. This way, environment variables are controlled uniformly, and multiple variable setups are allowed.

Port Forwarding Restriction: no-port-forwarding

To disable port forwarding, the no-port-forwarding option should be used in the authorized_keys file as shown in Listing 6-7. This option is commonly used when restricting commands, because even with command restrictions, it is possible to forward a port. See Chapter 7 for more details on port forwarding.

Listing 6-7. *A Public Key That Disables Port Forwarding in Addition to Restricting Commands*

```
command="/usr/bin/uptime",no-port-forwarding  ssh-rsa
AAAAB3NzaC1yc2EAAAABIwAAAIEAyvgrASy
8VI5FzO4pTVNw49PGFD3B1QiRRsQzN3p4J49O2P96NMZOBiBQz8e5D1HCwIhb2WRywB6WIQN
WZLZK1gLUZuGaSxCsOdBsCvWF3J5gJrRRtFK/mw+tOtIcg398fGrjm4Tf6GjrGdPOhslBtrUOYAPxmV
q4ORcu3pcfUdU= stahnke@rack
```

X11 Forwarding Restriction: no-X11-forwarding

If X11 forwarding is not desired, perhaps in high-risk environments, use the no-X11-forwarding keyword. This will result in an error for any attempts made to forward X11 applications across SSH.

Agent Forwarding Restriction: no-agent-forwarding

Agent forwarding (which is covered later in the section "Agent Forwarding") allows remote boxes to use public key authentication credentials forwarded from a source server to additional targets. This can be a time-saving task, but for some accounts it might not be desired.

TTY Restriction: no-pty

By default, sshd allows clients to request a PTY, or pseudo terminal, for all connections. If a user should not have a TTY, use the no-pty option.

Specific Port Forwarding Enabled: permitopen="host:port"

To restrict local port forwarding, you can use the option permitopen. The syntax requires a host:port with IPv4 or host/port with IPv6. This specifies the hosts and ports through which local forwarding is permitted. The host must be exact; regular expressions are not parsed. Multiple permitopen options are permitted.

This option is very rarely used. Normally, port forwarding is allowed or denied via the sshd_config file and then controlled again using the no-port-forwarding restriction if required.

Tracing Public Keys to Users

Public keys need to be related back to the user for two main reasons. The first reason is for accountability, auditing, and task management. The second reason is to ensure no rogue public keys have been placed into an authorized_keys file. An attacker or malicious user can easily obfuscate his or her identity by changing the default comment on a rogue key to a trusted user@host format. For example, if someone added or replaced a key in my authorized_keys file with the comment stahnke@rack, I would not notice it during a manual edit or review. However, if I validate the key using the ssh-keygen fingerprint display option, and match it back to a log, the rogue key will not match any key distributed and then be removed.

authorized_keys files are valuable targets for attackers and users looking to somehow escalate privilege. This is why it is of the utmost importance that such a file be accessible only to the owner.

Catching a public key that has been placed into an authorized keys file can be done with the aid of SSH key fingerprints. Each key is given a unique fingerprint, which can be used to verify the integrity of the public key used to authenticate. The following syntax will provide the fingerprint for a public key:

```
stahnke@rack: ~> ssh-keygen -l -f /home/stahnke/.ssh/id_rsa.pub
1024 b9:23:7c:cb:34:e6:3f:95:e5:f0:f0:43:68:39:7f:a1  stahnke@rack
```

When sshd has its LogLevel setting at VERBOSE or higher, the fingerprint of the key used to authenticate is logged. By comparing the key fingerprint in the logs to the key fingerprint of the original public key, imposter keys can be found. A rogue key will have a different fingerprint than the expected value from the original public key provided by user. This technique can be used to match keys back to users if several keys are valid for a single account.

```
root@www: # cat /var/log/secure
...
Mar 16 00:45:53 www sshd[3556]: Found matching RSA key:
b9:23:7c:cb:34:e6:3f:95:e5:f0:f0:43:68:39:7f:a1
...
```

The key fingerprint from the log can be tracked to an individual user. Using ssh-keygen -l to display the public key fingerprint can verify the authentication is from the proper key. Best practices for key management include keeping a fingerprint repository of known-good public keys for verification purposes. Key management is discussed in detail in Chapter 8.

Key Generation Information

The tool provided with OpenSSH to generate keys is called ssh-keygen. On most systems, key generation occurs in just a few seconds; however, when using larger key sizes, generation of the key pair can take longer. ssh-keygen includes options that allow users to manage several aspects of their key pair, including the comments associated with the key, the passphrase, or the names of key files.

> **Tip** If you are using SSH Communications Security's SSH Tectia line of products, key generation normally takes much longer than in OpenSSH. SSH Tectia uses 2048-bit keys by default, which really increases the generation and authentication time, though any smaller bit lengths can be specified. Additionally, if you need to connect to systems using SSH Tectia Server, you can export your public key into the commercial SSH2 format by running the OpenSSH ssh-keygen with the -e option. Chapter 10 will cover more about the interoperability between OpenSSH and SSH Tectia.

ssh-keygen is designed to create private and public keys simultaneously. The public key can be derived from the private key, so if a public key is lost, it can be regenerated. Internally, OpenSSH uses ssh-keygen to create host keys the first time sshd starts on a system. Host keys are created without passphrases to enable anyone attempting a connection to use the host key, which proves the identity of the server. User keys can be generated without passphrases, but this is considered against best practice.

The following switches are available to ssh-keygen. Many switches available to ssh-keygen involve Diffie-Hellman group exchange (DH-GEX). Diffie-Hellman group exchange, in this context, allows a mechanism of the SSH client and server agreeing on secret keys to encrypt a session. It is based on using large prime numbers and their moduli to agree on a secret key. The prime number information is stored in /etc/moduli.

-a trials

Normally, 100 tests are performed when testing prime numbers for potential usage in DH-GEX. The -a allows specification of how many tests should be performed. This switch is used in conjunction with the -T option.

-b bits

The number of bits can be specified. By default, 1024 bits are used. This number can be as low as 512 bits. The bit length determines the difficulty in cracking the key, so longer bit lengths are more secure; however, they also require more computational processing to work with them. If you are experiencing performance issues utilizing 2048-bit keys, perhaps lowering them to 1024 could increase speed. On many systems, the difference is negligible, as in Listing 6-8, but on some systems it can make a noticeable difference.

Listing 6-8. *A Time Trial for a Command Using 1024-bit Keys and 2048-bit Keys*

```
#using 1024 bit key
stahnke@rack: ~> time ssh  www uptime
 10:14:17 up 11:58,  1 user,  load average: 0.06, 0.06, 0.02

real    0m0.215s
user    0m0.013s
sys     0m0.005s

# Using 2048 bit key
stahnke@rack: ~> time ssh  www uptime
 10:15:07 up 11:59,  1 user,  load average: 0.02, 0.05, 0.01
```

```
real    0m0.218s
user    0m0.013s
sys     0m0.006s
```

Tip My experience has been that using large keys (larger than 1024 bits) with SSH Communications Security's SSH Tectia line of products is much slower than keys with similar size using OpenSSH. Keep this in mind when choosing key sizes if interoperability is required.

-c

The -c option is used to change the comment in the key pair for a protocol 1 RSA key. The example provided changes the comment on the protocol 1 public key.

```
stahnke@www: ~> ssh-keygen -c
Enter file in which the key is (/home/stahnke/.ssh/id_rsa):
/home/stahnke/.ssh/identity
Key now has comment 'root@www'
Enter new comment: This is my protocol 1 key.  I never use it.
The comment in your key file has been changed.
stahnke@www ~/.ssh> cat identity.pub
1024 35 10621362740706387178170706714006571881392778237725351122900054
292815098185403782452808576394898861111042949896172615479302591172915
778019376735514076051474863811164643257038503776091517435294591194419
964230283548592605762286273901086721760428442386765143003234179853970
31263024442685968678673831124793454070007 This is my protocol 1 key.  I never use it.
```

-e

The -e option exports an OpenSSH key file to the SECSH Public Key File Format specified in the drafts at the Internet Engineering Task Force website (http://www.ietf.org). If a key is exported to the SECSH format, the key can be used by commercial implementations of SSH, including the Tectia line of products from SSH Communications Security. When working with multiple SSH implementations, this option is very useful. More about interoperability between OpenSSH and commercial implementations is covered in Chapter 10. Normally, the output is redirected into a public key file. The following example exports an OpenSSH private key to SECSH format.

```
stahnke@rack: ~/.ssh> ssh-keygen -e
Enter file in which the key is (/home/stahnke/.ssh/id_rsa): <enter>
---- BEGIN SSH2 PUBLIC KEY ----
Comment: "1024-bit RSA, converted from OpenSSH by stahnke@rack"
AAAAB3NzaC1yc2EAAAABIwAAAIEAyvgrASy8VI5FzO4pTVNw49PGFD3B1QiRRsQzN3p4J4
9O2P96NMZOBiBQz8e5D1HCwIhb2WRywB6WIQNWZLZK1gLUZuGaSxCsOdBsCvWF3J5gJrRR
tFK/mw+tOtIcg398fGrjm4Tf6GjrGdPOhslBtrUOYAPxmVq4ORcu3pcfUdU=
---- END SSH2 PUBLIC KEY ----
```

-f

The -f option specifies a file to perform an action on. When adding comments, changing passphrases, or performing other key management tasks, ssh-keygen normally prompts for a file. Instead, this file can be specified on the command line, thus allowing a less interactive interface into key management. The earlier example where a key is exported into SECSH format can be done in one line using the -f option.

```
stahnke@rack: ~/.ssh> ssh-keygen -e -f /home/sthanke/.ssh/id_rsa > SECSH_pub
```

-g

The -g option instructs ssh-keygen to print the SSHFP resource records in generic format. SSHFPs, or SSH FingerPrints, allow the public host key to be stored as a resource record in DNS. This enables the ssh client to perform a lookup of the host key and verify it against the public key being provided by the remote server. If the SSHFP in DNS matches the key provided by the server, the user will not have to verify the public key provided by the server. For more information on SSHFP, see Chapter 8. The following syntax displays how to generate a generic resource record:

```
root@www: # ssh-keygen -r www -g
Enter file in which the key is (/root/.ssh/id_rsa): /etc/ssh/ssh_host_rsa_key.pub
www IN TYPE44 \# 22 01 01 5c7779a620fc38aa4348d954cfe40ca5752e5bfd
root@www: #
```

-i

The -i option will import a key matching the SECSH key standard to an OpenSSH format. The results are then placed on stdout. More information about importing and exporting keys is covered in Chapter 10. The following example uses the -i option to import a SECSH public key into the OpenSSH public key format.

```
stahnke@rack: ~/.ssh> ssh-keygen -i -f SECSH_pub
ssh-rsa AAAAB3NzaC1yc2EAAAABIwAAAIEAyvgrASy8VI5FzO4pTVNw49PGFD3B1QiRRsQzN3p4J49O2P96
NMZOBiBQz8e5D1HCwIhb2WRywB6WIQNWZLZK1gLUZuGaSxCsOdBsCvWF3J5gJrRRtFK/mw+tOtIcg398fGrj
m4Tf6GjrGdPOhslBtrUOYAPxmVq4ORcu3pcfUdU=
```

-l

The -l option will list the fingerprint (md5 checksum) of the public key file. This can be used to verify key integrity and to match up keys to specific users and accounts. Fingerprints can be listed for protocols 1 and 2. The following example lists the fingerprint of an RSA public key:

```
stahnke@rack: ~/.ssh> ssh-keygen -l -f id_rsa.pub
1024 b9:23:7c:cb:34:e6:3f:95:e5:f0:f0:43:68:39:7f:a1  stahnke@rack
```

-p

The -p option allows the user to change the passphrase on a private key file. To change the passphrase, the old passphrase must be known. Passphrases must be at least four characters. If the key previously had no passphrase, only the new passphrase is asked for. The first example shows changing a passphrase on a key that originally had no passphrase. The second example shows changing a passphrase on an already protected key.

```
stahnke@rack: ~/.ssh> ssh-keygen -p -f id_rsa
Key has comment 'id_rsa'
Enter new passphrase (empty for no passphrase): <new passphrase>
Enter same passphrase again: <new passphrase>
Your identification has been saved with the new passphrase.

stahnke@rack: ~/.ssh> ssh-keygen -p -f id_rsa
Enter old passphrase: <old passphrase>
Key has comment 'id_rsa'
Enter new passphrase (empty for no passphrase): <new passphrase>
Enter same passphrase again: <new passphrase>
Your identification has been saved with the new passphrase.
```

-q

The -q option enables quiet mode for key generation. This option is used when OpenSSH generates host keys for the first time. The first example shows key generation in quiet mode. The second example shows the normal key generation process for comparison purposes.

```
stahnke@rack: ~/.ssh> ssh-keygen -q -t dsa -b 2048
Enter file in which to save the key (/home/stahnke/.ssh/id_dsa):
Enter passphrase (empty for no passphrase): <new passphrase>
Enter same passphrase again: <new passphrase>

stahnke@rack: ~/.ssh> ssh-keygen  -t dsa -b 2048
Generating public/private dsa key pair.
Enter file in which to save the key (/home/stahnke/.ssh/id_dsa):
Enter passphrase (empty for no passphrase): <new passphase>
Enter same passphrase again: <new passphrase>
Your identification has been saved in /home/stahnke/.ssh/id_dsa.
Your public key has been saved in /home/stahnke/.ssh/id_dsa.pub.
The key fingerprint is:
7d:fd:4d:16:d0:19:4c:fe:2f:a6:01:f6:7a:87:a4:1d stahnke@rack
```

-r hostname

When using SSHFP in DNS, it is necessary to generate the resource records to put in the DNS entry. To do this, the hostname should be specified using the -r option. The following code generates an SSHFP-specific resource record:

```
www: # ssh-keygen -r www -f /etc/ssh/ssh_host_rsa_key.pub
www IN SSHFP 1 1 5c7779a620fc38aa4348d954cfe40ca5752e5bfd
```

-t type

The -t option, which is required, has already been demonstrated. It specifies the type of key to generate. The only option available for protocol 1 is rsa1. dsa and rsa are available for protocol 2.

-v

The -v option enables verbose mode when using ssh-keygen. For maximum verbosity, use -vvv.

-y

The -y option will regenerate the public key when provided with a private key. This can be useful if the public key was accidentally deleted or overwritten.

```
stahnke@rack: ~/.ssh> ssh-keygen -y -f /home/stahnke/.ssh/id_rsa
Enter passphrase: <passphrase>
ssh-rsa AAAAB3NzaC1yc2EAAAABIwAAAIEAyvgrASy8VI5FzO4pTVNw49PGFD3B1QiRRsQzN3p4J49O
2P96NMZOBiBQz8e5D1HCwIhb2WRywB6WIQNWZLZK1gLUZuGaSxCsOdBsCvWF3J5gJrRRtFK/mw+tOtIc
g398fGrjm4Tf6GjrGdPOhslBtrUOYAPxmVq4ORcu3pcfUdU=
```

-B

The -B option reads a private or public key and outputs the bubblebabble digest. *Bubblebabble* is another method to verify integrity of a key, and is used in commercial implementations of SSH. This option is for compatibility with those SSH implementations. The bubblebabble digest is not shown in the logs generated from sshd. The following code demonstrates generating the bubblebabble digest of a public key:

```
stahnke@rack: ~/.ssh> ssh-keygen -B -f /home/stahnke/.ssh/id_rsa.pub
1024 xizih-bovep-kypom-hocih-vumal-cutez-limav-gynin-ryfem-hekiz-fuxox  stahnke@rack
```

-C comment

When generating a new key, the comment can be specified on the command line using the -C option. The -C option is not used to change comments on existing keys. Comments are normally used to store dates, usernames, or policy information about the key. The following code demonstrates key creation with a comment:

```
stahnke@rack: ~/.ssh> ssh-keygen -t dsa -C "Mike Stahnke's Key"
Generating public/private dsa key pair.
Enter file in which to save the key (/home/stahnke/.ssh/id_dsa):
Enter passphrase (empty for no passphrase): <passphrase>
Enter same passphrase again: <passphrase>
Your identification has been saved in /home/stahnke/.ssh/id_dsa.
Your public key has been saved in /home/stahnke/.ssh/id_dsa.pub.
The key fingerprint is:
f0:2a:b9:93:1d:f3:25:4c:54:2b:0d:e8:d6:00:a7:b5 Mike Stahnke's Key
```

-D reader

If your organization is using smartcard readers, the -D option will specify which device to download the RSA key from.

-F hostname

The -F option of ssh-keygen allows a user to search through a known_hosts file for a specific host. ssh-keygen will display a comment and the public key cached in the known_hosts file via standard output. This option works with hashed or traditional known_hosts files. The example that follows searches my known_hosts file for the workstation named rack.

```
stahnke@www: ~> ssh-keygen -F rack
# Host rack found: line 1 type RSA
|1|G9QHTAWYDyHzzi07iHNZ9i8XD2Y=|51eE9tiqH4GvGWLwGqNFrVlrxhg= ssh-rsa
 AAAAB3NzaC1yc2EAAAABIwAAAIEAsTPfu6u59cdCDO1wa7QgF+bUmOhGQNOU
Mrmv35LylovhaMSpDnj+hMFMi4ADfIUWAGW5tRQaYPhCxlb74bTCKx5+fS3geFp
XqpchU3frVlOtjHkniIyDMbrgWfnbMFaV+Hr1hotl4bwdaFZj8r9ZtrUXoqgZ8Dp+/2h3h
1kUCIO=
```

-G output file

The -G option will generate a list of primes designed for use during Diffie-Hellman group exchange. This output file should then be tested before using it in a production environment. Generation of the prime number candidates can take a significant amount of time. When generating these primes, the algorithm starts at a random point; this can be modified using -S. The following code creates a moduli candidate file:

```
stahnke@rack: ~> ssh-keygen -G moduli
Wed Mar 09 23:42:29 2005 Sieve next 16744448 plus 1023-bit
```

-H

The -H option of ssh-keygen will convert a known_hosts file into a hashed known_hosts file. A hashed known_hosts file stores a hash identifier instead of the system name in known_hosts as the first field of each line. The hash helps prevent attackers and users from being able to harvest known_hosts files and figure out several system names, yet is still usable by ssh and sshd. A known_hosts file can have some records in hashed format, while others can be in traditional format. The following example will hash my current known_hosts file:

```
stahnke@www: ~> ssh-keygen -H
/home/stahnke/.ssh/known_hosts updated.
Original contents retained as /home/stahnke/.ssh/known_hosts.old
WARNING: /home/stahnke/.ssh/known_hosts.old contains unhashed entries
Delete this file to ensure privacy of hostnames
```

-M memory

When using DH-GEX, moduli generation is required. The -M option can specify how much memory (in MB) should be used for this action, as normally it can take high amount of system memory.

-N new passphrase

When generating a key, the passphrase can also be specified on the command line. This can be done using the -N option. Specifying the passphrase on the command line can be a security risk if someone is looking over your shoulder or is looking at running processes on the hosts and happens to see your passphrase. It is recommended to enter them interactively. Changing a passphrase interactively for an existing private key requires use of the -p switch. The example that follows shows key generation with a passphrase specified on the command line:

```
stahnke@rack: ~/.ssh> ssh-keygen -N "My New Passphrase" -t dsa
Generating public/private dsa key pair.
Enter file in which to save the key (/home/stahnke/.ssh/id_dsa):
Your identification has been saved in /home/stahnke/.ssh/id_dsa.
Your public key has been saved in /home/stahnke/.ssh/id_dsa.pub.
The key fingerprint is:
f2:44:c8:e4:71:fa:96:2d:23:9e:b1:06:04:65:ed:0a stahnke@rack
```

-P passphrase

The -P option specifies the old passphrase on the command line. When used in conjunction with -p and -N, it is possible to change a passphrase in a noninteractive mode. As with the -N option, the -P option poses a security risk for users who can see your screen or view the process stack, because the passphrases are visible arguments on the command line. This example changes the passphrase of a key without interaction:

```
stahnke@rack: ~/.ssh> ssh-keygen -p -N "newphrase" -P "oldphrase" -f ~/.ssh/id_dsa
Key has comment '/home/stahnke/.ssh/id_dsa'
Your identification has been saved with the new passphrase.
```

-R

Running ssh-keygen -R with a hostname as an argument will remove a hostname from a user's $HOME/.ssh/known_hosts file. In this example, the hostname rack is removed from the known_hosts file. The next time a connection is attempted to rack, the public key will need to be validated. The -R option is useful if a system key has changed, or needs to be revoked.

```
stahnke@www: ~/> ssh-keygen -R rack
/home/stahnke/.ssh/known_hosts updated.
Original contents retained as /home/stahnke/.ssh/known_hosts.old
```

-S start

When generating prime number candidates for DH-GEX, it is possible to specify the starting point for the algorithm. The -S option requires a hexadecimal argument for a starting point.

-T output_file

Once a set of candidate primes has been generated for DH-GEX (using the -G switch), the primes must be tested. This is performed using the -T option. The example provided tests prime number candidates for Diffie-Hellman group exchange.

```
# moduli file previously generated
stahnke@rack: ~> ssh-keygen -T moduli-1024 -f moduli
Wed Mar 09 23:54:47 2005 Found 32 safe primes of 11701 candidates in 188 seconds
```

-W generator

When testing prime number candidates for DH-GEX, the -W option can be used to specify the specific generator. The generator has possible values of 2, 3, and 5. The following example tests prime number candidates with a generator:

```
#moduli file previously generated
stahnke@rack: ~> ssh-keygen -T moduli-1024 -f moduli -W2
Wed Mar 09 00:05:26 2005 Found 23 safe primes of 7033 candidates in 121 seconds
```

-U reader

The -U option allows a user to upload his or her private RSA key onto the smartcard at the specified device location.

SSH Agents

Public key authentication can offer authentication that is noninteractive, which is ideal for users connecting to remote hosts and automating tasks. With a passphrase, the need to remember multiple passwords has been eliminated, but typing the passphrase to gain access to any remote host still occurs. Luckily, OpenSSH includes a program called ssh-agent that stores your private keys used for public key authentication.

What Is an ssh-agent?

The concept behind an ssh-agent is that you store your identity (authentication information) at the beginning of a session, and then when remote connections are being established, they consult the agent behind the scenes. The program ssh-agent sets up a socket that stores authentication information normally in /tmp, and sets up some environment variables to make the ssh client and shell aware of the socket's existence.

The normal output from running ssh-agent is a few environmental variables. Just displaying their values provides little value. To properly invoke the ssh-agent, the ssh-agent output should be captured and directed to the shell, as in this example:

```
stahnke@rack:~> eval `ssh-agent`
 Agent pid 19254
```

To see which environment variables are set, you can use a set command.

```
stahnke@rack: ~> set | grep SSH
SSH_AGENT_PID=19254
SSH_AUTH_SOCK=/tmp/ssh-sJnvL19253/agent.19253
```

The SSH_AGENT_PID variable is the process ID of the running agent. The ssh-agent will run until explicitly killed (ssh-agent -k), which is often done by the shell at logout. The SSH_AUTH_SOCK is the socket created with the authentication information. This file is normally only readable by the owner of the ssh-agent process.

After an ssh-agent is created, a private key must be loaded into the agent. To load a private key, you use an OpenSSH utility called ssh-add. ssh-add with no argument will load private keys from the default locations of $HOME/.ssh/id_dsa and $HOME/.ssh/id_rsa for protocol 2 and $HOME/.ssh/identity for protocol 1. If other names are used for private keys, they must be specified as arguments. Upon running ssh-add, the user is prompted for the passphrase to unlock the private key. The unlocked private key is then stored in the ssh-agent. To load your private key into the ssh-agent, run the following:

```
stahnke@rack:~> ssh-add
Enter passphrase for /home/stahnke/.ssh/id_rsa:
Identity added: /home/stahnke/.ssh/id_dsa (/home/stahnke/.ssh/id_rsa)
stahnke@rack:~>
```

Once the key is added, connections to remote hosts with the proper user's public key installed in the authorized_keys file require no interaction. When I attempt to ssh to my remote system named www, I will not be prompted for a passphrase because I have already set up and loaded my agent.

```
stahnke@rack:~> ssh www
stahnke@www: ~>
```

Now with my ssh-agent, I can connect with the ssh client from rack (the host with my private key) to any host that has my public key in an authorized_keys file without entering my passphrase. This concept will be exploited heavily in later chapters covering scripting and administration, beginning in Chapter 8.

The connection to the system www is not the only connection that can be made using this agent. The stahnke account is also able to connect to other hosts on this network with the proper authorized_keys file installed. As an example, the small script in Listing 6-9 demonstrates logging in to multiple hosts without ever having to authenticate, from a user's perspective. This little script, called ssh_demo.sh, shows my account using the same agent to connect to multiple hosts.

Listing 6-9. *A bash Script That Connects via SSH to Several Systems*

```
#!/bin/bash
# ssh_demo.sh
for server in www zoom rack
do
  echo $server
  ssh  $server /bin/uptime
done
```

The output from running Listing 6-9 after starting and loading my ssh-agent follows:

```
stahnke@rack: ~> bash ssh_demo.sh
www
21:28:46 up 4 days, 23:12,  1 user,  load average: 0.15, 0.30, 0.08
zoom
 21:28:49 up 31 days,  4:53,  1 user,  load average: 0.04, 0.07, 0.04
rack
 21:28:48 up 1 day, 37 min,  7 users,  load average: 0.01, 0.02, 0.30
```

ssh-agent Hints

On systems that contain my private key(s), I normally start ssh-agent during login script execution. This traditionally involves modifying a .profile or .bashrc file by including the line eval `ssh-agent` in the file. This process also requires the use of ssh-agent -k in a .logout or .bash_logout file. When I am going to use an X session or an X11 program like Konsole, I run ssh-agent start-kde or ssh-agent konsole from the command line. This invokes the X11 application inside of ssh-agent, so every process spawned from it is aware of the ssh-agent. This means that multiple terminal windows in KDE, for example, can use the same agent and not prompt for passphrases again.

I normally do not execute ssh-add at login time, though some administrators prefer this method, because I often just need a new shell on the local system, and I am not planning to connect to additional hosts. It can become an annoyance to have to enter your passphrase every time a new shell is opened, if you open many terminals on the same server.

After working with ssh-agents for a while, you will probably hone in on some best practices for your environment. Of course, you can add ssh-add to your startup scripts for your shell if you see fit.

If you normally log in to your workstation or server via an X-Windows System, you can start an ssh-agent for your X session. Any new shells or utilities that use ssh will have knowledge of that agent. If you start your X-Windows System from the command line, you can prefix your command with ssh-agent. This code shows how to start an X session with an ssh-agent command:

```
# Normal Way
stahnke@rack: ~> startx
# Way to invoke ssh-agent
stahnke@rack: ~> ssh-agent startx
```

If you normally log in to your X11 desktop via a window manager, starting the agent can be tricky. Many Linux distributions include code to automatically start ssh-agent if it is in /usr/bin. If this is not the case for you, starting an agent usually involves editing an .xsession or .Xclients file. The syntax and methods can vary greatly depending on the desktop environment and the operating system.

There is also a tool called Keychain from Daniel Robbins, formerly of Gentoo, that can assist with managing SSH agents. For more information on Keychain, see the discussion in Chapter 8.

ssh-agent

The ssh-agent can control your ssh sessions. It is designed to be run at the beginning of your session, either inside your shell or at your X-Windows System login.

-a bind_address

By default, the ssh-agent creates a UNIX domain socket at /tmp/ssh-XXXXXXXX/agent.pid. If this is not desired, the agent can create the socket elsewhere using the -a option. The following code creates a UNIX domain socket at an alternative location:

```
stahnke@rack: ~> eval `ssh-agent -a /home/stahnke/socket`
```

-c

If you use a C shell instead of a Bourne shell derivative, the output of ssh-agent needs to be different. Usually, ssh-agent can tell how to output the environment variables based on the $SHELL variable. To explicitly specify using C-shell-style environment variables, use the -c option. In this example, the ssh-agent is started with C-shell-style parameters:

```
stahnke@rack: ~> eval `ssh-agent -c`
Agent pid 27492
```

If the $SHELL environment variable is not a C-shell-style shell, the output is in the Bourne shell format. To specify the Bourne shell format, use the -s option.

```
stahnke@rack: ~> eval `ssh-agent -s`
Agent pid 27499
```

-k

The -k option will kill the agent defined in the $SSH_AGENT_PID environment variable. Sometimes this is executed by placing it in an exit script for your login sessions.

```
stahnke@rack: ~/.ssh> eval `ssh-agent -k`
```

-t life

By default, an agent stays alive until killed or the system is rebooted. This timeframe can be changed by using the -t option and specifying a number of seconds. For example, if an hour-long life span is desired for an agent, the following can be executed:

```
stahnke@rack: ~/.ssh> eval `ssh-agent -t 3600`
Agent pid 27598
```

-d

The -d option will enable debug mode. This can be used for troubleshooting. When -d is used, the agent does not fork into the background, so feeding its output to an eval statement will cause the process to hang. The debug mode can be useful to see what the environment variables being passed to the shell look like. This example shows ssh-agent in debug mode:

```
stahnke@rack: ~/.ssh> ssh-agent -d
SSH_AUTH_SOCK=/tmp/ssh-PAyAj27613/agent.27613; export SSH_AUTH_SOCK;
echo Agent pid 27613;
```

ssh-add

In addition to adding keys to your identity, ssh-add can be locked and unlocked just as a screen saver would be when you walk away from your computer. While locking saves you no time if you have only one private key, if you have multiple, you only have to enter one password to unlock all of them, even if the passphrases are unique. There is no method to automatically lock an agent if it has not been used for some period of time, so user education or agent timeout is recommended. The following examples will assume that you have an ssh-agent invoked.

-l

The -l option will list the fingerprints of the keys currently loaded into the agent. To see which keys you have loaded, execute ssh-add -l.

```
stahnke@rack: ~/.ssh> ssh-add -l
1024 b9:23:7c:cb:34:e6:3f:95:e5:f0:f0:43:68:39:7f:a1 /home/stahnke/.ssh/id_rsa (RSA)
```

-L

Whereas the -l option shows only the key fingerprint, the -L option displays the public key files corresponding to all private keys loaded in the agent. To see your public key in the agent, enter ssh-add -L.

```
stahnke@rack: ~/.ssh> ssh-add -L
ssh-rsa AAAAB3NzaC1yc2EAAAABIwAAAIEAw1aE6MP6Dxvv+wvLJf+6O/FCygxta+xEJpvwdt7eVBywuWwta
eJXj/68+bj36isSqfQHN7S1nPbxRbQchu41lWiPmcMLl7QUqWRXoJMO9ZpgGAZEhPBKWkiItQkPtnANGM+
NVGXLIDnV2uzrGqEUpYYi+nWJah1ye44/JszuZrc= /home/stahnke/.ssh/id_rsa
```

-d

When using multiple keys inside of a single agent, it can be useful to remove a key when it is no longer needed. To do this, use ssh-add -d. If only one identity is present, there is no need to specify which key file to remove from the agent. To remove an identity from the agent, run the following:

```
stahnke@rack: ~/.ssh> ssh-add -d /home/stahnke/.ssh/id_rsa
Identity removed: /home/stahnke/.ssh/id_rsa (/home/stahnke/.ssh/id_rsa.pub)
```

-D

To remove all keys from the agent, use the -D option. This is not the same as killing an agent, as other keys can still be loaded into the agent at this point. To remove all keys from an agent, run ssh-add -D.

```
stahnke@rack: ~/.ssh> ssh-add -l
1024 f9:e5:2d:29:e2:1b:79:1f:b7:82:14:8c:ec:cd:a1:b8 /home/stahnke/.ssh/id_rsa (RSA)
1024 0a:04:01:30:c3:79:a7:b2:5e:fe:42:11:20:b5:c9:7b /home/stahnke/.ssh/id_dsa (DSA)
stahnke@rack: ~/.ssh> ssh-add -D
All identities removed.
```

-x

When walking away from the terminal or workstation with your loaded agents, it is best practice to lock it. This will prevent other users from using your agent to authenticate onto remote systems. In the following example, the agent is working when I run the uptime command. After locking my agent, an attempt to ssh to a remote host requires me to enter a passphrase.

```
stahnke@rack: ~/.ssh> ssh www uptime
 14:12:36 up 15:56,  2 users,  load average: 0.00, 0.00, 0.00
stahnke@rack: ~/.ssh> ssh-add -x
Enter lock password: <lock password>
```

```
Again: <lock password>
Agent locked.
stahnke@rack: ~/.ssh> ssh  www uptime
Enter passphrase for key '/home/stahnke/.ssh/id_rsa':
```

-X

To unlock a locked agent, use the -X switch. This prompts for the password specified when the agent was locked. If you have forgotten the password for the agent, you will need to kill the agent and start another. The following example shows locking and unlocking an agent:

```
stahnke@rack: ~/.ssh> ssh-add -X
Enter lock password:
Agent unlocked.
stahnke@rack: ~/.ssh> ssh www uptime
 14:24:29 up 16:08,  2 users,  load average: 0.00, 0.00, 0.10
```

-t life

Lifetimes for each key can be specified in seconds. If a key lifetime is set longer than the agent lifetime, the key lifetime will override the agent lifetime setting. Specifying time increments on agents is a protective measure against users who log in for days at a time. The following example shows an identity added for 600 seconds:

```
stahnke@rack: ~> ssh-add -t 600
Enter passphrase for /home/stahnke/.ssh/id_rsa:
Identity added: /home/stahnke/.ssh/id_rsa (/home/stahnke/.ssh/id_rsa)
Lifetime set to 600 seconds
```

-c

The -c option makes the ssh-agent ask for confirmation before using a key. If the agent is running from a terminal, the confirmation comes on the command line. If the agent is not assigned a terminal, the program defined in the SSH_ASKPASS environment variable will be invoked to prompt for a passphrase each time a connection is attempted. This option is rarely used, as it takes away the primary benefit of using an agent, which is to allow authentication without requiring user interaction; however, this option may offer some additional security surrounding exceptionally important keys. If SSH_ASKPASS is not set, you cannot use the -c option.

SSH ASKPASS

The SSH_ASKPASS program is designed to be an X11 Window application that prompts for a passphrase if the DISPLAY and SSH_ASKPASS environment variables are set. This can be used during initial login of an X11 Window System session. The program path stored in SSH_ASKPASS can vary widely depending on operating system.

The SSH_ASKPASS program is normally found in the libexec directory of your OpenSSH installation tree. If it is not installed, you may need to build it. To build an SSH_ASKPASS program is fairly straightforward. Listing 6-10 shows the installation of SSH_ASKPASS.

Listing 6-10. *Downloading and Installing the* x11-ssh-askpass *Program*

```
stahnke@rack: ~> wget http://www.jmknoble.net/software/x11-ssh-askpass/\
x11-ssh-askpass-1.2.4.1.tar.gz
stahnke@rack: ~> tar zxvf x11-ssh-askpass-1.2.4.1.tar.gz
stahnke@rack: ~> cd x11-ssh-askpass
stahnke@rack: ~>./configure
stahnke@rack: ~> xmkmf
stahnke@rack: ~> make includes
stahnke@rack: ~> make
stahnke@rack: ~> su
root@rack: # make install
root@rack: # make install.man.
```

Now you can set the SSH_ASKPASS variable to the program you just installed. On my workstation, it is installed at /usr/local/libexec/x11-ssh-askpass. The SSH_ASKPASS is useful when using X11 applications rather than terminal applications. If a passphrase is required, SSH_ASKPASS will invoke the program and allow the connection to be made, as you see in Figure 6-1. If this program is ever invoked on the command line, redirect its output to /dev/null to ensure the passphrase is not displayed on the screen.

Figure 6-1. x11-ssh-askpass *prompting a graphical user for a passphrase*

-s reader

The -s option will allow ssh-add to read in a card stored on the smartcard reader device.

-e reader

The -e switch instructs ssh-add to remove the key stored in the smartcard reader device.

Agent Forwarding

ssh-agent forwarding relies on configurations in both the client and server configuration files. If enabled, a user can make multiple ssh connection hops without returning to the server on which his or her private key resides.

As an example, you have a workstation on which your private key is held, called john. Your public key is in your authorized_keys file on paul, george, and ringo. With agent forwarding enabled, you can use ssh to go from john to paul to george to ringo without ever returning to john. This can be useful when you are working on a particular box and realize it needs patches or updates that are stored on another host. You can use scp/sftp to copy the data from george to paul using an agent running from john. Figure 6-2 illustrates this example.

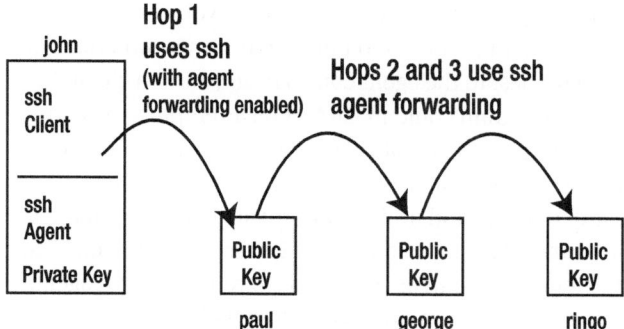

Figure 6-2. *Agent forwarding allows a single private key to be used to authethenticate to multiple hosts without returning to the original source node.*

Agent forwarding can greatly increase the usability of public key authentication for power users and administrators. Enabling agent forwarding involves changes to the client configuration file (either the user-specific config file or system-wide ssh_config file). Agent forwarding requires that the same public key (unless you are using multiple private keys) be installed on each host.

In the client configuration, add the following line to config or ssh_config to enable agent forwarding. This can be for a specified host or for all hosts depending on placement relative to the host * block.

ForwardAgent yes.

The following block of code demonstrates agent forwarding. First, I start an agent and load my private key. From there, I connect to the remote host www, and then to another host, zoom, without returning to my source node, named rack.

```
stahnke@rack: ~> eval `ssh-agent`
Agent pid 6580
stahnke@rack: ~> ssh-add
Enter passphrase for /home/stahnke/.ssh/id_dsa:
Identity added: /home/stahnke/.ssh/id_dsa (/home/stahnke/.ssh/id_dsa)
stahnke@rack: ~> ssh www
stahnke@www: ~> ssh zoom
stahnke@zoom:~ $
```

How Does the ssh-agent Work?

SSH agents store your private key information in a cache. They do not send your private key information to other hosts when agent forwarding is occurring. The ssh-agent handles inquiries about authentication on the local host and from remote forwarded agents via cryptographic challenges. This is important because it means your private key data is never transported from the host on which it resides.

Once you have your private key loaded in the agent and you attempt to authenticate to another server, the ssh client will pass the authentication challenge to the ssh-agent and await the result. If the result is as expected, you are authenticated; if not, further authentication methods may be attempted.

While SSH agents are secure and do not pass private key information, you need to keep in mind some considerations about using them in less-trusted networking environments. For example, the agent does not know that a request to the agent comes from your ssh client. In a hostile environment, a malicious user or program could make several attempts to beat the agent by sending it data in hopes it will pass the mathematical computations. Additionally, on a compromised host, or a server with a malicious root user, a user can simply point his or her environmental variables to your forwarded socket and utilize your private key for authentication. The malicious user is able to use your private key in this type of attack, but not obtain it. That is to say, he or she could connect to remote systems as you, but once you killed your agent, he or she could not connect to remote hosts as you anymore. As an additional security measure to minimize the risk for this type of attack, lock the ssh-agent or unload the private keys when the agent is not in use.

Summary of Public Key Authentication

From a user's point of view, public key authentication is a very fast procedure. While still slower than rsh, rlogin, and even SSH-1, public key authentication employing protocol 2 uses rsa/dsa digital credentials to provide the best security for a connectivity suite on the UNIX/Linux platforms.

Public Key Security

Public key authentication enables higher levels of security than traditional password authentication. Password guessing is often easy, especially if you are in an environment with hundreds or thousands of stand-alone servers. Oftentimes default accounts (whether from the system or your organization) remain on the servers with default passwords for months or years at a time. Any malicious or curious party can start guessing passwords until they are granted access. Password cracking utilities are often able to find passwords within minutes or hours. Utilities do not exist (that I am aware of) that can crack 1024-bit and higher keys within a timeframe of several years.

By removing password authentication and using only keys, some of the threats encountered with password authentication are eliminated. Because public key authentication can control what hosts users come from, you can block untrusted networks or systems as a further method of security and access control.

Public Key Hints

Using only public key authentication comes with a few caveats of its own. On many systems, having a valid password is required for authentication, regardless of whether or not you are using it. With modern versions of OpenSSH, public key authentication will fail if an account is locked. To disable password authentication but still allow public key authentication to occur, the password hash should be set to something other than the lock value of the operating system. The OpenSSH manual recommends a hash of *NP*, which represents "no password."

Because of the importance of the root account on UNIX and Linux systems, many organizations (and some operating systems) do not allow expiration or lockout of the root account. If there is no lockout policy for root, an attacker can try 10,000 times to gain access as root to a system, assuming he or she is not caught before then. Setting PermitRootLogin to without-password in the sshd_config file ensures that no matter what password is supplied from the attacker, access to the system will not be gained.

User-based public key authentication is one of the foundations for the rest of the material in this book. Because of its inherent security and speed, public key authentication is the basis for scripting, power administration, and working quickly while utilizing SSH.

Host-based Public Key Authentication

Key-based authentication can also take place between hosts. Under most circumstances, I am extremely opposed to any form of host-based authentication because this allows another host's authentication policies to be applicable to any system that trusts it. For most jobs, commands, and scripts, I recommend using public keys for users. However, there are some instances when I have found host-based authentication via OpenSSH to really shine.

The following are scenarios in which I sometimes use host-based authentication:

- Inside parallel computing clusters on separate isolated networks (high-performance computing).

- Inside high availability clusters (IBM HACMP, Veritas Cluster Server, HP MC Service Guard) so that scripts and manual failover procedures can execute if the failover was not hostile.

- When the data on the systems has low value, such as in labs or test environments.

- When someone else has accepted the risk. Many times a customer or client will say they are willing to live with the consequences of host-based authentication because its ease of use outweighs the administration costs, user education, etc. While I still do not recommend this situation, I have been in it and have delivered what I was asked to do. This can include systems where a legacy environment has been moved from an rsh environment. Host-based authentication via SSH is much stronger than traditional trust relationships.

Host-based authentication relies on knowing the public key of the host you want to trust. If you have that key cached, you can be fairly certain you are not connecting to a rogue host the next time you connect, because if the keys mismatch, ssh will balk. When using host-based authentication, I encourage you to take a look at the rest of your security settings to minimize the risks you are taking. The example that follows uses only the SSH-2 protocol.

First, you can use ssh-keyscan to populate a file with the lists of hosts you wish to trust. A common problem in host-based authentication is when a client specifies the short name of a host when the server is expecting fully qualified, or visa versa; for this reason, use a fully qualified domain name if it exists. This example will populate, and overwrite, the system-wide ssh_known_hosts file:

```
root@rack: # ssh-keyscan -t dsa,rsa -f file > /etc/ssh/ssh_known_hosts
```

Please note that host-based authentication is not allowed when using the root account in this scenario. To use the root account, it is best for it to have its own key pair.

After populating the ssh_known_hosts file, you need to populate the /etc/shosts.equiv file, which allows secure host-based authentication to take place. I use a simple cut command to grab the same hosts I got results from for ssh-keyscan and place them into my shosts.equiv file. If the ssh_known_hosts file contains more entries than are desired candidates for host-based authentication, populating the shosts.equiv file should be done manually. The following code will populate the shosts.equiv file for all hosts cached by the system-wide /etc/ssh/ ssh_known_hosts file:

```
root@rack:# cut -d' ' -f1 <  /etc/ssh/ssh_known_hosts |sort \
                    | uniq > /etc/shosts.equiv
```

From there, system-wide setup is in place, but OpenSSH-specific settings are still required. Inside the server configuration file, you need to add/change the following value and then restart the server:

```
HostbasedAuthentication yes
```

From a client perspective, you need to enable host-based authentication also. From OpenSSH versions after 3.7, there is a program called ssh-keysign normally found in the lib/ssh under your OpenSSH installation tree. This program is a helper program invoked when using host-based authentication. You should not have to run it manually, but it must be enabled in the system-wide ssh_config under the host * block.

```
HostbasedAuthentication yes
EnableSSHKeysign yes
```

After this setup, a nonprivileged (nonroot) user should be able to use ssh to go from the client to the server without providing passphrases or passwords, or having a public key. If you have problems getting this to work, try ssh -vvv to ensure that all of your hosts have the same specified domain names.

Types of Authentication Inside of OpenSSH

OpenSSH allows for several different types of authentication. The discussion thus far has covered normal password, public key, and host-based authentication. Kerberos and GSSAPI are also allowed; however, because of the infrastructure required to enable those options, they are outside the scope of this book.

Keyboard-interactive authentication is the last method to cover for OpenSSH authentication. Keyboard-interactive authentication and password authentication (in OpenSSH 3.9p1 and above) methods allow the usage of Pluggable Authentication Modules (PAM) supported in modern Linux, Solaris, HP-UX, AIX, and FreeBSD. PAM can basically be thought of as an authentication broker. When a system, whether it is telnet, ssh, xdm, sudo, or something else, requires authentication, it passes all requests to PAM. PAM can be configured to allow passwords, authentication, Lightweight Directory Access Protocol (LDAP), or other methods (such as SecureID or other token-based authentications). PAM is nice to use because you can change your system-wide authentication settings in one spot, and have all services change the way authentication information is processed.

Enabling PAM inside of OpenSSH is done by default on most Linux distributions if you are using the vendor-provided OpenSSH. Traditional UNIX systems may include PAM as an option, but some do not always enable it by default. After your system is configured to use PAM, you can begin to set up OpenSSH to do so.

OpenSSH must be configured with the --with-pam option to work with PAM. If OpenSSH is built with PAM, PAM is then enabled/disabled with the UsePAM keyword in the sshd_config file. If UsePAM is set to yes, password authentication is handled via PAM. If no, password authentication is handled via OpenSSH in versions later than 3.9p1.

Tip For more information about Linux-PAM, be sure to check out `http://www.kernel.org/pub/linux/libs/pam/`. Linux-PAM is sometimes thought to be very different from other PAM implementations. The Open Group has a site describing PAM, found at `http://www.opengroup.org/onlinepubs/008329799/`, that is not exclusively aimed at Linux.

If you compiled your own OpenSSH from source, check the `contrib` directory for an `sshd.pam` file. The OpenSSH source provides specific PAM configuration files for many operating systems and a generic one. To use PAM authentication, the `UsePAM` directive must be enabled along with placing the proper lines or files into `/etc/pam.conf` or `/etc/pam.d`.

A Quick Reference to Authentication

When working with implementation and setup of OpenSSH, you may find it helpful to have a quick reference on hand for certain tasks that are normally performed many times. This section serves as just such a reference.

Reference: Setting Up User Public Key Authentication

1. Generate a key with a good passphrase: `ssh-keygen -t dsa -b 1024`

2. Install a public key file:

   `ssh user@remote_host cat < $HOME/.ssh/id_rsa.pub  ">>" .ssh/authorized_keys`

Reference: Using SSH Agents

1. Enter `eval \`ssh-agent\``.

2. Enter `ssh-add` and then your passphrase.

3. Enter `ssh $REMOTE_HOST -l $REMOTE_USER`.

Reference: Host-based Authentication

1. Build the `ssh_known_hosts` and `shosts.equiv` file:

   ```
   ssh-keyscan -t rsa,dsa $FULLLY_QUALIFIED_DOMAIN_NAME > \
   /etc/ssh/ssh_known_hosts
    cut -d ' ' -f1 < /etc/ssh/ssh_knonw_hosts  | uniq > /etc/shosts.equiv
   ```

2. Edit `sshd_config`:

   ```
   HostbasedAuthentication yes
   ```

3. Edit `ssh_config`:

```
HostbasedAuthentication yes
EnableSSHKeysign yes
```

4. Restart `sshd` on the remote host.

Summary

In this chapter, I covered the types of authentication that are possible inside of OpenSSH, with special attention paid to public key authentication. Public key authentication is very secure and efficient, and its advantages become even more obvious when utilizing SSH agents and agent forwarding. While managing key-based authentication and educating your user base about keys can be difficult, the end result is a more secure environment, with fewer calls for password resets.

The next part of the book dives into scripting and management of multiple systems scaling from 3 to 3,000 using SSH scripts. The next part also will cover some additional features included with SSH such as tunneling and forwarding your X11 traffic to secure additional clear-text protocols.

PART 3

■■■

Advanced Topics

CHAPTER 7

TCP Forwarding

The advantages of the SSH protocol discussed previously focused on replacing legacy tools with their OpenSSH counterparts. Sometimes it simply is not possible to remove all clear-text or weakly authenticated applications. To mitigate the risk these applications pose on your network, their network communication can be *forwarded* through an SSH connection.

OpenSSH offers an advanced set of features that allow users and administrators to forward, or *tunnel*, otherwise insecure protocols inside a secure SSH connection. Tunneling can be used in many different situations and can become especially effective when working with hosts that have firewalls in between them.

Introduction to Forwarding

With tunneling, the original protocol travels inside of another protocol, in this case SSH. This means that the benefits of SSH are now leveraged by the originating protocol, and multiple layers of authentication could exist. If a protocol normally requires username and password for authentication, when tunneled inside of SSH, it still will require this authentication. SSH will also require some form of authentication to create the tunnel; therefore, weak authentication mechanisms can be overcome by tunneling their protocols inside of SSH. SSH also will encrypt, and optionally compress, the network transmissions of the original protocol.

If you recall, this is not the first instance of forwarding discussed with regard to SSH. In Chapter 6, you learned about agent forwarding, which utilizes UNIX domain socket forwarding. Forwarding protocols inside of SSH uses TCP forwarding.[1] In addition to providing the obvious advantages such as encryption and strong authentication, SSH can forward many of these weaker protocols in a transparent manner, allowing users to continue using their otherwise insecure applications in the typical manner while at the same time capitalizing on these secure features.

Some reasons forwarding through SSH should be considered are as follows:

- The protocol you are using is less secure than SSH.

- Firewall(s) allow TCP port 22 but not the port for the application you are using.

- The protocol you are using could take advantage of SSH features including compression.

---

1. SSH can secure TCP/IP connections via tunneling. Unfortunately, securing UDP protocols such as Syslog, DNS, and TFTP is not possible using SSH tunneling.

SSH forwarding, while easy to set up, requires some configuration changes in the applications using the forwarded SSH connection instead of the primary TCP port(s). For example, if you tunnel Telnet traffic onto port 6123, you would have to change your `telnet` connection command to `telnet localhost 6123`.

Because SSH forwarding occurs at the application layer, each application has to set up for tunneling inside of SSH. If you require a more robust solution, especially for out-of-network access, Virtual Private Network (VPN) is a better option. IPSEC tunnels also work very well and occur at the network layer. That being said, if you only require that few applications use tunneling, then SSH can provide a very low-cost and secure option without significant overhead spent in setup and administration.

SSH forwarding, while one of the least understood features of SSH, is not that difficult. Once some initial setup has been done, end users may never realize they are using a forwarded connection. Before we get into implementing forwarding, however, first let us discuss what forwarding really means.

How Does Forwarding Work?

Forwarding, at least with SSH, involves an application passing traffic that it would normally use over the network to OpenSSH. OpenSSH then encrypts that traffic and sends it to an SSH server that decrypts the traffic and passes it to the locally listening application counterpart from the originator, as shown in Figure 7-1. The client application and the server portion in this model are completely unaware their traffic is being forwarded. This means applications behave as expected.

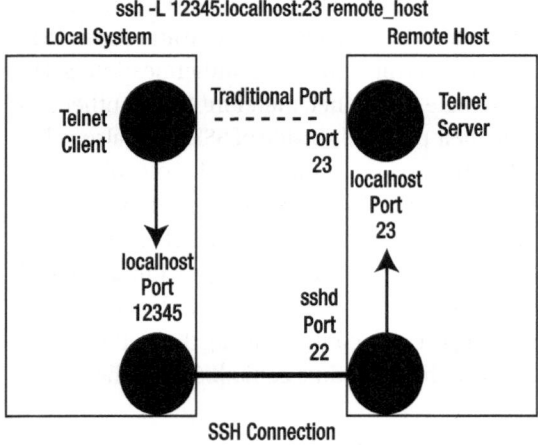

Figure 7-1. *Tunneling an application inside of SSH*

The SSH protocol uses Transmission Control Protocol (TCP) by default on port 22 for the listening daemon. With SSH port forwarding, SSH will encrypt and decrypt any TCP/IP stream, thus securing it while in transmission. This is achieved through port forwarding. Most TCP applications can be forwarded with little issue. IMAP, LDAP, HTTP, NNTP, POP, and Telnet can be forwarded with ease. The obvious omission from this list is FTP. Unfortunately, due to the way FTP is designed, forwarding the entire FTP data stream is very difficult, and oftentimes not possible. It is possible to forward the username/password transmission, but not the data; and even encrypting the authenticating mechanism introduces new problems in FTP. Most new FTP daemons will not allow forwarding because the IP address connecting to the source appears to be invalid. For encryption of FTP data traffic, I recommend using vsftpd (http://vsftpd.beasts.org/) with OpenSSL support. Keep in mind, however, that SFTP is a great alternative to using the FTP protocol.

■ **Note** FTP can be forwarded using DynamicForward for SSH if the FTP client and server run in passive mode and the FTP client supports SOCKS. This is not a common occurrence, and is still rather messy to set up. To transfer data securely, use SFTP or FTP over SSL.

The best way to understand SSH tunneling is to try it yourself. I started by tunneling telnet, because of the need to continue using several Perl scripts that require telnet. Normally, the telnet service accepts connections on port 23. To set up port forwarding of telnet over SSH, sshd must allow TCP forwarding.

To enable forwarding, navigate to the following directive in your sshd_config file, and set it to yes. You will need to restart sshd if this configuration is changed in your sshd_config.

```
AllowTcpForwarding yes
```

■ **Note** In this chapter, when a configuration change is made in the sshd_config file, I will assume you are reloading the configuration by restarting OpenSSH or HUPing it.

Port forwarding requires knowledge of the original port (23 in the case of telnet) and an open port. In this example, port 12345 will be used, which was chosen arbitrarily. It is important that the chosen port is not already in use.

When the port forwarding setup is complete, anyone who connects via telnet to the localhost on port 12345 will connect to the remote system on the Telnet protocol, which is inside the SSH protocol.

Port Investigation

While going into detailed discussion of network ports is outside the scope of this material, there are a few key points to keep in mind. If you choose to bind to ports lower than 1024 on a UNIX/Linux system, you must be root. These ports are known as *privileged ports*.

When using ports above 1024, you have free rein with the only caveat being you cannot use a port that is already in use. There are several methods available for determining whether ports are in use. lsof and netstat normally ship with UNIX and Linux distributions; however, to get the most accurate information, root access is normally required, and the output can vary depending on system type.

For an easy method of determining what ports are open, the netstat command can be used. The following portion of code shows me which ports are open on the remote server named www.

```
stahnke@www: ~> netstat -an | grep LISTEN
tcp        0        0 0.0.0.0:32768              0.0.0.0:*                    LISTEN

tcp        0        0 0.0.0.0:3306               0.0.0.0:*                    LISTEN
tcp        0        0 0.0.0.0:111                0.0.0.0:*                    LISTEN
tcp        0        0 0.0.0.0:23                 0.0.0.0:*                    LISTEN
tcp        0        0 127.0.0.1:5335             0.0.0.0:*                    LISTEN
tcp        0        0 127.0.0.1:25               0.0.0.0:*                    LISTEN
tcp        0        0 127.0.0.1:6010             0.0.0.0:*                    LISTEN
tcp        0        0 127.0.0.1:6011             0.0.0.0:*                    LISTEN
tcp        0        0 :::80                      :::*                         LISTEN
tcp        0        0 :::22                      :::*                         LISTEN
tcp        0        0 ::1:6010                   :::*                         LISTEN
tcp        0        0 ::1:6011                   :::*                         LISTEN
tcp        0        0 :::443                     :::*                         LISTEN
```

netstat will show TCP connections on the system. Look for the ports open by searching for the string after the colon. This example of netstat shows that several ports are open on all addresses; (0.0.0.0) and a few are bound specifically to the localhost address. Just be sure that you do not use a port already in use when forwarding connections.

As an alternative, you can always use the Network Mapper, known as nmap. Please note that some organizations, especially ones with strict intrusion detection setups, may frown upon using nmap because of its longtime association as the probing tool to begin an attack. You can download nmap from http://www.insecure.org/nmap. nmap has many options, but for this test, running nmap with no options is adequate for determining which ports are actively listening. In this example, nmap is run against a remote server on my network, named www.

```
root@www ~> nmap www
Starting nmap 3.70 ( http://www.insecure.org/nmap/ ) at 2005-01-30 12:39 CST
Interesting ports on www (192.168.1.109):
(The 1652 ports scanned but not shown below are in state: closed)
PORT     STATE SERVICE
22/tcp   open  ssh
23/tcp   open  telnet
80/tcp   open  http
111/tcp  open  rpcbind
443/tcp  open  https
3306/tcp open  mysql
Nmap run completed - 1 IP address (1 host up) scanned in 0.492 seconds
root@www ~>
```

This example shows that a few ports are open, so when forwarding connections, those ports cannot be used. The only port above 1024 is 3306. Normally when forwarding, ports above 1024 are used because then root access is not required to set up the forwarding.

TCP Connection Forwarding

Now that a bit of background has been established around forwarding with SSH, it is time to move into examples. I encourage you to work through these examples while you read, as it is a nice exercise to try it on your own, and it will only increase your understanding of the subject. If you are not running many services that require tunneling, for the purposes of examples, you might try forwarding web traffic or opening a telnet server.

Setting Up the Tunnel

Before you can start tunneling your TCP connections over SSH, you need to edit your remote host's sshd_config. Ensure that TCP forwarding is allowed by the remote system. The following line will enable TCP forwarding. By default, TCP forwarding is also enabled.

```
AllowTcpForwarding yes
```

My server named www runs a telnet server, at least in this example. From my workstation named rack, I will run a command to forward telnet connections securely to www.

The syntax is as follows:

```
ssh -L<local port>:<local system>:<remote port> <remote system>
stahnke@rack: ~> ssh -L12345:localhost:23 www
```

Because I have public key authentication set up already and my ssh-agent running, I am not asked for a passphrase. Using this set of options, I am logged in to my remote server www. This tunnel will stay open as long as this session to www stays alive. To verify a forwarded connection, from my workstation I will telnet to port 12345.

```
stahnke@rack:~> telnet localhost 12345
Trying 127.0.0.1...
Connected to localhost.
Escape character is '^]'.
login: stahnke
Password: <password>
[stahnke@www ~]$
```

From here, I could start running shell commands, just as if I had established a traditional telnet connection on port 23 of www. This configuration of forwarding will kill the forwarding mechanism when the initial session is closed. To avoid this, you can specify the -N option with your ssh command. -N does not execute remote commands and allows port forwarding with SSH protocol 2 only. The -f tells ssh to fork a new process, therefore you get to keep your terminal session on the host you started. After you log out of your initial session, which kills the existing tunnel, try this:

```
stahnke@rack: ~> ssh -f -N -L12345:localhost:23 www
```

Now you should be able to connect via telnet on port 12345 at localhost. Take notice that so far I have only established connection to localhost and not to the hostname rack. For security reasons, I specify localhost and allow the port forwarding to only bind on the loopback (lo0, 127.0.0.1). If you have a need to allow other systems to connect to the forwarded port, you can specify a -g option. The -g option enables gateway ports, which basically means binding to all addresses and not just the loopback. You can also specify this in your sshd_config file with the following directive:

```
GatewayPorts yes
```

The forwarded connection looks just like a standard `telnet` application server to my clients from other hosts as well with the -g option.

OpenSSH is forwarding in the following manner:

1. The user requests a `telnet` session via the command `telnet localhost 12345`.

2. The OpenSSH client on `localhost` reads all traffic coming to port 12345, encrypts it, and then sends the data through the preestablished SSH tunnel.

3. The OpenSSH server, in my case on www, receives the traffic, decrypts it, and passes it to the `telnet` server on the `localhost`. The connection is two-way.

If you run a who command when you are logged in through the forwarded `telnet` connection, you will see that the source host is `localhost`. This is an indication that `ssh` port forwarding is occurring. If it was a normal `telnet` connection, the remote hostname would be visible.

Now to make this forwarding useful, I need to instruct my colleague to modify his `telnet` scripts to now use `localhost` and the new port number. A myriad of options is available when doing port forwarding like this; for example, because many of the systems in my network do not normally run `telnet`, I could forward the connection on port 23 on `rack` to connect to www. Of course, you have to be root to set up a port binding on 23, but that would then allow traditional `telnet` clients and scripts to `telnet` port 23 on my workstation `rack`, but really be tunneled to www. Remember, however, that if a remote host is using `telnet` to connect to `rack`, that traffic is unencrypted, even if connecting to the tunnel.

Tunnel Setup via ssh Client Escape Sequence

Recall from Chapter 5 that the `ssh` client has escape sequences that can modify the behavior of an established SSH connection. Using the ~C command-line option when connected via `ssh`, a tunnel can be created. The syntax is very similar to the command-line syntax used when at the command prompt of the client host.

In this example, I have established an `ssh` connection from my workstation named `rack` to the remote system named www. From there, I can create the tunnel of port 23 as shown in the previous examples.

```
stahnke@www: ~> ~C
ssh> -L12345:localhost:23
Forwarding port.
```

After using the ~C escape sequence, the -L command option is used just as if I were on the command line. Remember that typing **help** at the ssh> prompt will also provide syntax examples. Now, if I have another session open on the workstation `rack`, I can connect to the `localhost` via `telnet` on port 12345 and be forwarded to the www system.

VNC

Virtual Network Computing (VNC, http://www.realvnc.com) is a remote administration tool that allows a user to assume command of a desktop environment. VNC works cross-platform and can be very valuable to help desks and support staff, or if you have computers with headless displays.

The reason VNC is used as an explicit example is because it is one of the most common applications tunneled through SSH. By default, VNC listens on port 5900. Once again, VNC is clear-text protocol. VNC can be tunneled inside of SSH to create a secure remote desktop environment that works on all sorts of platforms. Using VNC, I am able to control a Windows desktop from my Linux workstation and visa versa.

So to connect to the desktop on www, from my workstation rack, I will run the following:

```
stahnke@rack: ~> ssh -L 5900:localhost:5901 www
```

Normally, to use VNC, you run something like this:

```
stahnke@rack: ~> vncviewer www:0
```

Instead, now that I have forwarded the port, I can run vncviewer on the localhost and have encrypted connections.

```
stahnke@rack: ~> vncviewer localhost:0
```

Tunneling Through Firewalls

Tunneling with OpenSSH is a fairly straightforward process. As you have seen so far in this chapter, securing many TCP-based protocols can be done with only minor modifications to configuration of clients, but what happens when those clients want to interact with servers behind firewalls?

If port 22 is open on your firewall, even just outbound, you are in luck, OpenSSH can help you tunnel various forms of TCP traffic though that firewall using port 22. I have been in many situations where tunneling traffic on port 22 was a better solution than opening another port on the firewall. Also, because working with policy organizations that regulate firewall rules often means dealing with red tape, which can hold up a project, tunneling in this manner can be quite useful.

In my previous example, where I mention a colleague of mine who has an abundance of Perl scripts making use of telnet, tunneling once again can ease his pain. His firewalls will not allow telnet anymore, but with forwarding his scripts still work.

The next time you are working with firewalls, you should try to weigh the situation and see if a tunnel utilizing OpenSSH will suffice. For a tunnel to be a good solution, it should typically adhere to the following criteria:

- The tunnel will be used by technical end users. Configuring applications such as mail clients and LDAP clients to use tunnels is not very hard, but if something does go wrong, less technical end users can become confused when it appears that network traffic is configured to connect to the localhost, and if they have any type of administrative authority, often their investigations can lead to additional problems.

- The tunnel will be temporary, or used for testing. Tunneling is probably not a good long-term solution for critical applications. For proof of concept, or an occasional call to a data container, tunneling is wonderful, but because of the persistent connection required, tunnels can have issues when servers reboot, networks fail, or firewalls drop connections after idle periods.

- Tunneling is approved by your security organization. Some security organizations do not like tunneling for anything other than X11. (X11 forwarding is covered in the next section.) Tunneling, especially in a hostile network, does provide a way onto your other hosts for everyone, not just you. Security organizations that do not recommend tunneling are usually in fear of tunneling that leads to other tunnels or goes several hops and is not very traceable. Please consult your information security staff before tunneling.

- If the connection will be reestablished, thus allowing for a new tunnel to be created, it is easier to manage and track. Once again, because a persistent connection is difficult to keep, having to reconnect often can help your tunnel in terms of manageability. If you set up your tunnels only when needed, their reliability will be much higher than if you just leave them open always. Additionally, limiting the amount of time the forwarding is enabled helps minimize the opportunity potential attackers have to use your tunnels.

Tip Remember to use `ServerAliveInterval` in your `ssh` client configuration to ensure the firewall does not find idle connections.

Pass-through Forwarding

Forwarding can be done between two machines as shown previously using a local forwarding mechanism provided by OpenSSH. Besides tunneling between two systems, the SSH protocol allows tunneling through a host. This can offer maximum value when dealing with a firewalled environment. Many firewalls allow SSH connections to pass through (many also depend on where the connection originates, however). Because of this, tunneling traffic on port 22, the default port for OpenSSH, will allow two otherwise segregated computing environments to talk to each other.

As an example, consider a host named john that is running LDAP on port 389. paul is on the same side of a firewall as john, and is the only host that allows in-bound connections from the DMZ where ringo sits. ringo can then tunnel traffic via SSH through paul to john. This allows encrypted LDAP queries through firewalls.[2]

```
stahnke@ringo: ~> ssh -L12345:john:389 paul
```

This command run from ringo will set up a tunnel starting at ringo, ending at john, and having paul in the middle. When you `nmap` the systems, both ringo and paul will have port 12345 open. To use my forwarding connection across the firewall, I will direct traffic at the `localhost` port 12345. My LDAP calls are now successful. Figure 7-2 illustrates the architecture of this setup.

---

2. Normally, I would recommend running LDAP in conjunction with SSL or TLS.

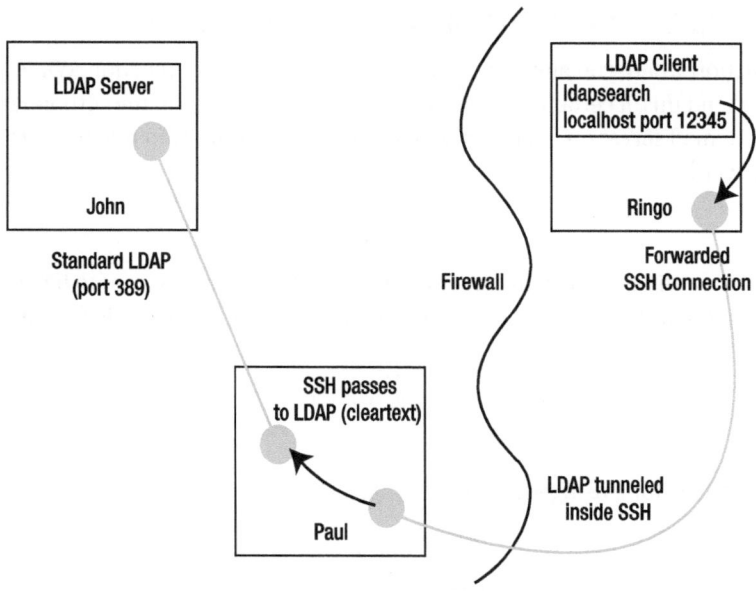

Figure 7-2. *The host Ringo uses a forwarded connection on Paul to send* ldapsearch *data to John.*

▪**Caution** When performing a tunnel-through operation, the traffic between the middle point and end point can be unencrypted, as it is in this example.

Remote Forwarding

So far, the discussion has covered local forwarding and traditional SSH forwarding. All the commands utilized thus far have been with the -L options indicating a local forwarding is taking place. An -R option is also available that allows remote forwarding.

As in one of the previous examples, host www runs a telnet server. However, I would like to encrypt that traffic. If I am on the server www, I can begin forwarding by issuing the following command:

stahnke@www: ~> **ssh -R12345:www:23 rack**

This sets up port forwarding in the exact same manner as earlier—meaning I must be on rack and telnet to the localhost on port 12345 to be forwarded to www's telnet server. The only difference is that I set up the forwarding remotely.

▪**Tip** Use remote forwarding when you are on the machine that has the application server you are trying to forward to. Use local forwarding when the intended target is off the localhost.

Creating Forwarded Connection via $HOME/.ssh/config

Suppose you have a situation where you always want to create a forwarded connection. While I do not normally recommend this, it certainly is possible. Suppose I had a host on my corporate network that had an IMAP mail server on it. I could set it up so that if I connect to that host via SSH, it automatically forwards IMAP.

Configuration

To configure automatic forwarding upon login, you must add a few items to your config file in ~/.ssh, not the system-wide setup, unless everyone wants to do this. In this case, I will forward IMAP from www.

```
#In ~/.ssh/config
LocalForward 12345 www:143
```

Remote forwarding can be done using very similar syntax:

```
RemoteForward 12345 rack:143
```

A tunnel will not be allowed on a low-numbered port (below 1024) unless a user has root authority. Unprivileged users can create tunnels to low-numbered ports, but not create the forwarded connection point below TCP port 1024.

Forwarding Collisions

If you have established a connection to a remote host with port forwarding already enabled and configured to be set up at login time via your config file, attempting to log in a second time will produce an error. The connection will still be established, but the forwarding will fail. The following command-line option will eliminate that problem:

```
-o ClearAllForwardings=yes
```

The option clears new forwardings, it does not remove existing forwarded connections. To provide an example in this situation, a tunnel must already be set up or configured to be established upon login.

Here is a portion of my $HOME/.ssh/config file:

```
Host www
Localforward 12345 www:389
```

Normally, this would forward port 389 on www to my localhost port 12345. However, what if I connect to www in multiple terminal windows simultaneously? An error is produced because each connection attempts to create the tunnel on port 12345, as shown in Listing 7-1.

Listing 7-1. *Connecting to a Host When the Port Requested Is in Use*

```
# After a forwarded connection has been set up
rack:~ # ssh root@www
root@www's password: <password>
bind: Address already in use
channel_setup_fwd_listener: cannot listen to port: 12345
Could not request local forwarding.
root@www ~>
```

In Listing 7-2, the `ClearAllForwardings` option has been enabled. This means the `ssh` client will not attempt to create the locally forwarded tunnel, even though the `$HOME/.ssh/config` file requests it.

Listing 7-2. *The* `ssh` *Connection Will Not Attempt to Create a Tunnel*

```
#With '-o ClearAllForwardings=yes' option
rack:~ # ssh -o ClearAllForwardings=yes root@www
root@www's password: <password>
root@www ~>
```

Using SSH As a Transport

Discussion of forwarding thus far has covered typical TCP applications such as IMAP, SMTP, Telnet, POP3, and LDAP in a variety of ways. Other applications have different features that use SSH as the encrypted tunnel to communicate through. Some of these applications, such as rsync (http://samba.anu.edu.au/rsync/) and Concurrent Versions System (CVS, http://www.gnu.org/software/cvs/), are well aware of SSH and the way it works. Configuration options inside these programs allow them to use SSH as the transport for communication with their application servers. This provides the same advantages of tunneling over SSH, such as encryption and working through firewalls, and is very simple to set up. For example, modern versions of rsync assume the transport mechanism is SSH unless explicitly told otherwise. CVS requires the environment variable `CVS_RSH=ssh`.

Dynamic Forwarding

Another type of TCP forwarding that is available when using the SSH protocol is *dynamic forwarding*. Using standard TCP forwarding, the connection ports are explicitly defined. With dynamic forwarding, the SSH client acts as a SOCKS proxy server, which means that the remote application will negotiate which ports to open, with the SSH client acting as a SOCKS server. Client applications using dynamic forwarding must be SOCKS aware. SOCKS proxies are normally used in conjunction with firewalls.

To demonstrate dynamic forwarding, some background information is required. Suppose you have a system on LAN that cannot make HTTP connections to addresses external to the LAN. You do, however, have an account on a system external to the LAN that has no HTTP access control in place.

To browse HTTP content, you can set up dynamic forwarding in the form of a SOCKS proxy, make an SSH connection to the remote host from your workstation, configure your web browser to use a SOCKS proxy, and now you can surf the web.

This may seem complicated, but I assure you it is not very difficult if you break down the steps for dynamic forwarding. First, you must ensure the remote `sshd` server allows TCP forwarding. After that, you establish a connection to the remote system and set up the dynamic forward tunnel, as in this example:

```
stahnma@lan_host: ~> ssh -D 1080 external_host
```

This creates a dynamically forwarded connection on port 1080 of the `localhost`.

The next step is to configure your browser on the LAN host to use the SOCKS connection at `localhost` port 1080. Start by bringing up the Preferences dialog box and clicking the Connection Settings button, shown in Figure 7-3.

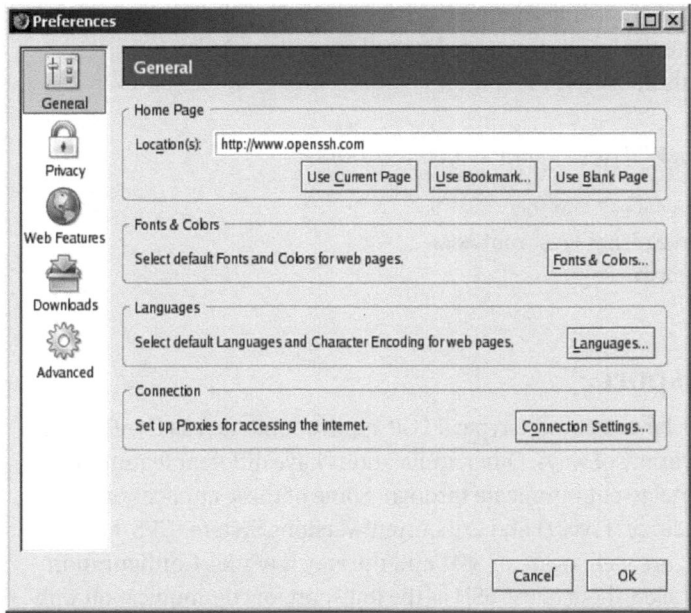

Figure 7-3. *Click the Connection Settings button inside the Preferences dialog box to configure your browser.*

Inside the Connection Settings dialog box, select Manual proxy configuration, and fill in the appropriate host and port values, as shown in Figure 7-4.

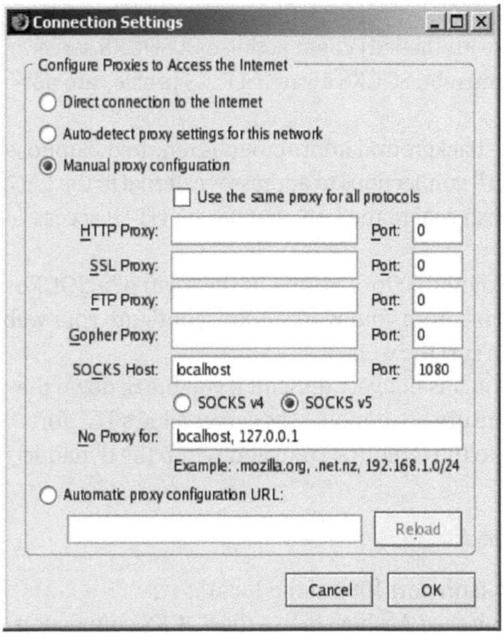

Figure 7-4. *Set up the SOCKS proxy by assigning the* localhost *and proper port.*

After the configuration setup is complete, try surfing to external websites. In this case, I tried a page on www.openssh.com, as you can see in Figure 7-5.

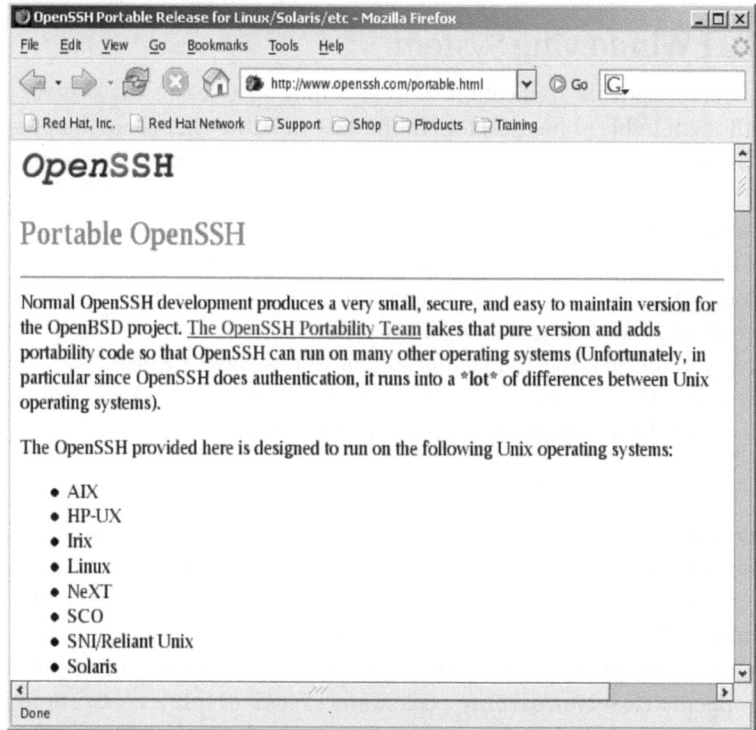

Figure 7-5. *Browsing using a SOCKS proxy*

X11 Forwarding

X11 has its advantages over other display techniques because it was designed to be network transparent, which means users running an X server on their desktop can receive windows from other hosts. This is useful when you need to run a Graphical User Interface (GUI) utility or application from a remote system. In some enterprise applications, X has even saved companies money by allowing several users to share a single server and having X served to their local system, thus sparing those companies from having to buy additional UNIX capacity and software licenses.

Administrators find the command-line interface to suffice for most tasks. However, even for those users with a particular affinity for the command line, the occasion sometimes arises to use an X11 GUI. For instance, suppose corporate backup software is managed through a GUI. It's still possible to securely interact with that software even from the other side of a firewall by using X11 via OpenSSH.

X11 security is susceptible to several eavesdropping mechanisms if the X server is not protected. Unfortunately, many X server products are configured for usability out of the box and not for security. Poor security configuration of X11 servers can leave an entire desktop available to attackers. Attackers can take screen captures of the entire desktop where the poorly configured X server is running in addition to keystroke logging and interjection.

Many X11 issues can be combatted by tunneling the connection over SSH. However, if the X server is configured to allow connections from any remote host (xhost +), even SSH X11 forwarding will not protect the X server desktop.

A Primer in the X11 Windowing System

X11, as is SSH, is a client/server network application. A user running an X desktop or X server can view X protocol traffic sent to his or her desktop. In the case of X, the clients are the programs, such as the Firefox browser, xterm, and xclock. The server portion services the requests of the X clients and draws material on the screen.

This architecture makes X inherently insecure. The X protocol calls for all of this data to be sent in an unencrypted format. Unfortunately, because this data contains keystrokes and mouse movements, it is a common target for attackers. Such deficiencies make it a perfect candidate for tunneling via SSH, resulting in the encryption of all X11 traffic.

X11 calls for a DISPLAY variable to be set. While many applications allow the display to be specified dynamically, almost without exception, users set DISPLAY upon login and never think about it again. The DISPLAY variable is composed of the following components:

```
<hostname>:<display number>:<visual number>.
```

The hostname component can be an IP address or a name resolvable from /etc/hosts or DNS. The hostname component can also be blank, which implies the localhost. The display number component determines the identifying number of the destination X server. Most of the time, a system is only running a single X server; however, if you are running more than one, you should set this component accordingly. Finally, the visual number component determines the screen inside of the specified X server. display number and visual display number both start at zero. For example, when I log in to www from my workstation rack, I can export my display like so:

```
stahnke@www: ~> export DISPLAY=rack:0.0
```

I now have the ability to forward X11 windows back to my workstation, rack, meaning that if I launch xterm or some other application from www, it appears on my workstation screen. However, at this time, the X traffic is still not protected with SSH.

The X server also can perform some access control over what hosts can be an X client. This is done by the command xhost. The xhost command allows you to specify what hosts are either allowed or denied connection rights. For example, if I am on my workstation rack and want my server www to have access to the DISPLAY, I can run the following:

```
stahnma@rack: ~> xhost +www
www being added to access control list
```

To remove www from the access list, a minus sign is used. Many people run an X server with xhost +, meaning all X clients are allowed. This can cause additional security problems. If the previous exercise of setting your DISPLAY variable and trying to run xterm or some other X application did not work, you might have to allow the remote host. Also note that many Linux distributions now ship with root's ability to accept remote X connections disabled. This was done for security reasons.

X controls access using host-based authentication via the xhost command. More advanced authentication mechanisms are available, however. xauth, which creates user-based access control to an X server, is one such mechanism. xauth uses cookies generated for each user to use, normally stored in $HOME/.Xauthority. The problem with xauth is that it can still be tampered with because the cookie transmission takes place over an insecure channel.

When SSH forwards X11 connections, it uses xauth as the X server access control mechanism. However, it has overcome the challenge of key distribution, because the transmission medium is encrypted.

Making OpenSSH Work with X11

X11 forwarding is not enabled by default. There are a few possible vulnerabilities that can exist if using X11 forwarding. For example, users who can access an .Xauthority file (due to poor home directory permissions, or if they have root) can use an existing X tunnel. If your users do not need X11 forwarding, it is best to keep the defaults

OpenSSH provides X11 forwarding without much setup. All you have to do to enable it is change a few directives in your sshd_config and your client configuration files.

Inside sshd_config

There are four parameters inside the sshd_config that require some examination:

- X11Forwarding yes: The default for this setting is no in OpenSSH. Security concerns can arise when forwarding X. Most organizations find that the security gained by encrypting X sessions far outweighs the concerns of X inside of OpenSSH. If a client (remember the client for X is where sshd is running) is configured to set the DISPLAY variable to something other than localhost, like a gateway system, anyone could interject traffic into your X session.

- X11DisplayOffset 10: By default, OpenSSH starts with the X display forwarding of localhost:10. If you need this setting higher than 10 because you run legitimate X servers, or have another application in this port range, you can adjust this number.

- X11UseLocalhost yes: This specifies whether SSH should bind only on the localhost (loopback), or bind to all addresses on the host. This prevents interjection into X sessions and prevents remote clients from connecting to the X11 tunnel created by SSH.

- XAuthLocation /usr/X11R6/bin/xauth: This specifies the location of xauth, which is used for authentication inside of X systems. Your path could be different from this one. You have the option of not including this line in the sshd_config file, and OpenSSH will take the default if it found xauth in your path at compile time, which is probably the case.

Inside ssh_config

Remember, you can specify per-host configurations in the client file, so if you have policy about X forwarding, you should be able to comply with it.

- `ForwardX11 yes`: This token by default is set to no. When set to yes, it tells the server that you wish to enable X11 forwarding for this connection.

- `ForwardX11Trusted no`: If this is set to yes, trusted xauth cookies are used to connect to the X display. If it is set to no (the default setting), X clients are not trusted, which prevents tampering with data belonging to trusted X11 clients. The default of no is a good security practice, as it prevents attacks against X11 forwarding; however, certain X applications do not behave well when the X cookie is untrusted. xterm, for example, will crash if it is running on Linux when large amounts of text are highlighted. This behavior depends on how the X server is configured.

- `XAuthLocation /usr/X11R6/bin/xauth`: Just as on the server, this specifies the path for xauth. If you set it on the server, you probably do not need to worry about it here, unless you know the server is set up incorrectly.

Example Connection

Here, I will demonstrate making a connection with X11 forwarding enabled. If you are following along and this is the first time you connect to a system with X11 forwarding enabled, you will see that xauth runs and creates an ~/.Xauthority file. After that, you check your DISPLAY to ensure that it is automatically set by OpenSSH, and then run a simple xterm command, which pops up on rack, and close it. Figure 7-6 shows how this appears on my system.

```
stahnke@rack:~> ssh root@www
/usr/X11R6/bin/xauth:  creating new authority file /root/.Xauthority
root@www ~> echo $DISPLAY
0:1
root@www ~> xterm &
[1] 10359
```

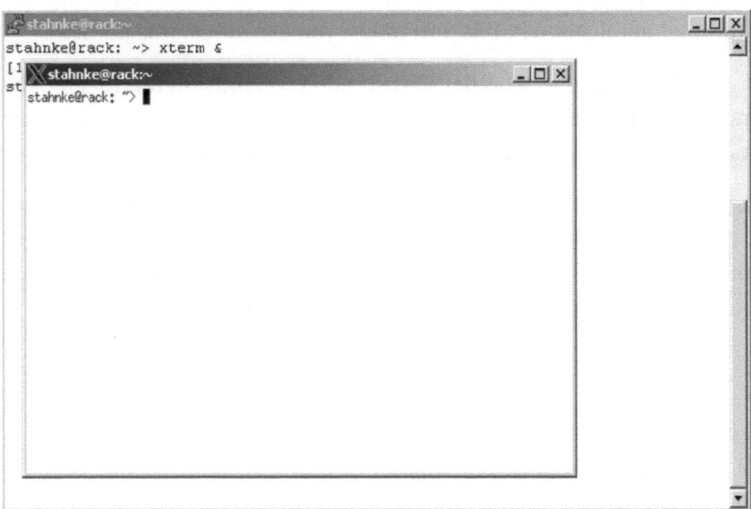

Figure 7-6. *Forwarding X11 traffic through SSH,* xterm *is launched*

■**Caution** If you set your DISPLAY variable manually, or through a .profile (or any login script), you have just bypassed X11 forwarding over SSH. Setting your DISPLAY variable reverts to standard unencrypted X connections. Also, if you need to mess with xauth, you probably are not working within the realm of SSH forwarding.

X Authentication

The X server (that is, your desktop) authenticates the X client and determines whether that client should be allowed to connect to the X session that server is managing. Traditionally, you use xhost to create an X host or deny a rule set. This allows any user from the X client to connect to your display.

The xauth method of X authentication is a key-based authentication that authenticates the X client system and the user. The ~/.Xauthority file contains keys for X clients. This allows the X client to authenticate to the X server in a more trusted fashion. The keys are still normally (without SSH) transmitted in the clear. The keys in this case only provide authentication; that is, the session is still clear-text. When using X over SSH, that xauth key exchange is encrypted and secured.

Notes on X11

Many users rely on X11 as a way of life. Changing their login habits can be nearly impossible. I worked with an engineer once who claimed that if we removed the ability to log in directly over X (via xdm), his team would lose 5 minutes per person per day, and that added up to thousands of dollars a year. Working with your organization to help them understand and then contain X can be challenging.

I have found that many end users who are used to logging in via xdm, gdm, or kdm are willing to change to using ssh to access a host and then launch their X application if an administrator takes the time to explain the security benefits of doing so and offer instruction on how to make it work. Many users think the only way to work on UNIX systems is to log in to a UNIX desktop environment and then launch a few terminal clients. Once you show them they can launch terminal clients without having a whole desktop enabled, and that it can be done over SSH, they will be happy.

Also remember that if you or your administration staff commonly use X to pull up desktops (oftentimes by opening a number of xterms), if the connection between the workstation and the initial X desktop is not encrypted, SSH will not help.

As a final caveat, if users or administrators are using xhost + on their workstations, all traffic can be monitored, including keystrokes sent and applications in use (even those that are not X11 applications). Tunneling through SSH will not prevent keystroke logging and other forms of eavesdropping on sessions. Several native UNIX tools can take a screenshot of open X servers, and many more malicious tools are available.

I encourage you to look for SSH clients that run on your client architecture, whether it is a Microsoft Windows product or a Linux/UNIX variant. Having the right client tools can enable good usability and security. Client tools are covered in more depth in Appendix A.

Summary

This chapter dug deep into the technical realm of SSH that extends beyond a simple Telnet replacement. From the beginning of the chapter, where I discussed insecure TCP connections, until the end, where we conquered X11, you saw how OpenSSH provides wonderful solutions for legacy security problems.

SSH tunneling might not save your organization millions of dollars, but it will provide you some piece of mind about the connections occurring on your network. As with any major product or implementation change, SSH tunnels, architectures, and setups take careful planning. If you plan and implement correctly, OpenSSH will save you time and make your life easier.

■ ■ ■

## CHAPTER 8

Managing Your OpenSSH Environment

If you rely on OpenSSH's default settings, rely on a fairly straightforward security policy, and are not trying to implement many of the advanced features afforded to you by OpenSSH, your implementation can be designed and deployed without a significant time investment. Indeed, this is how most SSH implementations begin. Usually, a few administrators start playing with OpenSSH, either on their home systems or at work, and decide it is a viable secure connectivity product their organization should be using. After installing it on a few development servers, they provide an informal introduction to their peers about the technology. From there the SSH policy and practices are developed until the organization is happy with the results OpenSSH is delivering for them.

However, to maximize your investment of time and resources, it is important to carefully plan your environment and administrative strategy. This chapter will examine several important topics regarding proper policy development, operational usage, OpenSSH security, and finally server and key management.

Planning Your Environment

When interacting with users and administrators interested in maximizing the benefits of their SSH implementation, I commonly begin with a few basic questions:

1. What are your goals with OpenSSH?

2. Are you considering eliminating other protocols?

3. What type of user education will you be providing?

4. Will you permit key-based authentication?

5. What practices are already defined surrounding key management?

Questions 1, 2, and 3 are all related. More often than not, the reason for introducing OpenSSH into the environment is to initiate a migration path away from legacy clear-text protocols with inadequate logging and authentication practices. This migration often puts organizations in a transition state after they have enabling OpenSSH on hosts, but have not yet turned off the legacy commutation mechanisms. This is where user education is critical, yet is often under-estimated. Just because port 22 (or wherever you decided to enable OpenSSH) is listening does not mean users have motivation to use OpenSSH, until it is their only choice. Providing educa-tion and a calendar for disabling older protocols is of paramount importance to a successful OpenSSH implementation.

Choosing whether or not to permit key-based authentication, as in question 4, will help decide the level of understanding needed by system administration and security staff surround-ing OpenSSH technology. Password authentication is simple to troubleshoot, and normally is easily understood by end users. Key-based authentication requires at least a simple under-standing of how key-based authentication works and some form of key management.

Question 5 only applies if key-based authentication will be permitted. Most organizations already have password policies such as how often passwords must be changed, what levels of complexity are required, and so forth; however, oftentimes there is no policy about private and public keys. Setting policy on keys and authentication mechanisms must be done if keys are being used in the infrastructure.

Establishing Security Guidelines

The architecture of OpenSSH should involve representatives from several areas of your organization. System administrators need to provide the hands-on technical knowledge of what works and is necessary in a working environment. Security administrators should be able to state a case for avoiding exploits and misconfigurations that can otherwise dearly cost your organization.

If you are wondering what types of policy questions there are to consider, consider these examples:

- Will you use a source code–based or binary distribution?

  Binary and source distributions of OpenSSH have their place. Using a source-based distribution normally requires a deeper level of technical expertise than that of a binary distribution. When using source, various options can be compiled in or specifically disallowed. This can allow for fine-tuning and customization to create an OpenSSH implementation that is perfect for your environment. However, as a disadvantage, when a new patch is available, source must be recompiled for each architecture your organization is supporting. Additionally, source code OpenSSH installations are nor-mally not supported by third-party vendors that provide binary alternatives.

  Using binary distributions offers the advantage of premade packages designed for a spe-cific operating system. They can normally be added, removed, and queried through a package manager. Additionally, vendors that provide an OpenSSH binary will often support it for their specific platform (at least on a best-effort basis). The disadvantages of using a binary distribution come into play when a patch, especially if it is a critical security alert, is released. Oftentimes third-party vendors take weeks or months to incorporate the latest patches and releases into their binary packages. Because of the time lapse with certain vendors, several new powerful features might be left out of a binary distri-bution for extended periods of time.

I will not recommend using source or binary packages in general. Both have merit as secure infrastructure components. Patching OpenSSH is discussed later in this chapter in the section "Patching OpenSSH."

- Will you allow SSH protocol 1 traffic?

  In its infancy, SSH protocol 1 had several security exploits. All known exploits in the OpenSSH implementation of SSH protocol 1 have been patched, but some of the specifications inherent to this version of the protocol are subject to exploitation and misuse. Most security consultants and Internet sources recommend using SSH protocol 2 only, as it provides a more robust feature set and is believed to be more secure.

  SSH protocol 1 sometimes must still be used if connecting to legacy embedded devices that cannot be upgraded. In this case, only specific clients should have protocol 1 communication enabled. On configurable sshd servers, only protocol 2 should be used. This topic is also discussed in Chapter 1.

- Will the SSH server listen on all IP addresses on a host?

  If you have systems with multiple IP addresses such as web hosting systems, do you want the SSH daemon to listen on all addresses? Some organizations restrict sshd to an infrastructure management network, and others allow sshd to bind to all addresses. In risk domains, such as DMZs or extranets, limiting the number of listening IP addresses is desired.

- What port will sshd reside on?

  Normally port 22 is used for SSH traffic. In high-risk environments, sometimes alternate ports are used to avoid simplistic attacks and scans. Moving the port that sshd listens on is commonly called *security through obscurity*, as it provides no additional security to a system, but may deter someone only using default configurations. If the port is changed, client configurations should be updated.

- Will you allow TCP connection forwarding?

  TCP connection forwarding can sometimes enable traffic to move where it is not desired, especially if you are bridging firewalls or tunneling across different networks. In a trusted environment, this is ideal; in an insecure environment, tunneling over OpenSSH may outweigh the problems of spanning networks, or it may not. Generally this discussion point generates many tests and reviews from network security staff and system administrators. If you do not think your organization will use TCP forwarding, the easiest thing to do is to leave it off. But also note that users can install/use external forwarders to perform TCP forwarding. Forwarding is covered in detail in Chapter 7.

- Will you allow X11 forwarding?

  I am a firm believer in X11 forwarding. Normally, X11 applications are used to make connectivity to UNIX/Linux servers very simple. Unfortunately, the clear-text nature of X11 technology allows for eavesdropping and poor authentication practices. Because

I have had no luck in convincing users to not use X11 applications, I enable X11 forwarding. This requires the usage of OpenSSH for authentication, which also protects against eavesdropping.

If using X11 technologies is required to enable business and application usage, use it in an encrypted manner that is not subject to interjection attacks. X11 forwarding is covered in Chapter 7.

• Will you allow SSH agent forwarding?

If compromised, SSH agents can allow an intruder to use that agent to authenticate on different hosts. I usually recommend allowing agent forwarding within trusted networks because of the productivity gains and disabling it in risk areas. SSH agents and agent forwarding is covered in Chapter 6.

• What logging parameters should you use?

OpenSSH provides logging through syslog. Do you want OpenSSH to provide its own log via the local syslog facilities, or do you want to use the standard syslog and auth log files? The facility that OpenSSH uses to log to is completely up to the administration staff. I often like separate AUTH or AUTHPRIV logs so application users viewing a standard syslog file do not see authentication information; other system administrators prefer a single log for everything occurring on a system.

What verbosity levels will you require? I normally log OpenSSH to the AUTH or AUTHPRIV syslog facility and keep it at the VERBOSE level. The VERBOSE level will cause a log file to grow more rapidly, but it also contains the fingerprints of public keys used for authentication. This is important for accountability among users of shared accounts.

• Will you force strict host key checking?

This is another heated subject of debate. If your user base does not understand host keys and system identification, getting a message that a key changed is probably just a hassle to them, as they will have to edit a $HOME/.ssh/known_hosts file. However, disabling it removes a layer of authentication from OpenSSH. If you just accept a host key change, you are not protected against man-in-the-middle attacks.

If your organization is more concerned with proper security than with usability, forcing strict host key checking should be enabled. User education is required when/if users see a host key change. Normally they should contact a help desk or security administrator to verify the host key change is legitimate. Additionally, the usage of SSHFP (covered later in this chapter) could help ease the host key management issue.

If host key checking causes too many incident calls and your organization is willing to accept the risk of man-in-the-middle attacks, or your host keys change because your network relies heavily on DHCP, disable strict host key checking. This is discussed in more detail in Chapter 4.

- What types of authentication will be permitted?

    Password authentication is normally allowed because of its ease for end users. The benefits and disadvantages of password authentication versus other authentication methods are covered in Chapter 6.

    Key-based authentication offers the benefits of automation with secure authentication, but introduces some more complex issues involving key management. Key management is discussed later in this chapter in the section "Key Management."

    Host-based authentication introduces a risk because multiple servers trust the authentication of other computers. However, SSH host-based authentication is far stronger than the connectivity provided by rsh. Normally, host-based authentication is not recommended.

These are just a few of the issues that are involved in setting policy for OpenSSH in your organization. At the biggest OpenSSH implementation I have done, the security and administrative staff had well over a month's worth of meetings and architecture designs before everyone found the usability and security of OpenSSH agreeable. That same organization used that thought-out OpenSSH framework for some of the most sophisticated scripting and security analysis of UNIX systems I have seen.

Ensuring the Proper Checks and Balances

After setting policy with your security and administrative staff, remember to run it past your auditors, whether they are internal or external to your organization. Sometimes a third-party sanity check can clear up discrepancies or unclear wording on some statements, particularly if you are using external auditors—they might have familiarity with OpenSSH and have some best practices to share with your organization.

Auditing also will examine your policy for separation of duties. If a single root user can control every SSH public key and every system, that person might be too powerful. Perhaps key management will be done per user, or on a server that the system administrators must check out the root password for. These types of checks and balances are important, but because they vary widely among different organizations, the discussion is limited. Consult your auditors for best practices and more information.

Staff Commitment

From the start, you need to strive for commitment from your administrative staff to use OpenSSH. If they are not using it on regular basis, how will you convince the user base of your systems it is the right thing to do? This can be a much bigger challenge than expected.

Many UNIX administrators are very resistant to change. When they learn that they should not be using rlogin and xdm to pull up an X desktop every time they log in, they get mad. I have had several administrators tell me their productivity will be significantly reduced if we remove rsh or xdm logins. After struggling with some education on OpenSSH and the security behind it, most reluctantly accept the new direction is the right way to go and their productivity does not drop. Sometimes administrators may hold out until rsh, xdm, and telnet are shut off, and if that is the case, be sure to communicate those changes to them well in advance. Scripts and batch jobs need to be changed too when moving from legacy protocols to OpenSSH, and that is covered in Chapter 9.

Additionally, be sure not to be the only one who is pushing and using OpenSSH. To help your peers, create keys for them on a few systems, or have them try out forwarding X11 applications with it. You will engage them and make them feel like part of the SSH implementation as well as create other knowledge administrators on staff. Most likely the UNIX administrative staff will be supporting, patching, and configuring OpenSSH.

OPENSSH SUPPORT

Many times companies, especially those not directly involved in the technology sector, are very hesitant to use an open source product, particularly in an enterprise-wide capacity. It is true that OpenSSH comes without commercial support, but help is available. If your organization's stance is firmly against open source software, SSH Communications Security does offer a commercial product, which is covered in more detail in Chapter 10. However, OpenSSH is fairly intuitive, and many troubleshooting scenarios are documented on the Internet.

Simple searches on your favorite search engine will likely lead you to a solution for your inquiry faster than you could open a problem ticket with many vendors. Because OpenSSH is so widely used in the UNIX/Linux communities, forums and articles are available on the Internet.

Additionally, because of the growing popularity of OpenSSH, most of the major UNIX/Linux vendors will support OpenSSH if it is the version they supply for their OS.[1] With Red Hat Linux, for example, several bugs have been opened, tracked, and fixed via their technicians in conjunction with the core development team of OpenSSH. The open source community is there to help everyone, including you, so just ask.

Asking for help with an open source product normally means that you have done some investigation of your own before posting a query. Some message boards and mailing lists are very friendly to repeated questions and people who did not read the fine manual (RTFM), but other places tend to expect a certain level of diagnosis ahead of time.

The official OpenSSH website provides an FAQ at http://www.openssh.com/faq.html. They also provide the instructions for reporting and tracking problems via http://www.openssh.com/report.html.

The official OpenSSH mailing list is openssh-unix-dev@mindrot.org. This list has many developers and power users as contributors.

If you believe you have found a bug in OpenSSH, after discussing it with the mailing list, bugs can be reported at http://bugzilla.mindrot.org.

news://comp.security.ssh is a Usenet news group devoted to SSH. If you are posting a question, be prepared to provide logs, configuration files, and other information.

OpenSSH Secure Gateway

Any strategy for developing an architecture for secure system administration should balance the need to adhere to rigorous security policies while maximizing the efficiency of those individuals tasked with managing the infrastructure. Over the years, one of the most effective methodologies I have encountered is using a secured gateway server. An OpenSSH gateway architecture offers numerous advantages, including the following:

---

1. Sun actually ships SunSSH with Solaris, which is a forked project from OpenSSH. OpenSSH can still be installed on Solaris, but is not supported from Sun.

- A common workplace for sharing scripts, programs, and informative messaging, such as outage windows, events, or patching dates

- An infrastructure built for scripting and thus performing flexible administrative tasks on large volumes of systems

- A central system for maintaining pristine OpenSSH settings and a mechanism to distribute those settings to the rest of the infrastructure

- A monitoring/logging location for administrators using OpenSSH as their administration connection method

In this section, I will introduce this concept, showing you how to effectively create, configure, and manage a gateway host.

Introducing the Gateway Server

The OpenSSH gateway system acts a pass-through for administrators by creating a central point of administration using public key-based authentication per user. When properly utilized, an OpenSSH gateway system quickly becomes a critical part of infrastructure management, and therefore availability of the server becomes critical.

Normally, one or more system administrators will store their private key on a server. After that, administrators will install their public key on the rest of the system population, as shown in Figure 8-1. What this provides is a central point of administration for system administrators. From this central server, an administrator can gather information about any number of hosts, resulting in significant time savings. Additionally, using keys will allow the administration staff to stop using potentially dangerous and weaker password-based authentication techniques.

The benefits of using a gateway are numerous:

- *Script reuse and collaboration*: If the entire administration is using the same server to run scripts and batch jobs, other administrators can learn from those scripts. For example, if a senior administrator has created scripts that perform complex administration tasks, others can take those scripts and run them, or modify them to meet their own needs. This normally involves a common script directory or open group permissions of home directories.

- *Automation*: Through the gateway, connections can be established to other systems on the network. SSH allows the use of remote commands to automate many tasks. Scripting is covered in detail in Chapter 9, but some examples could include file system monitoring, configuration management, application monitoring, adding user accounts, and password resets.

- *Known network behavior*: Because the gateway server is used for specific tasks, intrusion detection staff, auditors, and other security personnel may become comfortable with the node names for the gateway and have a better understanding of the logs from the remote systems. For example, if several privileged accounts were accessed from systems other than the gateway, this could be cause for further investigation.

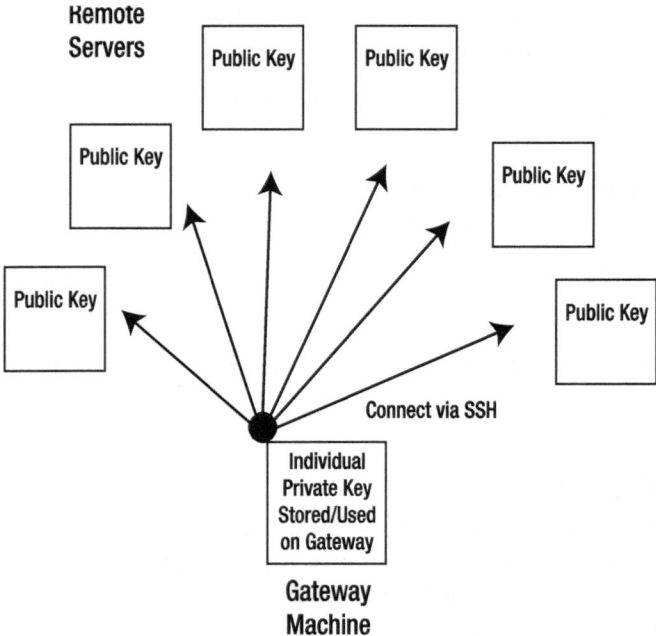

Figure 8-1. *The gateway system in the OpenSSH gateway architecture*

Setting Up the Gateway

Setting up a gateway server is trivial. Most organizations will choose a system that is not serving other purposes. Having a dedicated system will aid in securing the box and probably also help with availability. If the box does have other duties, they should lie within the control of the system administrators, as extra traffic on the box only opens the system to security risks.

The first task of creating an OpenSSH administrative gateway is to secure the box. It is best to secure the operating system before creating any private keys, as you do not want them to be compromised. Because securing this system involves removing legacy services such as telnet, ftp, the r-utilities, NFS, NIS, and anything else that is clear text, you want to be sure your OpenSSH server is behaving as expected before accidentally locking yourself out of a box.

- Does sshd start on reboot?

- Is sshd being monitored so that if it dies (or is killed) it will be restarted?

- Is sshd configured to allow connections for your administrative staff?

If your sshd on the gateway server is set up, then you are ready to remove the legacy services from it. While I realize that NIS and NFS have not been involved in the earlier discussions about legacy services, their inherently weak authentication and clear-text nature make your administrative gateway server better off without them. Pay special attention to NFS-mounted home directories because they are subject to compromise, and by default, private keys are stored in home directories.

Normally an administrative gateway will have port 22 open (or whatever port you have chosen for sshd) and possibly a port for backup software; although if your backup software uses TCP connections, it can be tunneled via SSH. If you are comfortable running other services on the gateway server, that is up to you.

After removing legacy services and configuring `sshd` to your liking, it is time to generate OpenSSH key pairs for each administrator. I do not recommend using key lengths less than 1024 bits. 2048-bit keys are exceptionally strong but can cause performance issues during authentication on older hardware. It is best to give each private key a passphrase. You can either generate the keys for your administrative staff or let each user create his or her own keys. Remember that passphrases can (and should) be changed by the key owner.

The public keys then should be distributed to the rest of the systems. These keys can be installed in a few different ways. If your organization allows administrative staff to log in directly as root, you can place an `authorized_keys` file containing all the public keys from your gateway in root's `.ssh` directory. Remember that allowing root access via OpenSSH does not mean root access is available via other services such as `telnet`. It is also wise to protect your hosts from brute-force password guessing attacks (and possibly administrators not following policy) by setting the following keyword in `sshd_config`:

```
PermitRootLogin without-password
```

By removing root's ability to authenticate with a password, you have ensured that over SSH only keys authentication will work. It also a best practice to ensure that the `authorized_keys` file specifies which keys can be used from where. That way, if a key is compromised, source node restrictions prevent use from other systems.

In my work, I have found that allowing remote root access provides the most flexibility for the administrators. Most often if they are troubleshooting or on a system, they are using root access, either directly through `su` or through `sudo`. However, if root logins are enabled, a single private key that is compromised will literally get you the keys to the kingdom. Securing the administrative gateway server is a must.

■**Caution** On AIX versions 4.3 and 5.x, accounts are allowed to log in remotely via a single `rlogin=true` line in the `/etc/security/user` file. Because of this, it is difficult to allow remote login of an account via SSH, but not with `telnet` or `rlogin` if they are enabled. This can be done by modifying the source of OpenSSH, but could have unintended consequences, such as losing failed login lockout policies, etc. The best option, if connections are desired only via SSH, is to remove the other methods of connectivity. As a final caveat on AIX, the `PermitRootLogin` setting in `sshd_config` will take precedence over the operating system settings when using OpenSSH. This means you could allow root logins over SSH, but not via Telnet.

The private key that each administrator keeps on this system should stay there. If key-based authentication is desired for an administrator to connect to the administrative host, ensure it is a different key. In this example, two different passphrases are needed to compromise the environment.

The scenario plays out like this. If I have an administrative gateway server named AGS (A Gateway Server), a workstation named WS, and many other hosts named host1, host2, etc., I would log in to AGS from my workstation WS via `ssh`. On AGS I have a nonprivileged account; I do not have `sudo`, nor know the root password. From there on AGS, I invoke `ssh-agent` and add my private key to it. After that, from AGS I can move to any system host1, host2, etc., all using SSH.

Security Concerns

Though OpenSSH provides secure solutions to several connectivity quandaries, poor configuration and management of the tool can still lead to security compromises. Accidentally allowing blank passwords in the `sshd_config` or having administrators leave default passwords on accounts can allow compromises that OpenSSH cannot stop.

Furthermore, be sure to use different strings for your password on the system (if you have password authentication enabled) and your passphrase for your private key. While this may seem like a usability hassle, adversaries will have to compromise two pieces of data instead of only one to assume your identity on the network.

Physical Security

The server should be kept in a locked room. This also discourages the use of workstations as gateways, because workstations normally reside on somebody's desk. Servers can be racked in a secured room to restrict console access.

Physical access to the hardware can allow for attacks or data corruption. Additionally, sometimes the cleaning staff will unplug a cable from the power strip to plug in a vacuum cleaner, which also hurts the availability of this critical server.

Authentication to the Gateway

Administrators need connectivity to the gateway server. How this connectivity occurs is subject to discussion. SSH is the preferred method of connectivity to the server; the debate normally involves whether or not key-based authentication should be used to connect to the gateway.

The main argument for key-based authentication to the gateway server is security (keys should be more difficult to compromise than passwords). The opposition argues that key-based authentication to a gateway node requires a key be available to an administrator at all times. If an administrator is vacationing and is needed on a support issue, he or she would need a private key to access the gateway. This presents the difficulty in distributing keys. Keys can be distributed on USB flash devices, floppy disks, or other media. For more information on key management, see the section "Key Management" later in this chapter.

If key-based authentication is permitted to gateway server, the key must be different from the one stored on the gateway. If the keys are not different, any host with the private key loaded effectively becomes a gateway.

Root Access to the Gateway

Root access to the administrative gateway system should be guarded with the utmost care. If you have a separate security administrative staff, perhaps having them keep the password in a locked filing cabinet or other measures could be arranged. Having root access controlled by a group other than the system administrators offers a separation of duties. If you do not have a process set up to remove all system administrators' root access from a host, allowing only two or three individuals that access can help reduce the problems that can occur if every administrator has root on this box.

Tip Remember, securing root access on the gateway server also means that the administrator's public keys should not be installed in root's home directory on the gateway server.

With root access, logs can be tampered with and keys can be compromised. If several people have root access to the gateway, the exposure to shoulder surfing or unlocked screen attacks becomes higher. Normally, the logs on the gateway server can be read by any system administrator without invoking root access.

Services

While having insecure services on the gateway server has been discussed, there are a few additional points that should be covered. If you authenticate users via LDAP or some other account repository, be sure the communication between the gateway server and that data source are encrypted. I have seen servers using OpenSSH authenticate via an LDAP over port 389, which is normally clear-text. Someone sniffing that traffic flow could then have your passwords.

Additionally, if you or your organization utilize any type of host-based intrusion detection software, it is wise to place an agent on the gateway server.

User Restrictions

Allowing administrators access to the gateway, assuming their public key has been installed on remote systems, gives them a great responsibility. They will be operating as root on remote systems when they log in. If you have less experienced administrative staff, installing their public keys remotely using normal user accounts will enable learning without the negative consequences of root-level mistakes.

Remember that you also can deny or allow users inside of the sshd_config file.

I oftentimes have end users asking me if they can use the gateway server because they have 30 web server systems or 45 application-rendering hosts. Because these users do not require root access to perform most of their daily tasks, I help them set up keys from either their work-station or their favorite server and create for them a type of gateway server for their group.

These systems that assist application groups then become their home for application logs, reporting tools, and of course their private keys. I have seen the system administrators and application analysts share gateway severs, and in small environments, this seems to work fine. In larger environments, having separate control areas, especially if disk space is an issue, becomes key.

Network Location

When creating an administrative gateway server, its network location is critical. The server should not be placed on a hostile network or be accessible from untrusted networks. A system on an internal network is best, assuming SSH is allowed to the other segments of the network you need to access to perform administrative tasks.

Ideally, the administrative gateway server can initiate an SSH connection to any other remote hosts on your network. If you have isolated networks, setting separate administrative gateways is required.

Firewall considerations should also be made when selecting placement for an SSH gateway. Some companies place firewalls around the SSH gateway because of its importance; other companies require authentication to firewalls before outbound traffic is allowed. If firewalls require interaction to allow outbound traffic, many automation tasks will probably not work.

Avoiding a Single Point of Failure

Though the administrative gateway model may not seem life changing, after a few months of using it, you will wonder how you ever got along without it. The administration staff will have built up dozens of scripts and may only have one way into most systems because of their reliance on keys and OpenSSH. The gateway is the hub for nearly all administration activities. When an admin needs to resolve a problem ticket, work on changes, automate tasks, or monitor services, the gateway server is used. If this system is down, it can (and undoubtedly will) leave your administrators sitting idle until the service is restored.

If the gateway system is down, your staff will feel it. Even taking down the gateway server after hours can be catastrophic if it provides the only avenue to production hosts. To avoid single points of failure, you can cluster the system with another. You also can just copy everyone's .ssh directory to a different system if the outage is planned. Depending on the number of users you have on your administrative gateway server, you might want to have more than one.

Using rsync over SSH provides a low-cost way to replicate data between gateway servers and sites. Keep in mind, however, that rsync is unable to handle multiple masters—meaning that an update on the master can overwrite files on a client. rsync over SSH is covered in Chapter 7.

In a recent implementation of an admin gateway that I did, there was no budget available for clustering, so the keys were backed up to a CD-ROM that was locked in a fire safe. That way, if the gateway server was down, they could install the keys on another server and use it.

Managing the Gateway

The OpenSSH administrative gateway can require some unique practices to ensure security and usability are maintained. Working in an environment without root access can be extremely difficult for those who have been using it for years. A gateway system should provide a repository of scripts, a host list, a list of unavailable systems, and the cached public host keys of those systems.

File Permissions

For administrators to share data, ensure they are in the same group and their directories allow the group to read, execute, and possibly write to their files. So many administrators get used to just using root to copy a script or file from a coworker's directory that they often forget the basics of file permissions and ownership and will instantly request, or complain about not having, root-level access. By allowing collaboration between user files and scripts, this situation can hopefully be avoided.

If you do not want to have every administrator sharing files, you can create another location for common scripts that much of the staff might utilize. I normally have some form a remote host node-name generation scripts in a repository for use.

If each administrator can generate system lists by operating system or IP address using the same algorithm, duplicate efforts should be cut to a minimum.

Ability to Generate System Lists

A user on a gateway server is made powerful by his or her ability to log in to remote hosts without further authentication after loading an ssh-agent. For tasks that encompass the entire environment, this user needs to ensure that he or she is covering the right system base.

In small environments such as home networks and many small businesses, maintaining a list of hosts is quite easy. In larger environments, using some form of data store such as a relational database or LDAP directory is desired to retrieve hostnames. This way, if a system is decommissioned, your list is automatically updated.

Although the details of asset and configuration management are well beyond the scope of this material, having the ability to generate accurate host lists will only improve the productivity of everyone using the administrative gateway approach.

Creating Unavailable Lists

If you have the ability to create a host list, are all of them available? It is also a common practice to somehow maintain a list of systems that you are unable to connect to, for example because they are unpingable, the sshd port is not open, or ssh is misconfigured. Sometimes, however, it is more effective to create fault-tolerant scripts that can handle systems being unavailable.

If you set the client's ConnectTimeout to a small value, needing to ping all hosts ahead of time, and thus creating an unavailable list, is not always required. However, if your processes require tracking of down systems, or if you are using SSH Communications' Tectia product, which does not have a ConnectTimeout setting, pinging the system before attempting a connection may be desired.

The following is a list of systems that will be verified for connectivity:

```
stahnke@rack: ~> cat list
#system list
rack.example.com
www.example.com
zoom.example.com
slack.example.com
mo.example.com
```

The script, shown in Listing 8-1, will read each line from that list and connect to the systems via SSH public key authentication. To ensure no password prompts are given, -o "BatchMode yes" is specified. Because -o is normally interpreted by the shell to mean "or," the command is stored in a variable and then piped to sh. The script also assumes that all commands are in your $PATH variable.

Listing 8-1. *A Simple Script to Find Unavailable Systems*

```
#!/bin/bash
user=stahnke

for server in `cat list | grep -v ^\#`
do
  echo $server
  cmd="ssh -o \"BatchMode yes\" $user@$server true 2>&1 "
  echo $cmd | sh
done
```

This was the output from my workstation rack, which in this case is acting as the administrative gateway. I purposefully turned off sshd on this workstation to show an error. The system named slack is not currently online. The name mo is not found in DNS. In this example, only the systems named www and zoom are available.

```
stahnke@rack: ~> ./check_available.sh
rack
ssh: connect to host rack port 22: Connection refused
www
zoom
slack
ssh: connect to host slack port 22: Connection timed out
mo
ssh: mo: Name or service not known
stahnke@rack: ~>
```

As a simple enhancement, I could output the available systems into one list and the unavailable systems into another, as you see in Listing 8-2.

Listing 8-2. *Enhanced Availability Script Creates Availability Lists*

```
#!/bin/bash
user=root
> available
> unavailable
for server in `cat list | grep -v ^\#`
do
  echo $server
  cmd="ssh -o \"BatchMode yes\" -o \"ConnectTimeout 3\" $user@$server true 2>&1 "
  echo $cmd | sh
  if [ "$?" = "0" ]
  then
    echo $server >> available
  else
    echo $server >> unavailable
  fi
done
```

After running the script from Listing 8-2, I have two files, available and unavailable. From here on, if I want to perform actions on several different systems, I can use the available file.

```
stahnke@rack: ~> cat available
www
zoom
stahnke@rack: ~> cat unavailable
rack
slack
mo
```

■**Tip** The code for this script can be downloaded at http://www.apress.com.

Caching Host Keys

When using the administrative gateway server, it can be annoying to have to enter yes each time you connect to a new system. Keys can be cached at the system level by using the ssh-keyscan utility included with OpenSSH.

After you have ensured the systems are available, execute this command:

```
root@rack: # ssh-keyscan -t dsa,rsa `cat available` > \
/etc/ssh/ssh_known_hosts
```

■**Caution** Running this command removes keys that were previously in the system-wide public key cache. Additionally, if you do not trust the public keys for the remote systems, this command will not report differences between yesterday's public key and today's.

Backup Policies

If most of your systems have a backup system, your gateway server should be no different. However, you should not back up the .ssh directories unless the backup system is extremely trusted. Most backup systems I have had contact with communicate in clear-text and have very limited security. An administrator, either backup or system, could restore your key pair to another system to crack or remove the passphrase fairly easily in many cases. To avoid this, I normally place .ssh directories on an exclude list. Of course, if the authorized_keys files used remotely restrict source nodes, only the original location can be used.

Excluding the .ssh directory provides protection against malicious administrators who normally can touch your private key due to root access restrictions. It also prevents an administrator who has had his or her key revoked due to job movement or separation from your organization to restore that key and instantly have root access to remote hosts.

Do You Need a Gateway?

This section has focused on an administrative gateway server using public key authentication to remote systems. If you have a secure environment or are comfortable enough calling your environment secure, an administrative gateway might be a bit much to deploy and maintain.

Other Choices

In large-scale environments, an administrative gateway (or several of them) is normally the most efficient workflow design to enable an administrative staff to perform tasks on multiple hosts. If policy or resources prevent a gateway model, you have other options.

Ad Hoc Administration

If you want to have keys in several spots or you have no drop-off point to put your files and scripts, ad hoc administration can be a simple solution. You can simply connect to any remote system from your workstation and begin your administrative tasks.

Small administrative shops generally prefer this method, as each user can tweak the workstation account settings according to his or her needs and then log in from there. Usage of keys from a workstation or from other hosts is still highly encouraged in this design.

No Keys Allowed

If your organization does not allow users to have keys, what options do you have? You can script all of your logins using Expect (http://expect.nist.gov) or accept that you are probably not going to be able to automate and therefore streamline your work processes. Most organizations that oppose keys are not necessarily against them in principle, but rather are unable to justify the overhead of managing them. Keeping track of which key belongs to what individual can be a daunting task. Several tips and ideas about key management are included later in this chapter.

The benefits of keys versus password-based authentication are covered in detail in Chapter 6.

Educating your end users about key-based authentication is a daunting task. After a few of them see the speed at which you are able to log in to systems and get results, they will want to use keys. Be sure to educate them about securing their private key. Additionally, you should make certain their keys have a passphrase by trying to load their keys into your agent and just hitting Enter.

Securing OpenSSH

As mentioned earlier, OpenSSH can be configured in several ways that can impact the overall security of the environment. Securing OpenSSH is mainly rooted in policy. And of course, security policy is normally created by weighing the risks versus the cost to mitigate that risk, which could entail lowering the overall usability of a system or a monetary investment.

The commitment required for securing OpenSSH is ongoing. Because the technologies behind OpenSSH are changing, so are the security practices. Whether it be new tokens in configuration files under consideration to address certain scenarios or patching new versions of OpenSSL, securely maintaining an OpenSSH infrastructure should be emphasized.

Much of the security for OpenSSH is set in the server-wide configuration files. As explained in Chapters 4 and 5, these settings establish the baseline for your OpenSSH implementation.

Setting Up Authentication Methods That Make Sense

Selecting authentication methods for OpenSSH involves choices between host-based, public key, password, or keyboard interactive authentication. There are a few other options such as Kerberos and the GSSAPI that are not covered in great detail in this text.

It is strongly suggested that password-based authentication be phased out where possible. Passwords are normally weak and easy to remember, or written down in an insecure location. Using keys with passphrases can provide better usability and security at the same time.

If your organization has made a significant investment in LDAP, Kerberos, or some other form of directory service, it is probably wise to continue using that infrastructure. Additionally, OpenSSH can be configured to read smart cards, which enable a wonderful Public Key Infrastructure (PKI) setup.

When using any form of network authentication, ensure that the communication between the remote host and the authentication source is encrypted. In simpler terms, do not connect via Telnet or XDMCP to your gateway server. If you connect to the gateway server this way, the encrypted tunnel is broken, thus leaving passwords available to a network sniffer.

Securing the Root Account

The root account accessing an sshd server requires special attention because of the power and authority that is provided with its usage. As stated earlier, allowing root to log in remotely, contrary to several security documents, is not always a bad thing. Accountability behind the root account is paramount to the success of an OpenSSH implementation. In the log files, when root logs in, the fingerprint of the public key is shown.

```
stahnke@rack: ~> ssh root@www
root@www ~> tail -2 /var/log/secure
Feb 20 21:48:39 www sshd[31456]: Found matching DSA key:
d3:4a:1f:71:ae:79:66:35:31:d9:30:78:63:1f:94:13
Feb 20 21:48:39 www sshd[31456]: Accepted publickey for root from 192.168.1.101
port  33032 ssh2
```

The fingerprint can be verified from my account named stahnke on rack by issuing the ssh-keygen -l command. The ssh-add -l command is also available if the keys are loaded in an agent.

```
stahnke@rack: ~> ssh-keygen -l
Enter file in which the key is (/home/stahnke/.ssh/id_rsa):/home/stahnke/.ssh/id_dsa
1024 d3:4a:1f:71:ae:79:66:35:31:d9:30:78:63:1f:94:13 /home/stahnke/.ssh/id_dsa.pub
```

Upon inspection, it is clear that stahnke's key is the one in use. The IP address from the client is shown, and this should lead to the host that key is on.

Note For key fingerprints to show up in a log file, the LogLevel token of the sshd_config file must be set at VERBOSE or higher.

The root account also has some unique tokens in the sshd_config file itself.

PermitRootLogin has four available options: yes, no, forced-commands-only, and without-password.yes enables any type of authentication sshd would normally allow. The value no will deny any attempts to access the root account directly. The without-password token will work for any authentication method other than password authentication. This is ideally used for key-based authentication. The forced-commands-only token requires commands be specified in the authorized_keys file.

Choosing the Logging Level and Facility for sshd

By default, sshd logs at the INFO level. This will provide information about a public key-based authentication. Listing 8-3 shows the logging from a Linux system at the INFO level. Listing 8-4 shows the VERBOSE level, and Listing 8-5 demonstrates the DEBUG level of logging.

Listing 8-3. *Lines Provided by* sshd *at the* INFO *Level*

```
Feb 20 22:32:28 www sshd[32112]: Accepted publickey for root from 192.168.1.101
 port 33043 ssh2
Feb 20 22:32:28 www sshd(pam_unix)[32114]: session opened for user root
by root(uid=0)
```

Listing 8-4. *Lines Provided by* sshd *at the* VERBOSE *Level, Which Displays Public Key Fingerprints*

```
Feb 20 22:34:53 www sshd[32187]: Connection from 192.168.1.101 port 33044
Feb 20 22:34:53 www sshd[32187]: Found matching DSA key:
 d3:4a:1f:71:ae:79:66:35:31:d9:30:78:63:1f:94:13
Feb 20 22:34:53 www sshd[32187]: Found matching DSA key:
d3:4a:1f:71:ae:79:66:35:31:d9:30:78:63:1f:94:13
Feb 20 22:34:53 www sshd[32187]: Accepted publickey for root from 192.168.1.101
 port 33044 ssh2
Feb 20 22:34:53 www sshd(pam_unix)[32189]:session opened for user root by
 root(uid=0)
```

Listing 8-5. *Lines Provided by* sshd *at the* DEBUG1 *Level, Which Can Impact Privacy for Users and Generally Fills Logs Too Quickly*

```
Feb 20 22:37:04 www sshd[32239]: debug1: Forked child 32280.
Feb 20 22:37:04 www sshd[32280]: debug1: rexec start in 4 out 4 newsock 4 pipe
6 sock 7
Feb 20 22:37:04 www sshd[32280]: debug1: inetd sockets after dupping: 3, 3
Feb 20 22:37:04 www sshd[32280]: Connection from 192.168.1.101 port 33046
Feb 20 22:37:04 www sshd[32280]: debug1: Client protocol version 2.0;
client software version OpenSSH_3.9p1
Feb 20 22:37:04 www sshd[32280]: debug1: match: OpenSSH_3.9p1 pat OpenSSH*
Feb 20 22:37:04 www sshd[32280]: debug1: Enabling compatibility mode for
protocol 2.0
Feb 20 22:37:04 www sshd[32280]: debug1: Local version string SSH-2.0-OpenSSH_3.9p1
Feb 20 22:37:04 www sshd[32280]: debug1: PAM: initializing for "root"
Feb 20 22:37:04 www sshd[32280]: debug1: PAM: setting PAM_RHOST to "rack"
Feb 20 22:37:04 www sshd[32280]: debug1: PAM: setting PAM_TTY to "ssh"
Feb 20 22:37:04 www sshd[32280]: debug1: Miscellaneous
failure\nNo such file or directory\n
Feb 20 22:37:06 www sshd[32280]: debug1: temporarily_use_uid: 0/0 (e=0/0)
Feb 20 22:37:06 www sshd[32280]: debug1: trying public key file
/root/.ssh/authorized_keys
Feb 20 22:37:06 www sshd[32280]: debug1: matching key found: file
 /root/.ssh/authorized_keys, line 1
```

```
Feb 20 22:37:06 www sshd[32280]: Found matching DSA key:
d3:4a:1f:71:ae:79:66:35:31:d9:30:78:63:1f:94:13
Feb 20 22:37:06 www sshd[32280]: debug1: restore_uid: 0/0
Feb 20 22:37:06 www sshd[32280]: debug1: ssh_dss_verify: signature correct
Feb 20 22:37:06 www sshd[32280]: Accepted publickey for root from 192.168.1.101
port 33046 ssh2
Feb 20 22:37:06 www sshd[32280]: debug1: monitor_child_preauth: root has
been authenticated by privileged process
Feb 20 22:37:06 www sshd[32280]: debug1: Entering interactive session for SSH2.
Feb 20 22:37:06 www sshd[32280]: debug1: server_init_dispatch_20
Feb 20 22:37:06 www sshd[32280]: debug1: server_input_channel_open: ctype session
rchan 0 win 65536 max 16384
Feb 20 22:37:06 www sshd[32280]: debug1: input_session_request
Feb 20 22:37:06 www sshd[32280]: debug1: channel 0: new [server-session]
Feb 20 22:37:06 www sshd[32280]: debug1: session_new: init
Feb 20 22:37:06 www sshd[32280]: debug1: session_new: session 0
Feb 20 22:37:06 www sshd[32280]: debug1: session_open: channel 0
Feb 20 22:37:06 www sshd[32280]: debug1: session_open: session 0:link with channel 0
Feb 20 22:37:06 www sshd[32280]: debug1: server_input_channel_open: confirm session
Feb 20 22:37:06 www sshd[32280]: debug1: server_input_channel_req: channel 0
 request pty-req reply 0
Feb 20 22:37:06 www sshd[32280]: debug1: session_by_channel: session 0 channel 0
Feb 20 22:37:06 www sshd[32280]: debug1: session_input_channel_req:
session 0 req pty-req
Feb 20 22:37:06 www sshd[32280]: debug1: Allocating pty.
Feb 20 22:37:06 www sshd[32280]: debug1: session_pty_req: session 0 alloc /dev/pts/3
Feb 20 22:37:06 www sshd[32280]: debug1: server_input_channel_req:
 channel 0 request shell reply 0
Feb 20 22:37:06 www sshd[32280]: debug1: session_by_channel: session 0 channel 0
Feb 20 22:37:06 www sshd[32280]: debug1: session_input_channel_req: session 0
req shell
Feb 20 22:37:06 www sshd[32280]: debug1: temporarily_use_uid: 0/0 (e=0/0)
Feb 20 22:37:06 www sshd[32280]: debug1: ssh_gssapi_storecreds:
Not a GSSAPI mechanism
Feb 20 22:37:06 www sshd[32280]: debug1: restore_uid: 0/0
Feb 20 22:37:06 www sshd[32280]: debug1: PAM: setting PAM_TTY to "/dev/pts/3"
Feb 20 22:37:06 www sshd[32280]: debug1: PAM: establishing credentials
Feb 20 22:37:06 www sshd[32282]: debug1: Setting controlling tty using TIOCSCTTY.
Feb 20 22:37:06 www sshd(pam_unix)[32282]: session opened for user root by
root(uid=0)
Feb 20 22:37:06 www sshd[32282]: debug1: PAM: reinitializing credentials
Feb 20 22:37:06 www sshd[32282]: debug1: permanently_set_uid: 0/0
```

As you can see, each LogLevel increases the output placed in the log. Normally, logging at VERBOSE is thought to be a best practice because of the ability to trace key fingerprints back to their owners. DEBUG logs are useful when experiencing an SSH problem, such as an authentication mechanism not behaving as you expected.

Patching OpenSSH

Besides not wanting to adopt an open source product, some organizations have been hesitant to use OpenSSH because of the frequency in which patches were needed a few years ago. If you have key-based authentication set up on your systems running OpenSSH, patching OpenSSH can be done in a very short amount of time. The last time an OpenSSH security vulnerability came out, I was able to patch 230 systems in under two hours using keys and OpenSSH's ability to remotely execute commands. This included troubleshooting on a few systems.

Patching OpenSSH can be critical if a flaw is discovered that allows an exploit of your system. You need to be ready. Additionally, you should monitor OpenSSL and Zlib for security updates, as they provide some of the foundation for OpenSSH.

The track record for OpenSSH overall is very good. The benefits of an open source community can be seen when a security exploit, whether it be theoretical or practical, is discovered. Patch delivery time often takes hours instead of weeks from commercial vendors.

Tip To receive to updates regarding OpenSSH, when new releases are available, subscribe to the announce list at `http://www.mindrot.org/mailman/listinfo/openssh-unix-announce`.

Considerations When Patching

When patching OpenSSH, be sure that your configuration files are kept intact. Most package management systems will provide these features, but if yours does not, or you are using a source-based configuration, be sure to have your pristine configuration files available.

Caution Many times security announcements are released pertaining to specific versions of software. Some companies such as Red Hat will back port a security patch into an older version of the software to ensure the rest of their software stack will remain compatible. So, if the official OpenSSH website says that OpenSSH 3.9p1 is the latest available, Red Hat Enterprise Server 2.1 has OpenSSH 3.1.p1–17 as the latest in that line of products. Their 3.1.p1–17 contains back ports of the relevant security patches from 3.9.

Core Operating Systems

Remember to monitor other patches available for your systems. Your vendor may provide an update to its packaged OpenSSH, or it may provide a patch for something in the operating system that could potentially change the behavior of OpenSSH.

Methods of Patching

If a security emergency hit your servers and you had to patch OpenSSH, you would want to be sure that the current OpenSSH on the system had not been compromised. This can be done via checksum verification in most package management systems. After verifying OpenSSH is stable, deploying a new patch for OpenSSH should be fairly easy. A script to distribute and execute files is covered in the next chapter. It can easily be used for rpms, pkgs, depots, and bff files.

Working with the Daemon

When patching OpenSSH locally, there a few things to keep in mind. If you stop sshd, connections already established to the remote host will remain, unless the stop script searches for existing sshd processes and kills them; but most init scripts are well behaved. Most of the time this is a very good thing, as you would not want your connection to drop. New connection attempts will not be established. If you restart the daemon while working on it, connections are also not dropped. Remember to verify your sshd_config file (sshd -t) after maintenance before restarting sshd.

Using the nologin Directive

The nologin directive can also be very helpful when performing maintenance on a system. If a user other than root attempts to connect to a host while the nologin file exists in /etc, the contents of that file will be displayed, and the login attempt will be denied. Root is allowed to log in.

In this example, I am working on the server www and I have created a /etc/nologin file.

```
stahnke@rack: ~> ssh www
www is undergoing network upgrades.
Service may be interrupted.
Please refrain from using www until 12:00 CST.
```

SSH Management

Managing OpenSSH takes some initial planning and can vary in degrees of difficulty depending on your organizational policy and culture involving security. Some facilities implementing an OpenSSH infrastructure perform a one-time setup and then do not change configuration files for years at a time. Another approach is to verify host keys, versions, and configuration files at regular intervals and correct any discrepancies. Luckily, most monitoring of OpenSSH can be done via ssh and can therefore be automated.

Creating Master Configuration Files

Having pristine configuration files is an excellent way to start with the maintenance of SSH infrastructure. The configuration files should be compliant with all relevant security policy that you or your organization has in place, and of course should be tamperproof. Keeping a good set of configuration files can be as easy as using the configuration files' setup on your adminitrative gateway server, which hopefully a very limited number of people have root access for. Creating a cron job once a period (week, month, year) to copy those configuration files to a less privileged location is trivial and should be done so the rest of the team can view and distribute good configuration files.

Note The master sshd_config file should be readable only by root; the ssh_config file can be readable by any user.

Distributing config Files

Distributing files via scp or sftp is an excellent way to use OpenSSH as a tool that enables a self-managing infrastructure. Sending out good configuration files only takes a small shell script. You can see the next chapter for file delivery examples.

Checking Versions

Keeping track of versions of OpenSSH and your configuration files is important. Simply placing comments in the configuration files as to what version or modification date the file is using is a great way to ensure your environment is consistent.

Keeping OpenSSH versions the same is more difficult, unless you compile all installations from source. As stated earlier, most major UNIX/Linux vendors provide OpenSSH in a native package format for their systems. The downfall of using these precompiled binaries is the speed at which they are updated. While most Linux vendors release patches rapidly (sometimes within hours of a critical update), the major UNIX vendors seem to lag behind, sometimes taking months to provide an updated package.

To potentially combat this, the OpenSSH source tree does include the options to make Solaris, AIX, and rpm packages in the contrib directory. However, keep in mind that creating your own package may not be supported by your UNIX/Linux vendor.

Checking Changes

Using a checksum mechanism of some type (sum, MD5, SHA-1) is a quick and extremely accurate way to check on the integrity of a file. As an example, in my configuration file, when PermitRootLogin is set to yes, the configuration file has the following hash:

```
440eff0739983efa196ba097bfb2322b  /etc/ssh/sshd_config
```

After changing it to my desired value, without-password, the MD5 sum is this:

```
43049866c243931064a1b6d036d0ea22  /etc/ssh/sshd_config
```

As you can see, small changes in a file change the hash of the file dramatically. While theoretically two different files could have the same hash value, the likelihood of that occurring is extremely low. SHA-1 is thought to have even lower collision rates.

MD5 (or any hashing algorithm) can tell when sshd_config files have been modified, as long as you know the original value to compare the hash against. These summing techniques can also be used to ensure OpenSSH binaries have the correct values. In Chapter 9, scripts are provided that use md5sum to determine file changes.

Tip The sum mechanism is generally thought to be an insecure checksum algorithm because it can be defeated using point-and-click tools that pad a file until a specific sum value is reached. Using MD5 or SHA-1 is encouraged. MD5 and SHA-1 both have had some press coverage recently exploiting possible flaws in their hashing algorithm. For maximum protection, use multiple checksum algorithms, as creating a rogue file whose MD5 and SHA-1 hashes match the original is nearly impossible.

Checking Host Keys

Host keys are generated upon the initial install of OpenSSH. Caching those host keys into a known-good location is a best practice. If the host key changes unexpectedly, you would then have reason to have suspicion and investigate the change.

Generally, security weaknesses have two main attributes: type of vulnerability and the length of time that vulnerability is exposed. In the case of host keys, there is some argument to change them on a semiregular basis (perhaps annually). While this may cause a great deal of pain to users having to recache system public keys, it can mitigate some risk of an attacker attempting to copy known keys onto rogue systems.

Another approach to host key management has been made available in Internet draft form called SSH FingerPrints (SSHFP, http://www.ietf.org/internet-drafts/ draft-ietf-secsh-dns-05.txt). OpenSSH 3.8 and newer support SSHFP, which allows fingerprints (checksums) of host keys to be placed in DNS. With this enabled, the ssh client can verify the host key provided by the remote host with its expected entry in DNS; if they match, the ssh client will accept the host key without prompting the user for verification. SSHFP is covered later in this chapter in the section "Key Management."

Monitoring SSH

If the sshd process becomes the main, and perhaps only, way into a system, it is critical that the daemon be running as expected. Monitoring the process for at least a listening sshd process is a good idea. Many monitoring tools in existence today, such as BMC Patrol for UNIX and Linux; IBM Tivoli Monitoring; Computer Associates Unicenter Network and Systems Management; or the Nagios, released under the GPL, easily allow monitoring of a process on a system.

Key Management

When I am asked about the greatest challenges surrounding an SSH implementation, I always respond with the same answer—key management. Ensuring keys follow policy, are used correctly, and can be tracked is an extremely challenging task. I have written the following sections to aid you in OpenSSH key management.

Introduction to Key Management

Why is key management important when it comes to OpenSSH? If keys are not tracked and managed correctly, the consequences can vary from being unable to log in to a host to an attacker using an ill-protected private key to wreak havoc on your environment, and almost any scenario in between.

Digital credentials, such as keys, require revocation under select sets of circumstances. Suppose an administrator separates from your organization under unfavorable conditions. Your account management procedures should remove his or her accounts from your systems. However, was his or her public-key entry removed from the authorized_keys files for other users such as root, dbadmin, webuser? If not, you still have a gap in your account deprovisioning processes.

Because of the difficulty in ensuring copies of private keys are not made, you will have no way of knowing whether that system administrator copied his or her private key to another location to use in case of separation from the company. This is why source node restrictions are important for `authorized_keys` files. You may now have a knowledgeable disgruntled ex-employee, who can pose a *very* serious threat to your organization.

Managing keys is built around two basic principles: the first being that you must have the ability to quickly add, verify, and disable keys from usage, and the second that you must have thought-out policy to ensure keys are handled correctly.

Key Policy

Keys and key policy relate to the overall picture of OpenSSH architecture because they play such a pivotal role in making SSH a success over legacy protocols. In many organizations, the security alone will not drive the behavior to make a switch away from familiar daemons and services. The productivity gains from using SSH while at the same time being secure will enable the change.

Key management and policy is critical in enabling an organizational-wide change. Policy surrounding key pairs might be in place if you have worked extensively with PKI on your network. If not, when developing the policies for keys, think about the important elements of SSH keys:

- Key size

- Algorithm

- Passphrases

- Comments

- Naming conventions

- Ownership

- Which systems should store private keys

- File permissions

- Public key restrictions

- Cron usage

Key Size

Choosing a bit length for a key is straightforward. While 768 bits is thought to be safe in most scenarios, 1024 is the default and recommended; however, starting with OpenSSH 4.2, the default key size will be 2048 bits. For added security, 2048 or 4096 bit lengths can be used, but this can impact performance during authentication. The time taken to generate keys can vary depending on entropy, system load, and speed of the processor. The minimum key length supported by OpenSSH is 512 bits.

Algorithm

The choices for key algorithms are DSA (Digital Signature Algorithm) and RSA (named after Ron Rivest, Adi Shamir, and Len Adleman). Internally these algorithms are quite different, but for security purposes, both are thought to be secure given an adequate (1024 or greater) key length. In the past, RSA was a patented algorithm, and thus may not have been used in certain security products because it required a license fee. That patent expired in the year 2000 (http://www.rsasecurity.com). If you are using SSH protocol 1, you must specify rsa1 as the key type. For protocol 2, you can specify either rsa or dsa.

Passphrases

Keys should have passphrases. Without them, they are left in the open, and an attacker or malicious user can easily assume your identity. Passphrases, as covered earlier, can be much longer than traditional passwords and can be easier to remember due to their linguistic structure. Minimum lengths on passphrases are encouraged because they are susceptible to brute-force attacks, as they cannot be locked.

Comments

Comments can be placed in key files, both private and public, by starting a line with the # character, either before or after the key, as shown in the following example. When a key is generated via ssh-keygen, the end of the key will have the user@system syntax. If your organization desired more comments, such as create date, approval number, or contact information, that information can be added manually or edited using the -c option of ssh-keygen. Keep in mind that because comments have no effect on the key ability to authenticate, changing comments from intruder@hacker.com to stahnke@rack can easily be done to make a public key look legitimate.

```
# Michael Stahnke RSA Public Key
ssh-rsa AAAAB3NzaC1yc2EAAAABIwAAAIEAtK8ltz+TOjNvYtaAu/69IuLqSNSVSIwlK4uV/x4rvpZXchxN
XhUofOzCSKKx5/wLKBD1yP6mHOTiP4V2MVBLbjnJ9OOCL4OzG5QeOcQkta6MEBdiJZpJOs3O
X+wG+O/c8d9RgvTtx+uWTZDYac1cSI/cBmvEpCmQAlpMu9XKhZU= stahnke@rack
# Generated March 15, 2005
```

Naming Conventions

How will the keys used be named? Normally, a private key (utilized in SSH protocol 2) is named id_rsa or id_dsa. While these names indicate they are keys, they do not tell an administrator much about them as a key pair. Conventions can include username.source-hostname.rsa/dsa and then appending a .pub to the public half of the pair or naming the keys an employee identification number.

Ownership

Ownership of keys is twofold. First off, whoever the key is generated for is obviously the owner; however, the more difficult question becomes who can share that key? Will a workgroup be allowed to use one key? Should individuals have their own key?

What accounts can be authenticated with this key? Can a user from an administrative server log in remotely as his or her standard account, as root, as another user? Pay particular attention to the root's authorized_keys file. Should keys in root's authorized_keys files originate from several sources or only one?

Best practice for key management ownership dictates that keys be assigned to an individual and not to groups of people. Host-based authentication could be an option when many people must connect between the same set of systems.

Which Systems Should Store Private Keys

Will you allow private keys to be used from any source node? Should all private keys be stored on a select group of systems? Oftentimes, once application users understand what using keys is about, they will set up keys between two nodes to synchronize data sets. Is that permitted or must they use gateway servers?

It is also highly discouraged to store a private key on an NFS mount due to the inherent insecurities of NFS. Storing public keys on NFS mounts, however, seems to be a sound practice, assuming you want a user to have the ability to log in on any host that can mount the exported filesystem.

File Permissions

The permissions of private keys should always be the least restrictive possible, which normally is only readable by the owner. The entire .ssh directory should also not be group-writable or accessible to the others in any way. If poor permissions are on remote .ssh directories where authorized_keys files are stored, public key authentication will fail, assuming you have StrictModes enabled in your sshd_config. If the .ssh directory is group/other writable, others can easily interject their public key in the authorized_keys file to assume that identity.

Public Key Restrictions

Public keys can be limited by adding some tokens to the beginning of the file. Using restrictions on keys, you can limit the source node, the commands performed, and the ssh options. For example, if I want to restrict my account named "script" to only run my backup job, I can use the public key file in Listing 8-6. Note that white space results in a syntax error, and the following string is one line in a UNIX editor.

Listing 8-6. *Limiting Public Keys Is a Good Way to Use Keys in Scheduled Tasks Such as cron*

```
no-agent-forwarding,command="/backup.sh",from="!hacker.com,*.example.com"
ssh-dss AAAAB3NzaC1kc3MAAACBAOdKR5Z5...
```

Cron Usage

The scripting framework that OpenSSH provides is truly powerful. To use this framework effectively, public key authentication must be enabled. Of course, automation of UNIX and Linux administration relies heavily on the cron and at facilities. Normally, cron is unable to load keys into an agent because it is noninteractive. Keys for a cron user need to be without a passphrase. This is less than desirable, but there is no good way to avoid it.

To secure cron jobs, several options are available. You can limit the public keys used for cron as mentioned previously. This would mean a private key used by another would only allow certain commands. The upside to this is limited command usage. The downside is that you will need separate keys for each cron task. You could allow the cron jobs to not function as root remotely, though this may take away critical infrastructure agility gained from the OpenSSH administrative gateway. You could place the private key on a very hardened operating system and accept the risk. Finally, you could use a tool to load an ssh-agent ahead of time. See the sidebar "Keychain: A Gift from Gentoo" for more information.

Note If you are using SSH Communications Security SSH Tectia, you can provide a passphrase to a private key via the `ssh-add2 -p` option. This is not always desirable, as a simple process stack listing could reveal the passphrase. Using OpenSSH, SSH_ASKPASS can be exploited to provide a passphrase via a noninteractive manner. This practice is not recommended.

Once you have selected a cron key pair methodology, your administrators will quickly realize the versatility of OpenSSH. In my main line of work, I have over a dozen cron scripts execute daily via `ssh` to populate databases, run reports, and monitor logs. Scripting techniques are covered in the next chapter.

KEYCHAIN: A GIFT FROM GENTOO

A technology called Keychain is really starting to gain acceptance in the open source community. It was originally developed by Daniel Robbins and is now maintained by Aron Griffis. The source is available from `http://dev.gentoo.org/~agriffis/keychain`. Keychain source is currently available for Linux, Solaris, BSD, Cygwin, Tru64 UNIX, HP-UX, and Mac OS X.

Keychain handles key-based authentication by fronting `ssh-agent`. Keychain enables a user to have a single long-running `ssh-agent` per system rather than per session. This will enable cron jobs to use keys with passphrases, as they only need to be entered after booting the system.

The best way to get to know Keychain is by using it for a little while. Once I started using Keychain, I quickly wondered how I got along without it.

Everything having to do with Keychain is easy. For installation, after downloading and unpacking the source, run the following:

```
root@rack: ~> install -m0755 keychain /usr/bin/keychain
```

From there you need to set up your Keychain. If you are in an X environment, simply enter `keychain keyfile`. If you are in a terminal environment without an X server, run `keychain -nogui keyfile` where `keyfile` is the name of your private key. In my case, I am using a file called `id_dsa`.

```
stahnke@rack: ~> keychain id_dsa -nogui
KeyChain 2.5.1; http://www.gentoo.org/proj/en/keychain/
Copyright 2002-2004 Gentoo Foundation; Distributed under the GPL

 * Warning: SSH_AUTH_SOCK in environment is invalid; ignoring it
 * Initializing /home/stahnke/.keychain/rack-sh file...
 * Initializing /home/stahnke/.keychain/rack-csh file...
 * Starting ssh-agent
```

Now I have an `ssh-agent` running. When I log out, this agent will still be running. I do have to add my keys to the agent once via `ssh-add`. After that, the only way to stop the Keychain is by rebooting or explicitly killing it by running the following:

```
stahnke@rack: ~> keychain -k all
```

> To get the most from Keychain, you should add the following line to your login script (`.bashrc`, `.profile`, etc.). Note that I use the Keychain `-sh` file because I use bash. C-shell users can use the file with the `-csh` extension.
>
> ```
> stahnke@rack: ~> echo "source \
> /home/stahnke/.keychain/rack-sh" >> .bashrc
> ```
>
> For more information about Keychain, you can try
>
> ```
> stahnke@rack: ~> keychain --help
> ```
>
> The official Keychain site is located at: `http://www.gentoo.org/proj/en/keychain`.

Key Distribution

Distributing public keys to the nodes in the environment is the final piece in the overarching discussion of OpenSSH architecture. Having a well-devised key distribution system will make managing keys a much easier task than you would think after reading the previous policy considerations about keys.

Advantages of a Public Key Repository

Managing public keys is a very difficult task without clean processes behind it. If you have five administrators each with their public key on 100 systems, and one leaves the group, how do you remove just his or her key and leave the other four? When you get a new person, how do you put his or her key on the remote systems?

In my experience as an SSH administrator, I have found, using an administrative gateway model, that having the least number of public key file sets available is the easiest model to manage.

If I have one public key repository, and I know it is updated and accurate, I can push out those keys to all nodes on my network. If there were public keys that were not authorized, they will be overwritten with correct ones. If a new administrator did not have his or her key on a subset of the hosts, it will be pushed with the rest. In this respect, managing keys is a lot like managing an NIS map. I update the key repository in one spot and then push it out to the networked system population. However, unlike NIS, this can be done more securely, and I can verify the files have not changed once they have arrived on a remote host.

Common Drop-off Point

To create a single `authorized_keys` file or sets of them, you need to start with a common base. To do this, on your administration gateway, you can create a drop-off where administrators must have their public key in order to be included in the next fileset push. From there, create a script that concatenates the public keys and the required comments into a pristine copy of the `authorized_keys` file for a particular user. Keep permissions on the newly created `authorized_keys` file as restrictive as possible.

You now have a complete `authorized_keys` file for a particular user. For the rest of the examples, I will assume the remote user is root because root requires the most care throughout the process.

Building a tar File

After building the authorized_keys file, you have a few tasks to perform:

1. Apply some means of version control to the authorized_keys file including date on which it was created. This can easily be done in your script.

2. Get hashes for the files you will be moving to root's .ssh directory. If you are just moving an authorized_keys file, record the known-good MD5 sum of the file. Keep the MD5 sum locally.

3. Move this file to an archive directory so you can show what keys had root access on a given date range. Your auditing policy may provide you with more or less restrictive guidelines on root access retention; follow them accordingly.

From there, you can package up files in a tar file or any other archive format. I normally use tar because I oftentimes overwrite root's entire .ssh directory to ensure permissions, any temp data, and anything else has been overwritten. After creating an archive, it is time to distribute that archive. File pushes are covered in the next chapter.

Building a Public Key rpm

After a few months of trying to manage an openssh_public_keys.tar file, I decided a more robust solution was needed. Because I manage mainly Linux systems, I built a noarch (unspecified architecture) rpm (rpm Package Manager) package containing root's .ssh directory and eventually keys for individual users as well. rpm (http://www.rpm.org) is available for several UNIX variants. While rpms must be built on each flavor of UNIX, the benefits remain the same. Instead of rpm, a pkg or depot could be used on their respective platforms to show similar benefits.

Tip Building advanced rpms can be difficult. For more information about building rpms, take a look at *Automating UNIX and Linux Administration* by Kirk Bauer (Apress, 2003).

Using an rpm to distribute and install OpenSSH public keys provides several benefits over a flat file distribution mechanism:

• Integrity verification is inherent to an rpm. I can verify the MD5 sum of file, the file sizes, the modification times, and file ownership via the rpm -q --verify command. Because of this, I no longer have to keep a local copy of the MD5 sums of the files. This implies that I trust the rpm database for integrity verification.

• Finding out what version of the keys are installed on a system can be done easily through rpm queries or any software delivery/patch management tool. A simple rpm -q openssh-openssh-public-keys will tell me what version I have installed on the system.

• Revoking old keys can be done via %pre scripts in the rpm spec file. This way, if I choose not to remove all files before installing them, upgrading the rpm will remove the explicitly specified files.

- The package is installable by any administrator, not just the primary OpenSSH administrators. If packages are pushed out via a tool or process, this rpm can fit into that process.

- rpms are easily versioned in their spec files.

Creating an rpm

Creating an rpm for the first time is exciting and can really upset you if things are not going well. For the following examples, a Red Hat/Fedora Linux distribution is assumed. SuSE systems are very similar; however, their path comparable to /usr/src/redhat is /usr/src/packages.

rpms consist of two main items: the source and a spec file. The spec file is where most of the energy is consumed, because you have already made the source. The following is a very simple spec file that will create an rpm based on an authorized_keys file that has been created and installed in /root/.ssh/authorized_keys. Note that in spec files, the ~ character to imply home directory is not interpreted.

Inside of /usr/src/redhat/SPECS create the following file. You must be root to perform this task. Normally, you can build rpms without root authority, but because this needs to incorporate files readable only by root, and for simplicity, this build requires root access.

```
/usr/src/redhat/SPECS> cat specfile
Summary: Administrator Public OpenSSH Keys
Name openssh-public-keys
Version: 0
Release: 1
License: Free
Group: Security
BuildArch: noarch
# If you are not using rpms of openssh, comment this line out
Requires: openssh
%description
openssh-public-keys is the collection of OpenSSH public keys maintained by the
 UNIX/Linux adminstration staff.
%pre
# If /root/.ssh exists, move it.
if [ -d /root/.ssh ]
then
  mv -f /root/.ssh /root/.ssh.rpmsave
  echo "/root/.ssh saved as /root/.ssh.rpmsave"
fi
#Package will contain the following files
%files
%defattr(-,root,root)
%attr(0700,root,root) %dir /root/.ssh
%attr(0600,root,root) /root/.ssh/authorized_keys
```

■Note Code for this chapter is available at http://www.apress.com.

Once you have created a spec file, it is time to build an rpm. To build an rpm, rpmbuild is required. Here is my output:

```
/usr/src/redhat/spec> rpmbuild -ba specfile
Processing files: openssh-public-keys-0-1
Requires(interp): /bin/sh
Requires(rpmlib): rpmlib(CompressedFileNames) <= 3.0.4-1
rpmlib(PayloadFilesHavePrefix) <= 4.0-1
Requires(pre): /bin/sh
Requires: openssh
Checking for unpackaged file(s): /usr/lib/rpm/check-files %{buildroot}
Wrote: /usr/src/redhat/SrpmS/openssh-public-keys-0-1.src.rpm
Wrote: /usr/src/redhat/rpmS/noarch/openssh-public-keys-0-1.noarch.rpm
```

From here, an rpm is created in /usr/src/redhat/rpmS/noarch. A simple install can be performed using the syntax shown in Listing 8-7.

Listing 8-7. *Installing the* openssh-public-keys rpm

```
/usr/src/redhat/rpmS/noarch>  rpm -Uvh openssh-public-keys-0-1.noarch.rpm
Preparing...                     ##################################### [100%]
   1:openssh-public-keys  ##################################### [100%]
```

The U option specifies upgrade. This means that if the package had already been installed at a lower version, its rpm would install the newer version of that same package. The v is for verbose, and the h provides hash marks during installation.

rpm Querying

Once you are on a box with rpm, to check and see if the keys file is installed, you can run the following:

```
root@rack: ~> rpm -q openssh-public-keys
openssh-public-keys-0-1
```

The system will return the package name and version if it is found. To get the file listing and package description, you can try the following:

```
root@rack: ~>  rpm -ql openssh-public-keys
/root/.ssh
/root/.ssh/authorized_keys
[root@rack SPECS]# rpm -qi openssh-public-keys
Name        : openssh-public-keys                Relocations: (not relocatable)
Version     : 0                                  Vendor: (none)
Release     : 1                         Build Date: Tue 22 Feb 2005 10:49:14 PM CST
Install Date: Tue 22 Feb 2005 10:49:41 PM CST    Build Host: rack
Group       : Security              Source rpm: openssh-public-keys-0-1.src.rpm
Size        : 616                                License: Free
Signature   : (none)
Summary     : Administrator Public OpenSSH Keys
```

```
Description :
openssh-public-keys is the collection of OpenSSH public keys maintained
by the UNIX/Linux adminstration staff.
```

rpm Verification

Once you distribute your rpm or tar file, you have the ability to verify integrity of the keys on the remote hosts. This is critical so that users with loose sudo permissions or with extensive UNIX/Linux knowledge are not able to install their public key into root's authorized_keys file without detection. To bypass the rpm verification check, a user would have to corrupt the rpm database or install a public key rpm of their own. While rpm verification will not tell you who has violated policy, it can tell if it has happened. Hopefully, fingerprint verification will enable system/security administrators to track down the owner of the rogue key.

To verify your rpm, run the following command:

```
root@rack: ~> rpm -q --verify openssh-public-keys
```

If this command returns nothing, then all files are as expected. Now try editing the /root/.ssh/authorized_keys file.

```
root@rack: ~> rpm -q --verify openssh-public-keys
S.5....T    /root/.ssh/authorized_keys
```

Now the output shows that the file has changed. The S means the file size has changed. 5 indicates the MD5 sum is different than it was at install time, and the T indicates the timestamp also differs from the installation base.

Revocation of Compromised Keys

If a private key has been compromised, removing all of the existing public counterparts to that key needs to occur in a very short amount of time. Simply remove the compromised key from your pristine authorized_keys file, copy it to /root/.ssh, increment the version in the rpm spec file, and rebuild the rpm. A simple distribution of the new rpm will remove old files containing the compromised key, and thus showing major value in OpenSSH.

Keys on CD-ROM/Floppy/USB Key

Administrators know that working only from one spot is not realistic. It seems as though administrators would like to be able to work from anywhere. If they take their private key with them, they can. Normally, I recommend that they take a private key that can authenticate them to the administrative gateway. From the gateway, the real key is used to work everywhere else. This way, a central point of administration still exits. Once administrators become familiar with logging into one or two systems to do all their work, their repository of scripts, tricks, and commands will build up, and they will not be able to work without them anyway.

SSHFP: Storing Public Host Keys in DNS

Working with OpenSSH can become somewhat of hassle to end users when dealing with acceptance of host keys. If a host key changes, or if a client has never connected to a remote host, the user is asked to accept or deny the key, assuming sshd is configured to run with StrictHostKeyChecking enabled. End users are often confused by this. The undereducated end user normally will just enter yes to allow the host key caching. If the host key has changed, they will call the help desk and tell the analyst they are unable to log in to their remote host. This is desired behavior, as it prevents rogue host interjection and creates a verification point between end users and key changes on systems. However, if a host key change is planned, and a user's client was not updated, this causes nonproductive downtime. To the end user who understands host keys, host key management can be more difficult. They will edit their local .ssh/known_hosts file and remove the offending host key.

This conundrum can be resolved using infrastructure your organization most likely has already invested in, DNS. DNS (Domain Name System) is the network service that resolves easy-to-remember hostnames, such as www.google.com, to an IP address so the request can be routed appropriately. OpenSSH can leverage DNS by allowing host key fingerprints to be stored in DNS as a resource record that relates to the host entry. This way, when a client wants to ssh to rack.example.com, DNS resolves the IP address of rack.example.com and provides the expected host key fingerprint. If the host key fingerprint presented by the server matches the host key found in DNS, the key is automatically cached, because it has been verified by two sources.

SSHFP, which provides an increase in usability and security, can be set up on the newest versions of Berkeley Internet Name Domain (BIND), which is the most common DNS name-server. When a client attempts a connection, a request is made to DNS for the IP address of the request and then for the SSH public key fingerprints.

This technology is still in its infancy but will likely prove to be very worthwhile. The original Internet Engineering Task Force (IETF) Internet Draft expired in March of 2004, but still has merit.

SSH relies on resource records inside the zone files of a DNS server. BIND 9.3.1 is the first version of BIND to support SSHFP as a resource record. Previous versions must use the generic resource record format.

SSHFP can be treated in two ways. If the DNS zone is not signed (DNSSEC), then the key is presented with the yes/no question similar to ask on StrictHostKey checking. OpenSSH will trust (automatically accept) an SSHFP record if the zone is signed, requiring the user to perform no action. Implementing DNS, BIND, and DNSSEC is outside the scope of this material, but for more information, see *Pro DNS and BIND* by Ronald G. F. Aitchison, (Apress, 2005).

SSHFP uses resource records to store the public key fingerprint information. A resource record is a bit of data that relates to an entry in a DNS zone file. BIND 9.3.1 and newer support a special resource record class called SSHFP. Other DNS servers and older versions of BIND should be able to use the generic form the SSHFP resource record.

Once a working DNS setup has been established, the SSHFP entry must be generated. The ssh-keygen utility provided with OpenSSH is used to generate SSHFP resource records. Listing 8-8 uses an SSHFP type of resource record that is supported only in the newest versions of BIND.

Listing 8-8. *Using* ssh-keygen *to Generate an SSHFP Resource Record*

```
root@www ~> ssh-keygen -r www.example.com -f /etc/ssh/ssh_host_rsa_key
www.example.com IN SSHFP 1 1 5c7779a620fc38aa4348d954cfe40ca5752e5bfd
```

Inside the resource record, each field has meaning. The first field is the hostname of the system. The IN indicates the record class. SSHFP, of course, designates it is an SSHFP resource record. The first 1 represents the key algorithm. A 1 indicates RSA, while a 2 represents DSA.

The second 1 means the key is an SHA-1 checksum representing the fingerprint of the host key. The final field is the checksum of the host key itself.

Generic resource records can also be used for compatibility with nameservers that do not explicitly have SSHFP defined as a resource record (see Listing 8-9).

Listing 8-9. *Generating a Generic Resource Record*

```
root@www ~> ssh-keygen -r www.example.com -f /etc/ssh/ssh_host_rsa_key -g
www.example.com IN TYPE44 \# 22 01 01 5c7779a620fc38aa4348d954cfe40ca5752e5bfd
```

A generic resource record is similar to the SSHFP specified record. Upon examination of Listing 8-9, you can see that the first field is the hostname, followed by the record class. TYPE44 means it is an SSHFP record. \# indicates it is a generic resource record. 22 is the number of octets in the record data (length).

The resource records can then be added to the zone file, and the nameserver can be reloaded. If your DNS server is not reporting errors about the resource records, the DNS setup is complete.

From a client perspective, /etc/ssh/ssh_config also should be edited so the client knows to attempt a host key lookup in DNS. In the configuration file, the following line should be present:

```
VerifyHostKeyDNS yes
```

This instructs the client to attempt a host key lookup in DNS. If it is found and matches the fingerprint presented by sshd, the connection continues without user intervention. If no matching fingerprint is found, users must either accept or deny the host key being presented.

SSHFP is a very new technology that will likely take off in the near future. Its usability and security benefits seem to make managing an OpenSSH infrastructure slightly easier.

Summary

This chapter saw the discussion of managing OpenSSH progress from technical details to overall strategies. The architecture and designs presented in this chapter are proven and have worked in several SSH implementations.

I encourage you to start with architecture and policy and then move into process definitions and security crisis procedures. I am sure process and procedures do not sound technical enough to excite everyone, but remember that without them, security crumbles. Behind these processes there is always a technical solution, whether it is for key management or gateway implementation.

As mentioned previously, the next chapter covers scripting via OpenSSH, which will utilize the key management and gateway architectures described in this chapter. Additionally, several new scenarios that administrators are likely to encounter will be discussed.

PART 4

■ ■ ■

Administration with OpenSSH

■ ■ ■

## CHAPTER 9

Scripting with OpenSSH

OpenSSH can appease many security concerns that are caused from the usage of legacy services, and that is a very good thing. However, once that security is in place, OpenSSH provides additional benefits to the system administrator. Through the use of password-free authentication, whether it be public key or host based, OpenSSH provides a framework for scripting several administrative tasks that can save you hours of work.

This chapter is not intended to be a complete lesson on automation, nor a complete guide to what is possible with a script and SSH. Rather, this chapter will focus on several key scripts and points mentioned in earlier chapters, as well as demonstrate some other matters to consider as you tailor your scripts to suit your needs.

The discussion will start with basic authentication assumptions and move into shell scripting with bash, Perl scripting, and finally some web-based scripting using PHP and bash.

Prerequisites

To effectively script tasks involving SSH, authentication must be automated. Through the use of an ssh-agent, a key without a passphrase, or a keychain (which also uses ssh-agent), this is easy to accomplish. If you need a refresher on how to set up public key authentication, see Chapter 6. Chapter 8 also discusses some best practices and other considerations regarding key-based authentication and protecting/distributing keys.

Automation

No matter the context, automation can be defined as the process of performing repetitive tasks in a batch-like format. In regard to programming, an automated task should require no user input, other than perhaps by way of the command line.

Input

Most scripts require some form of input. This input can be read on the command line, from a file, or via a web form. Having lists of systems on which to perform operations is a regular occurrence when scripting. Each iteration of the control stage of these scripts performs the same tasks on each target. If scripts are developed to use the same input parameters, such as a fully qualified hostname, the input section can be reused in additional scripts.

As an example, a network configured for the domain name `example.com` might consist of the following hosts:

```
rack.example.com
www.example.com
zoom.example.com
macmini.example.com
slack.example.com
```

Output

Capturing the output from an automated job can be accomplished in a number of different ways. You can open an output stream in Perl, echo the results to a file via a shell command, display them via a web page, or simply send them to `stdout`. Particularly during the development phase, sending output to `stdout` can reduce troubleshooting headaches. If having the output in a file is a requirement, using a simple output redirection operator is often much simpler than recreating a script.

■**Tip** Apress offers an outstanding book on automating administration through scripting, titled *Automating UNIX and Linux Administration*, by Kirk Bauer (Apress, 2003).

Shell Scripts

Shell scripts can get a job done quickly and effectively. Given the proper development effort, a shell script can even exhibit most characteristics of a more complex programming language, including functions, arrays, and flow control.

The shell scripts in this chapter will use bash (http://www.gnu.org/software/bash). bash is the default shell in most Linux environments and can be installed on most traditional UNIX systems. If bash is unavailable, ksh and sh perform in a similar manner—however, some commands and parameters may require adjustments.

Why Shell Scripts

The main advantages of the shell script are the speed at which it can be developed and the time it ultimately saves over performing a task manually. For instance, during my administrative duties I am often asked to confirm which version of package xyz is running on a given set of servers. Using a simple for loop and SSH, I can quickly whip up something to perform the task. In fact, most shell scripts I use have the same framework, involving a single for loop to control the script. From there, I either edit a line, or comment it out and create a new one. If a script has some special requirements, such as someone else needing to understand it, I try to write a cleaner and more understandable script.

To familiarize you with shell scripting, let's start with some examples mentioned in Chapter 8. During the discussion on public key distribution, it was mentioned that keys could be pushed easily using a shell script. Listing 9-1 provides this script, which is titled key_push.sh.

Tip Because of the quantity of scripts I write, I try to be sure I have an extension on every script: sh for shell, pl for Perl, etc. This can help avoid confusion later when looking for scripts that perform certain tasks. I also try to name the script something descriptive of the action it performs. Naming a file `script.sh` does not help much when reviewing code. The name `key_push.sh` tells me that this script pushes keys in some way.

Listing 9-1. *A Script Using a* for *Loop to Push an* openssh-public-keys *rpm*

```
!/bin/bash
# name: key_push.sh
for system in `cat list`
do
  scp openssh-public-keys-0-1.noarch.rpm root@$machine:
  ssh root@${system} "rpm -Uvh\
    public-keys-0-1.noarch.rpm;\
    rm -f public-keys-0-1.noarch.rpm"
done
```

Note Code from this chapter is available in the Source Code section of the Apress website, at http://www.apress.com.

This script is about as simple as it gets. Line 1 declares the type of script and the interpreter. Line 2 offers a comment, including the script name. Line 3 iterates through each line in a file called list, using a for loop for flow control. Each iteration of the loop pushes a file called openssh-public-keys-0-1.noarch.rpm from the current working directory to root's home directory on the remote host. Then, an SSH connection is made to install the rpm and remove the file.

Sample output produced from executing key_push.sh is found in Listing 9-2.

Listing 9-2. key_push.sh *Output*

```
openssh-public-keys-0-1.noarch.rpm                     100% 2750    2.7KB/s   00:00
Preparing...                        ###########################################
/root/.ssh saved as /root/.ssh.rpmsave
openssh-public-keys                 ###########################################
openssh-public-keys-0-1.noarch.rpm                     100% 2750    2.7KB/s   00:00
Preparing...                        ###########################################
/root/.ssh saved as /root/.ssh.rpmsave
openssh-public-keys                 ###########################################
openssh-public-keys-0-1.noarch.rpm                     100% 2750    2.7KB/s   00:00
bash: line 1: rpm: command not found
```

This script does not perform any type of error checking, nor does it ensure the data was transferred or let you know if anything wrong occurred. Also, you cannot tell which line of output is from which remote system. Because I know the setup of these systems, I know the first two rpm installations worked fine, but failed on the host named zoom. The zoom server runs the Debian Linux operating system, and thus does not use rpm as its default package manager.

This script can be improved upon without too much effort, as seen in Listing 9-3. If a small amount of error checking and some additional output were added, a user running the script would have a much better idea of what is happening.

Listing 9-3. key_push_2.sh—*an Improvement on the First Script*

```
stahnke@rack: ~> cat key_push_2.sh
!/bin/bash
# name: key_push_2.sh
for system in `cat list`
do
  echo "Copying to $system"
  scp  openssh-public-keys-0-1.noarch.rpm  root@$system:
  echo "Executing on $system"
  ssh root@$system " rpm -Uvh \
    openssh-public-keys-0-1.noarch.rpm  && rm -f \
    openssh-public-keys-0-1.noarch.rpm "
done
```

While Listing 9-4 is not much more complicated, it adds some helpful features. It tells the user which remote system the script is working on. Additionally, by switching the ; to the && operator, I have made sure that the host will not delete the rpm file unless it installed properly.

Listing 9-4. *The Results of Running* key_push_2.sh

```
Copying to rack
openssh-public-keys-0-1.noarch.rpm                    100% 2750    2.7KB/s   00:00
Executing on rack
Preparing...                    ###########################################
/root/.ssh saved as /root/.ssh.rpmsave
openssh-public-keys             ###########################################
Copying to www
openssh-public-keys-0-1.noarch.rpm                    100% 2750    2.7KB/s   00:00
Executing on www
Preparing...                    ###########################################
/root/.ssh saved as /root/.ssh.rpmsave
openssh-public-keys             ###########################################
Copying to zoom
openssh-public-keys-0-1.noarch.rpm                    100% 2750    2.7KB/s   00:00
Executing on zoom
bash: line 1: rpm: command not found
```

This script can still be improved upon by adding some logic to determine if a remote system uses rpm for package management, and possibly by adding a summary file at the end of the script, which is nice to have when working with large numbers of systems.

Redirection and Pipes

OpenSSH provides several nice ways to use redirection and pipes to obtain desired results for capturing input and working with files both locally and remotely. To begin, a simple one-line ssh command will direct the output to the screen.

```
stahnke@rack: ~> ssh root@www uptime
22:04:12 up 56 min,  0 users,  load average: 0.00, 0.00, 0.03
```

That same command can have the output redirected into a file locally. This is more useful in loops—but for simplicity, the following example uses just one command.

```
stahnke@rack: ~> ssh root@www uptime > file
stahnke@rack: ~> cat file
22:05:15 up 57 min,  0 users,  load average: 0.05, 0.01, 0.03
```

This time, I will run uptime and keep the file remotely.

```
stahnke@rack: ~> ssh root@www "uptime > file"
stahnke@rack: ~> ssh root@www "cat file"
22:06:30 up 57 min,  0 users,  load average: 0.01, 0.01, 0.02
```

Notice that the only difference between a local file and remote file is the usage of quotation marks. When using redirection and pipes, if a command is inside quotation marks, it runs remotely. If it is outside, it occurs locally. This seems fairly simple, but can get rather difficult when working with complex strings and programs. If you need to pass a double quote to the remote command, simply escape it with a backslash as you would on the command line.

Pipes

Suppose I want to determine whether two files differ on different systems. This can be done by using a *pipe* to direct stdin to ssh. In the following example, diff is running to compare the /etc/bashrc file from my workstation rack with the /etc/bashrc file on the remote server named www.

```
stahnke@rack: ~> cat /etc/bashrc | ssh root@www diff - /etc/bashrc
49d48
< /usr/bin/fortune
```

This output shows the user that the local file has an additional line running the fortune command. This diff command ran over the network and thus did not require me to copy a file to a remote location.

You can also use pipes to copy something bit for bit over the network. Suppose you want to create an iso file, but you are short on disk space on the local host.

```
stahnke@rack: ~> dd bs=2048 if=/dev/cdrom | ssh root@www dd of=my_cd.iso
```

This command creates an iso file from my local CD-ROM drive and sends its contents over the network to a system with more disk space. By doing this, the iso file is never saved on the local file system.

Pipes with Redirection

Pipes provide a nice mechanism for working with files on two different hosts without copying files between them. As shown earlier, redirection operators allow ssh commands to store stdout and stderr in files either remotely or locally. When pipes are combined with redirection operators, files can be moved over the network and operated on in single commands.

The following single line of code takes a local file, compresses it, and sends it over the wire to a remote file called zipped.gz. This type of redirection can come in handy during scripts—though oftentimes scp and sftp are simpler and more effective solutions.

```
stahnke@rack: ~> gzip < ~/.ssh/id_dsa.pub| ssh root@www "cat > \
zipped.gz"
```

As a rule of thumb, I use pipes and redirection if I want to make only one ssh connection to a remote system. If I have a file to move and operate on, using scp/sftp can take multiple network connections: one to move the file and one to work with it upon arrival. If bandwidth is not a big issue and authentication is automated, multiple network connections are not normally an issue.

Variables Within SSH Commands

Local variables in a script are referenced just as they are in any other shell script. If you want to use local variables inside of a remote command, this can also be done simply by using the variable name, because the variables—including variables inside double quotes—are evaluated before the command is sent. Variables in single quotes are not expanded before being sent to the remote command. For example, the following commands will display the remote /etc/passwd file:

```
stahnke@rack: ~> myfile=/etc/passwd
stahnke@rack: ~> ssh root@www cat $myfile
```

If I wish to use awk to print the username from the file, I need to be a bit more creative.

```
stahnke@rack: ~> myfile=/etc/passwd
stahnke@rack: ~> ssh root@www "cat $myfile | awk -F: '{print \$1}'"
```

In this example, I could have worked with awk remotely or locally. The example uses cat to display the passwd file and then send it to awk for parsing. This is carried out on the remote system. Notice that the $1 variable must be escaped to prevent the local shell from expanding it. Alternatively, the passwd file could have been displayed from the remote system and parsed by awk locally, using the following syntax:

```
stahnke@rack: ~> ssh root@www "cat $myfile" | awk -F: '{print $1}'
```

While pipes and redirection can be very powerful, it becomes extremely tedious to sort out which actions are occurring locally and which are happening remotely. Scripting with SSH allows for several methods of accomplishing the same tasks, depending on personal preference as well as familiarity with pipes, redirection, and shell scripting. Things can get even more complex when using variables locally and remotely.

The following examples will examine the /etc/passwd file and then run du -sh against each user's home directory.

Sending the Script as a Command over ssh

In the example shown in Listing 9-5, the script to execute is sent on the command line as an argument to the ssh command. This means that each variable and control operator must be escaped with backslashes. Quotation marks also need to be escaped, which makes debugging this command very difficult.

Listing 9-5. *A Script that Uses Local and Remote Variables with Control Statements*

```
#!/bin/bash
for system in `cat list`
do
  echo "${system}"
  ssh root@${system} "for user in \`cut -d: -f1 /etc/passwd\`;   \
      do homedir=\`grep ^\$user: /etc/passwd | cut -d: -f6 \` ; \
        space=\`[ -d \"\$homedir\" ] && cd \$homedir && du -sh . | \
        cut -f1\` ; echo \$user \$homedir \$space    ;   done"
done
```

Using scripts like this is not normally a preferred method of execution due to the complicated syntax.

Scripting Using a "Here Document"

Because of the numerous backslashes in the Listing 9-5 script, it is difficult to edit, troubleshoot, or maintain. As an alternative, a script using a "here document" can be used, which is shown in Listing 9-6. This example is obviously easier to read and write. The backslash preceding the EOD prevents interpolation of the content, which allows the script to be written without having to double-escape everything. With "here documents," syntax highlighting will not normally occur inside of an editor.

Listing 9-6. *An SSH Script Using a "Here Document"*

```
#!/bin/sh
for system in `cat list`
do
  echo "${system}"
  ssh root@${system} /bin/sh <<\EOD
    for user in `cut -f1 -d: /etc/passwd`; do
      homedir=`grep ^\$user: /etc/passwd | cut -d: -f6`
      space=`[ -d $homedir ] && cd $homedir && du -sh . | cut -f1`
      echo $user $homedir $space
    done
EOD
done
```

Locally Run Script

Another alternative is to write the script so it runs on a local system. Then scp can be used to transfer the file. A separate SSH connection can occur and call the script. While this takes two SSH connections, it may be worth the time trade-off to have a simple process.

Still another option for a script that is saved and run locally is to offer it as input to ssh on the command. With either of these methods, output can be captured. The script in Listing 9-7 can be used as input on the local system or executed remotely.

Listing 9-7. *A Locally Saved Script Named* disk_check.sh

```
#!/bin/bash
    for user in `cut -f1 -d: /etc/passwd`; do
      homedir=`grep ^\$user: /etc/passwd | cut -d: -f6`
      space=`[ -d $homedir ] && cd $homedir && du -sh . | cut -f1`
      echo $user $homedir $space
done
```

After saving the script locally, a simple calling program can be used. The script can be used as input rather than stdin, as shown in Listing 9-8.

Listing 9-8. *A Calling Program to Run Listing 9-7*

```
#!/bin/bash
for system in `cat list`
do
    echo $system
    ssh $system /bin/sh < disk_check.sh
done
```

Running this script or any of the previous examples in this section will produce the remote hostname, and then a line with the account name, home directory, and disk space usage. Listing 9-9 shows an excerpt from my systems.

Listing 9-9. *The Output from Listings 9-5 Through 9-8*

```
www
lp /var/spool/lpd 8.0K
sync /sbin 15M
shutdown /sbin 15M
halt /sbin 15M
operator /root 44M
games /usr/games 8.0K
ftp /software 19G
dbus / 21G
...
apache /var/www 15M
webalizer /var/www/usage 396K
ldap /var/lib/ldap 8.0K
stahnke /home/stahnke 392K
ntp /etc/ntp 20K
xfs /etc/X11/fs 16K
```

Capturing stderr and stdout

The script in Listing 9-3, key_push_2.sh, puts all stdout and stderr messages to the screen. This is fine when working with three hosts—however, when working on hundreds or thousands of systems, something a little more robust is needed.

As mentioned earlier, to capture stdout from an ssh command, you can simply redirect the output via the > operator. stderr can also be redirected using the 2> operator in Bourne shells and their derivatives. However, even these output files can be tedious to sort through.

With OpenSSH, scripts can be designed to be fault tolerant. Setting a low ConnectTimeout value for the client will help. Also, if BatchMode is enabled, any authentication failures or prompts for password will be suppressed, which allows the program to continue without user interaction.

Note OpenSSH has a client option called ConnectTimeout, which allows ssh to abort a connection attempt if no connection is established in the amount of time specified by the SSH client. The SSH Tectia Server from SSH Communications Security does not have this option and will wait to attempt an SSH connection to a remote host until TCP timeout occurs, which normally takes much longer than a few seconds. Because of this, I usually ping a system before attempting to make an SSH connection if I am using the SSH Tectia Client. This also assumes that ICMP is not filtered or blocked on your network.

A Simple Key Distribution Script Revisited

In the example shown in Listing 9-10, key_push.sh from Listing 9-3 is modified to encourage readability and error checking. It also now accepts any file name, as long as it is set in the proper variable. The output is still displayed on the screen, but the errors are sent to stderr. Redirection on the command line can still capture the results of this script.

Listing 9-10. *A Key Distribution Script Using* BatchMode *and* ConnectTimeout

```
#!/bin/bash
# Script will take any local file from a given loction
#   and place it on remote hosts using a simple scp.
#
#  Assumptions:   $SYSTEM_LIST is FQDN one host per line
#                 You have key exchange authentication setup for
#                        the remote file owner
#
 #!/bin/bash
SSH_PATH=/usr/bin
REMOTE_USER=root
LOCAL_FILE=~/openssh-public-keys-0-1.noarch.rpm
REMOTE_FILE=/root
SYSTEM_LIST=~/list
SSH_PORT=22
CONNECT_TIMEOUT=3
for system in `cat ${SYSTEM_LIST}`
do
```

```
 echo ${system}
# Copy local file
        if (${SSH_PATH}/scp -o \"ConnectTimeout ${CONNECT_TIMEOUT}\"\
          -P ${SSH_PORT} ${LOCAL_FILE}\
        ${REMOTE_USER}@${system}:${REMOTE_FILE})
        then
          echo "${LOCAL_FILE} distributed to ${system}"
        else
          echo "${system} scp failed" 2>&1
        fi
done
```

Listing 9-11 shows the execution and resulting output from Listing 9-10.

Listing 9-11. *The Output from Listing 9-10*

```
stahnke@rack: ~> ./ssh_push.sh
rack
openssh-public-keys-0-1.noarch.rpm                   100% 2750      2.7KB/s    00:00
/home/stahnke/openssh-public-keys-0-1.noarch.rpm distributed to rack
www
openssh-public-keys-0-1.noarch.rpm                   100% 2750      2.7KB/s    00:00
/home/stahnke/openssh-public-keys-0-1.noarch.rpm distributed to www
Zoom
openssh-public-keys-0-1.noarch.rpm                   100% 2750      2.7KB/s    00:00
/home/stahnke/openssh-public-keys-0-1.noarch.rpm distributed to zoom
```

Migrating Legacy Scripts

Because OpenSSH is largely used as a replacement for the r-utilities, some discussion on migrating these scripts is in order. The r-utilities rlogin and rsh serve two slightly different functions: rlogin is used to log in remotely and rsh is used to launch commands on a remote host. Both can easily be replaced with the ssh command—however, for readability, some users like to use slogin, which is normally a symbolic link to ssh, as the utility. rcp can normally be substituted with scp. The major hangup with migrating legacy scripts is the authentication for the users. In many environments in which rsh is used heavily, the trust relationship has grown to a very large number of systems, meaning that a single user can move from system A to system B to system C without ever authenticating, because B and C trust A's authentication. To replicate this in an OpenSSH environment, you either need to enable host-based authentication (which is discouraged, and discussed in Chapter 6) or create a key infrastructure that is compatible with the scripts.

Real-World Examples

Shell scripts serve my needs dozens of times per day. I normally have two scripts from which I can achieve the majority of my administrative tasks. I find that most of my workload comes in the form of either moving new files to remote hosts or executing a small series of commands on these systems. Whether I need to verify security settings or add a new user to a system, using a few simple shell scripts can normally get the job done without much of a hassle.

In this section, I will offer several examples that will hopefully provide some insight on just how useful SSH-based shell scripting can be.

Administrative Example

In the following examples, two simple scripts are presented. One is called ssh_push.sh and the other is ssh_exec.sh. These scripts are simplistic, but perform some error checking. When I introduce a user or administrator to OpenSSH, especially using a gateway model, I provide them with these two scripts. From there, specific tasks and duties can be developed for everyday usage and cron scheduling.

The ssh_push.sh and ssh_exec.sh scripts are quite similar, and this is intentional. The less code I have to support by giving it to others, the easier my job is. Additionally, the setup for any type of SSH command is nearly identical. These scripts can easily be combined into a single script, with an option for scp or ssh as the command of choice.

The second script, ssh_exec.sh, provided in Listing 9-12, looks remarkably like the example given earlier, in Listing 9-10. This script takes a few command-line arguments. The first is the remote command. If the command has spaces in it, the command should be surrounded by quotation marks. The second argument is the list of servers to connect to. The third argument is the remote username to connect as.

If you take a look at this script, you'll notice that the constants are defined first, and then the number of arguments is verified. From there, $SSH_COMMAND is built. The reason this command has to be echoed and then piped into sh is because, inside of a shell, a -o is normally interpreted as an or operator.

Listing 9-12 uses ConnectTimeout and BatchMode settings to ensure the script can run without requiring input from the user. It also does not require any changes to a user's $HOME/.ssh/config file. It will also handle errors by simply outputting a node name, rather than running the remote command, if the remote system is unavailable. The results listed in Listing 9-13 show that the system named slack is down.

Listing 9-12. *A Script to Run Remote Commands on a Number of Systems*

```
#!/bin/bash
# Name: ssh_exec.sh
#
# Script will take and execute a command string
#    remotely on multiple hosts.
#
#  Assumptions:  1. $SYSTEM_LIST is FQDN one host per line and
#                   specifed as the second command line argument.
#                2. You have key exchange authentication setup for
#                   the remote file owner
#
#
SSH_PATH=/usr/bin
REMOTE_USER=root
REMOTE_COMMAND=$1
SYSTEM_LIST=$2
REMOTE_USER=$3
```

```
SSH_PORT=22
CONNECT_TIMEOUT=3

#Check to ensure all command line arguments were given
if [ ! "$#" = "3" ]
then
  echo "Usage: $0 remote_command system_list remote_user" 1>&2
exit 1
fi

# Traverse the system list
for system in `cat ${SYSTEM_LIST}`
do
 echo ${system}
#Run Remote command
SSH_COMMAND="$SSH_PATH/ssh -p $SSH_PORT -o \"ConnectTimeout \
  ${CONNECT_TIMEOUT}\" -o \"BatchMode yes\"  -l ${REMOTE_USER} ${system} $1"
echo $SSH_COMMAND | sh
done
```

Listing 9-13. *The Results of Running* ssh_exec.sh *in Listing 9-12*

```
scripter@rack ~> ./ssh_exec.sh uptime list root
rack
 17:09:09 up 1 day, 19:27,  4 users,  load average: 0.41, 0.43, 0.37
www
17:09:09 up 1 day, 19:48,  1 user,  load average: 0.16, 0.03, 0.01
Slack
ssh: connect to host slack port 22: Connection timed out
zoom
 17:09:15 up 49 days,  8:45,  1 user,  load average: 0.00, 0.00, 0.00
```

More examples of scripts using SSH can certainly be provided, but I have found that administrators and users often have the need to distribute files and run commands remotely. Between Listings 9-10 and 9-12, this basis is covered. As you work with these scripts, you will probably find that minor modification will make them easier for you to work with. Initially, my ssh_exec scripts did not take command-line arguments, but I found myself using them so often that I modified the scripts so I could invoke them more quickly.

Security Examples

Here are a few more examples of bash scripts I use to verify some security settings. Using these scripts, I can verify integrity of packages, analyze system logs, and detect whether anyone is attempting to use host-based authentication via the placement of a .rhosts file in their home directory.

Verifying rpms

This rpm verification script, shown in Listing 9-14, is useful only if you trust that your rpm database is intact and has not been compromised. A feature of rpm is that you can verify the integrity of the files for things like date change, deletion, MD5 change, file length change, and so on. This can be utilized to ensure that public keys do not change, and to check on other important system files.

The script reads two parameters from the command line. The first parameter is the name of the system to verify the packages on. The second parameter is the package to be verified. The option all will check every package on the system. (Bear in mind that this will take a long time to execute.)

Listing 9-14. *A Script to Verify rpm Integrity*

```
#!/bin/bash
file=$1
option=$2
REMOTE_USER="root"
if [ "$file" = "" -o "$option" = "" ]
then
    echo "Usage: $0 filename  [rpm to verify| all] >"  1>&2
fi
for system in `cat $file`
do
  echo "$system"
  if [ "$option" = "all" ]
  then
    ssh ${REMOTE_USER}@${system} "rpm -qa --verify"
  else
    ssh ${REMOTE_USER}@${system} "rpm -q --verify $option"
fi
done
```

This script does not have quite the error-checking ability shown in earlier examples. Also, fewer options are set via constants in the file. This can make the script easier to work with. Constants are used in many files I work with because not all systems are set up the same, so ssh could be at different locations.

After running the script from Listing 9-15, I can see that a few files that are provided with the initscripts rpm have been changed.

Listing 9-15. *rpm Verification Output*

```
stahnke@rack: ~> ./verify_rpms.sh list initscripts
rack
..5....T  c /etc/inittab
www
S.5....T  c /etc/sysctl.conf
```

Working with System Logs

Sometimes, when working on servers in more hostile environments, it's good to have a separate storage area for logs. Log aggregation servers and log reporting tools are plentiful, and several that have been released under various open source licenses are quite nice; however, sometimes you may just want to retrieve logs and look at them quickly, without the time investment of setting up a complete log management infrastructure. To do this, once again, a very simple bash script utilizing OpenSSH will suffice.

As shown in Listing 9-16, redirection and pipes are used to provide a few more options via ssh. Note that if the "gz" is specified on the command line, the logs are gzipped. The input file for this script is just called list. This can obviously be modified to suit your needs.

Listing 9-16. *Log Retrieval and Compression Using SSH*

```
#!/bin/bash
thedate=`date +%b\ %e`
date_num=`date +%F`
log_file="/var/log/messages"
for system in `cat list`
do
  echo $system
  ssh root@${system} "cat $log_file | grep \"$thedate\"" > \
  ${system}.${date_num}
  if [ "$1" = "gz" ]
  then
    gzip ${system}.${date_num}
  fi
done
```

The script will retrieve a log file and then compress it on the local system. Listing 9-17 shows the results when it is run against a few of my systems. In this example, I have a ConnectTimeout value set in my $HOME/.ssh/config file.

Listing 9-17. *The Results from Listing 9-16*

```
scripter@rack ~> ./logging.sh gz
rack
www
slack
ssh: connect to host slack port 22: No route to host
zoom
```

Scanning for .rhosts Files

To prevent legacy host-based authentication using .rhosts files, the following example script in Listing 9-18 will find these files and report their location. I have elected not to have this script delete the .rhosts files, because I normally want to speak with users about the creation of these types of files and find out what tasks they are attempting to accomplish. (Host-based authentication via OpenSSH is covered in Chapter 6).

The structure of the script is the same as the others: a for loop executes on a set of remote hosts. I do not stray much from the for loop structure because I am often working on hundreds of systems at a time. There is one optional command-line parameter for this script: the home option. On systems with hundreds of thousands of files or more, doing a find from / would take hours or days. If the keyword home is used, ssh remotely finds the directories containing the word home, thus hopefully skipping application directories and saving time. If you have home directories in /users or some other place, this script should be modified accordingly.

Listing 9-18. *A Script to Locate* .rhosts *Files*

```
#!/bin/bash
for system in `cat list`
do
  echo $system
  if [ "$1" = "full" -o "$1" = "" ]
  then
    ssh root@$system "find / -name .rhosts -type f -print "
  elif [ "$1" = "home" ]
      then
        ssh root@$system "for home_dir in \`grep home /etc/passwd \
          | cut -d: -f6\` ; do find \$home_dir -name .rhosts -print ;done"
  fi
done
```

This script executes the find command to look for .rhosts files. Errors are provided from the find command if the home directory does not exist. This script also requires root access on the remote systems. Here is the output from a run of a few systems:

```
stahnke@rack: ~> ./rhosts_check.sh
rack
/home/stahnke/.rhosts
www
```

Shell scripting with SSH is rapid and oftentimes does not do very much error checking. The goal is normally to execute a task in the smallest amount of time possible. The scripts shown in this chapter are not designed to be complex, but to show that basic flow control using for loops and a few variables can accomplish many administrative tasks quickly and securely in conjunction with SSH.

Using Perl

Some UNIX administrators know very little Perl, but from my experience, the ones who do are able to do some amazing things that might not have been possible without it. This discussion of Perl in regard to OpenSSH assumes an installation of Perl version 5.8.x. Perl is included in nearly every UNIX/Linux operating system today. If you do not have it installed, fear not—Perl is open source and available at http://www.perl.com/CPAN/src/stable.tar.gz.

When is Perl a Good Idea?

This question can quickly become "When is Perl *not* a good idea?" The debate for superior programming languages often raises a near-religious argument from UNIX administrators and programmers. Perl, however, is thought to be the Swiss army knife of programming languages. It has several advantages, including its amazing ability to handle strings (character-type input), work on multiple platforms, and provide multiple ways of doing nearly every task imaginable.

The development from the open source community also makes Perl a wonderful tool. Hundreds of modules (shared-code libraries) are available for Perl that make interacting with nearly any application or protocol fairly simplistic.

Perl can be used on Microsoft Windows systems and from the command line on UNIX/Linux systems, and can even drive GUIs and web content. The discussion in the following section assumes a basic working knowledge of Perl. Perl code can easily become very unreadable, but the best programmers get around by using complex operators and implied variables. The examples in this chapter, however, stay away from such complexities in an effort to provide usable material.

Perl also has the advantage of being able to work with multiple applications and protocols simultaneously. While performing complex applications is out of scope for this material, a few small examples will be included. For instance, if you need a script that finds the kernel version of all Linux systems and updates a database, you might be forced to use several different shell scripts, or switch to an ODBC API (Open Database Connectivity Application Programming Interface), depending on your database choice. With Perl, you can use an SSH module and a DBI (Database Interface) module in the same script. Perl can also be compiled. Compiling code may help obfuscate sensitive information such as passwords or usernames from unwanted viewing.

The Net::SSH Module

Perl, in conjunction with a module from Comprehensive Perl Archive Network (CPAN, http://www.cpan.org), has a few different modules that work with OpenSSH. The modules are actually designed to work with the RFC spec for SECSH, which includes OpenSSH and SSH Tectia products from SSH Communications Security.

There are two primary modules for Perl that work with SSH. One is Net::SSH (and its derivatives), which uses the already installed ssh commands on the local system. The other is Net::SSH::Perl, which uses a Perl/C implementation of the SSH protocol so that no client commands are needed. Each module has some specific function, such as working with types of encryption or connecting to remote systems emulating a file system. The work in this section will use simply Net::SSH.

Perl modules are much like rpms from a packaging standpoint. It seems the package you need always requires another package, and that package has three dependencies, and so forth. Luckily, CPAN has come up with a way to install CPAN modules using Perl to account for dependency troubles.

Installing Net::SSH via CPAN

Installing Net::SSH is by far the most difficult part in working with Perl and SSH. Configuring CPAN the first time, retrieving the Pari module (which is required by Net::SSH to perform a collection of mathematic library calls), and then dealing with the rest of the SSH dependencies takes some patience. It also might take some troubleshooting on your system depending on what is currently or has been installed.

CPAN also has a module for Perl that will help with configuration and installation of additional Perl modules. Normally, CPAN is installed with Perl. If you are unsure whether CPAN is installed, try running the following command:

```
$ perl -MCPAN -e shell
```

If you are shown a cpan> command command>prompt or some questions about configuration, then CPAN is installed. If Perl provides an error, you need to install the CPAN module. If you need the CPAN module, you can get it from http://search.cpan.org/src/ANDK/CPAN-1.76/lib/CPAN.pm. After a basic configure, make, and make install, you should be on your way.

CPAN will be configured automatically the first time you run the following command. Accepting the defaults is normally fine—however, keep in mind that you may need to adjust them if your connection runs through a proxy server.

```
$ perl -MCPAN -e shell
```

After configuring CPAN, try to install Bundle::SSH. According to the site's documentation, you must perform some setup to download and install the Pari module before continuing with the Bundle::SSH install. Pari is an interface to the C Pari library, which is used for mathematic operations.

To download Pari, get the Pari tarball from the following location: ftp://megrez.math.u-bordeaux.fr/pub/pari/unix/pari-2.1.4.tgz. Following that, extract the command>contents to ~/.cpan/build. Next, run a ./Configure inside the Pari directory. From there, you can execute the following:

```
$ perl -MCPAN -e shell
cpan> force install Bundle::SSH
```

This will produce hundreds of lines of output while the configure and make commands are running. Near the end of the compilation (which can take some time on slower systems), you will be asked questions about which protocols of SSH you are interested in supporting. I picked choice 3, which is support for protocols 1 and 2, simply because I would not want to have to install this module again if I had to work with a legacy protocol 1 application. For encryption algorithms, I chose 2, 3, 4, and 5. I skipped the IDEA (International Data Encryption Algorithm) command>algorithm because it is patented,[1] and I do not want any trouble with patents when there are four other perfectly good ciphers to choose from.

Testing Your Net::SSH Installation

Listing 9-19 shows a Perl script slightly modified from the informational page on CPAN regarding Net::SSH. This script uses the ssh subroutine, which is very basic and allows a command to be executed remotely over SSH. After you set a user, system name, and command, the script executes. The results are displayed on stdout.

Listing 9-19. *A Basic Perl Script Utilizing* Net::SSH

```
#!/usr/bin/perl
use Net::SSH qw(ssh);
```

---

1. Because of intellectual property concerns, OpenSSH does not support the IDEA algorithm.

```
use strict;
my $user   = "stahnke";
my $system = "www";
my $command = "uptime";

  print "$system\n";
  ssh("$user\@$system", "$command") ;
```

After running the script, you should see the results from an uptime command. Net::SSH is indeed installed correctly if your results are similar to the following:

```
scripter@rack ~> perl test_ssh.pl
www
 19:07:50 up 1 day, 21:47,  1 user,  load average: 0.00, 0.00, 0.00
```

Using Net::SSH

As mentioned earlier, Net::SSH enables Perl to utilize the already installed ssh client on the system. This can produce a performance issue when it comes to forking multiple processes, but it was chosen here to keep the examples simple.

Net::SSH has very few features that surpass what's available by way of a traditional SSH client. For authentication to work correctly, you must have previously set up key-based authentication. Password authentication is not an option using this module. Once authentication is handled, you can pass commands as would normally be done on the command line.

Perl can then process any output received from your ssh command and work with it in various capacities. In my previous hypothetical example of finding kernel levels and then placing them into a database, some data sanitation might be required to prep the data for entry after the script retrieves the kernel level. Also, other actions might be taken based on retrieved data.

I use Perl mostly in bigger projects that have several specific tasks that will all eventually be connected via a database or reporting mechanism. One reason I choose Perl when I have several similar tasks is code reuse. If I have a Perl file that has things like database names, database users, and passwords, along with connection parameters, I can put the file in a .pm (Perl module) file and just reuse it, rather than reentering it. I also can call commonly used subroutines from .pm files. I normally have a .pm file that reads a server database for all host-names of a certain operating system type to perform maintenance or patching on. Unless you are a very experienced Perl programmer, the primary benefit of Perl comes when working with other types of IT infrastructures in conjunction with OpenSSH.

Function Walkthrough

The functions for Net::SSH are nearly identical to each other. The options are the parameters that can read, write, and report errors. If only basic command execution is needed, the ssh subroutine can easily be used. sshopen2 provides a read-and-write stream while sshopen3 adds an additional handle for stderr.

- ssh [USER@]HOST, COMMAND [, ARGS ...]: This basic function simply runs the remote command supplied by the script.

- issh [USER@]HOST, COMMAND [, ARGS ...]: This function displays the command it is preparing to run and waits for a user to confirm it before execution.

- ssh_cmd [USER@]HOST, COMMAND [, ARGS ...]: This is similar to the ssh function in that it executes a remote command. It will, however, deliver a fatal error if any data is sent to stdout.

- sshopen2 [USER@]HOST, READER, WRITER, COMMAND [, ARGS ...]: This function executes remote commands and connects via the file handles reader and writer, which work with streams of data.

- sshopen3 [USER@]HOST, WRITER, READER, ERROR, COMMAND [, ARGS ...]: This function executes remote commands and can handle stderr output as well.

Examples of Scripts in Perl

Perl really becomes more useful when you need to interact with other types of applications in a single script. In the following example using Perl, I will get a list of servers from a database and then run ssh commands to those hosts.

Retrieving Files and Updating a Database

The following script assumes you have a MySQL database called db set up on the database host. It also assumes you know the database username and password. If you are new to databases and especially MySQL, there is a plethora of wonderful material available to you, including *The Definitive Guide to MySQL 5, Third Edition*, by Michael Kofler (Apress, 2005).

To add MySQL functionality to Perl, CPAN can be used once again.

```
stahnke@rack: ~> perl -MCPAN -e shell
cpan> install Bundle::DBD::mysql
```

The script in Listing 9-20 performs a query on my system management database, looking for all systems currently running a variation of Fedora. After that, it performs an SSH command to each of them to see what version of Perl is installed. This is intentionally rather simplistic. This script is meant to illustrate concepts of using SSH in conjunction with Perl and other technologies.

Listing 9-20. *A Perl Script That Utilizes SSH and DBI*

```
#!/usr/bin/perl
use DBI; # Needed for database connection
use Net::SSH qw(sshopen2); # Needed for SSH
my $dbname="db";
my $dbuser="dbuser";
my $dbpass="password";
my $dbhost="www";
my $sshuser="root";
my $sshcommand="rpm -q perl";
```

```
# Connect to the database using DBI.
my $dbh = DBI->connect("DBI:mysql:database=$dbname;host=$dbhost",
                        $dbuser, $dbpass,
                        {'RaiseError' => 1});
#Prepare SQL Query looking for systems running Fedora
$sth = $dbh->prepare("SELECT node_name from server where
os='fedora'");
#Execute Query
$sth->execute();
#Perform Action on Results
#Work with each Row Returned
while( my @node = $sth->fetchrow())
{
     #Each row is a node name
     $sshhost=$node[0];
     #Establish SSH connection
     sshopen2("$sshuser\@$sshhost", *READER, *WRITER,
             "$sshcommand") || die "ssh: $!";
     #Process SSH results
     while (<READER>)
     {
       chomp();
       print "$sshhost: ";
       print "$_\n";
     }
     close(READER);
     close(WRITER);
}
#Close database connections
$sth->finish();
$dbh->disconnect();
```

The execution and output from this Perl script is as follows:

```
stahnke@rack: ~> perl dbi_ssh.pl
rack: perl-5.8.5-9
www: perl-5.8.5-9
```

Additional Perl-Driven Tasks

Perl, in conjunction with OpenSSH, is powerful toolkit. In addition to getting information from a database, Perl can easily update a database, interact with LDAP (Lightweight Directory Access Protocol), and work with XML (Extensible Markup Language) streams, email, SNMP (Simple Network Management Protocol), the AIM (America Online Instant Messenger) protocol, and nearly anything else you can think of.

Perl scripts oftentimes require modification to run perfectly in your environment. I have been at locations where using Perl with databases, LDAP, and SSH made automation in an environment very easy; and at others where the scripts from the first location would not have helped anything. Perl scripts are often more difficult and finely tuned than shell scripts. The ability to reuse code also makes Perl a nice language for larger projects.

Web Scripting

Web scripting, or programming, is certainly not a very new technique, but I do not see lot of usage with it in conjunction with SSH. The concept is fairly simple—having a web page that takes certain types of inputs and executing different SSH commands based on those inputs.

Introduction to Web Front Ends for SSH

A few years after a large SSH implementation, a group I worked with was just starting to understand the capabilities of SSH. At the same time, they wanted a help desk to be able to log in to remote systems and run a restricted set of commands, without having to do account maintenance for every worker on the help desk.

A few forward-thinking system administrators thought a web front end would be the best possible solution. This would allow restricted access via web access control, and allow for us to sanitize all input before processing. This would also benefit the system administrator who had the pager for the week, because the help desk could now run basic troubleshooting commands if the administrator was unable to get onto a computer immediately.

Setting Up an Account to Use a Web Front End

There is some setup required to make SSH work from a web-driven application. The account that the web server runs under needs to have public key authentication set up with the remote hosts the application is designed to use. If you are using Apache, the user is Apache by default. Other web servers and account names may vary.

After generating a key for this web account, you need to distribute the key. If you choose to use a passphrase, use Keychain to make sure an agent is loaded for the end user of your application. Also, the key can be set up to limit what commands that key can be used to perform. Depending on your security and situation, limited keys can greatly increase your peace of mind.

Additionally, because there is no interactive user to type yes if a new key is cached, you should modify the web user's ssh_config to set StrictHostKeyChecking to no. Alternatively, you could cache all the remote system's public keys. Remember that setting StrictHostKeyChecking to no defeats the normal protection SSH provides against an MITM attack. An example of a web user's ssh_config file follows in Listing 9-21.

Listing 9-21. *A* $HOME/.ssh/config *File for a Batch User*

```
Host *
    ForwardAgent no
    ForwardX11 no
    BatchMode yes
    ConnectTimeout 10
    StrictHostKeyChecking no
    Protocol 2
```

In addition to having a web account with an SSH key, it is also critical to have the ability to execute commands based on HTML markup. This can be done through a variety of methods, including CGI (Common Gateway Interface) and PHP (PHP: Hypertext Preprocessor).

Tip *Beginning PHP 5 and MySQL: From Novice to Professional*, by W. Jason Gilmore (Apress, 2004), is great book for information about MySQL (as covered earlier) and PHP. The PHP topics include a chapter called "Working with the File and Operating Systems," which can be a foundation for system administrators looking to use SSH inside of PHP.

Security Concerns

Working with web applications that can touch remote systems is dangerous. This is not recommended as a rapid implementation. As with all aspects of security, the access control and communication methods need to be well thought out before you move the code into a production environment.

Because the private key for the web user will be without a passphrase, or unlocked via Keychain, deciding which remote user to log in as is key. Certain tasks, of course, such as log reading, normally require privilege of the root user. If your operating system allows logs to be read by a lesser user, it is a good idea to use that user. The concept of least-privileged user is very important, especially in web design.

Input sanitization is probably the most important aspect of web scripting. Ideally, a drop-down menu is created so that users cannot inject any of their own commands into the application through the usage of && operators or ;. If a password is being used, be sure to keep that password encrypted also. Remember that normal HTTP traffic is not encrypted. Best practices use some form of SSL for communication encryption.

Using Web Front Ends

If you think the security and setup are feasible, writing a few PHP pages to get some dirty work done is not too bad. You can easily use Perl, bash, Python, Ruby, and a variety of other programming languages to enable these types of transactions. I chose PHP because of its simplicity and wide usage in the open source community.

The first file in the following two-file application is simple HTML—there is nothing fancy about it. Optionally, this could use a database to pull hostnames and perhaps other resources for commands, paths, locations, and policy information; but once again, for the sake of simplicity, I am presenting static content.

The code shown in Listing 9-22 assumes you have the user running the web server setup with public key authentication to the remote systems. None of the commands used in this example require root-level authority, so this can be done as a standard user. In the case of this example, I have a user called `scripter` that has public key authentication enabled to three remote systems.

Listing 9-22. *The HTML Form that Accepts User Input*

```
<html>
 <head>
   <title>PHP SSH example</title>
 </head>
<body>
  <form action=ssh_action.php method=post>
  Machine
  <select name="system">
    <option value="0">rack</option>
    <option value="1">www</option>
    <option value="2">zoom</option>
  </select>
  <br /><br />
  Command
  <select name="command">
    <option value="0">uptime</option>
    <option value="1">who</option>
    <option value="2">w</option>
    <option value="3">last</option>
    <option value="4">process stack</option>
  </select>
  <br /><br/ >
  <input type=submit value="Run Command">
  </form>
</body>
</html>
```

Listing 9-22 produces the following web page.

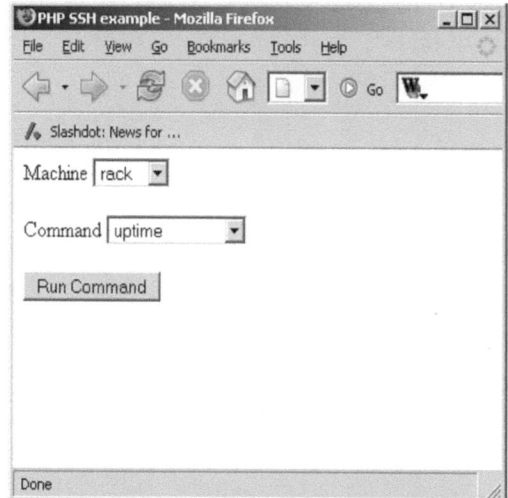

Figure 9-1. *A web application for selecting systems and SSH commands*

The HTML page acts as a front end for end users to pick the system and command they wish to run. The back end calls the standard ssh command provided by the system. It also sources the ssh_config file. Listing 9-23 also selects the command using a switch statement. This is to prevent someone injecting their own POST commands to the HTTP server. If someone tries to use commands other than the given options, they are simply given an error message.

Listing 9-23. *A PHP File that Executes Commands via SSH*

```php
<?php

$system=$_POST['machine'];
$command=$_POST['command'];

switch ($command)
{
  case 0:
  $command="/usr/bin/uptime";
  break;
  case 1:
  $command="/usr/bin/who";
  break;
  case 2:
  $command="/usr/bin/w";
  break;
  case 3:
  $command="/usr/bin/last";
  break;
  case 4:
  $command="/bin/ps -ef";
  break;
  default:
  echo "You have entered an invalid POST entry! <br/>";
  exit;
}

switch ($system)
{
  case 0:
  $system="rack";
  break;
  case 1:
  $system="www";
  break;
  case 2:
  $system="zoom";
  break;
  default:
```

```
    echo "You have entered an invalid POST entry! <br/>";
    exit;
}
  $REMOTE_USER="scripter";
  $SSH_PATH="/usr/bin/ssh";
  print "$REMOTE_USER@$system:> $command<BR>\n";
  print "<br/>\n";
  $results=shell_exec("$SSH_PATH $system -l $REMOTE_USER \"$command\"");
  print "<pre>";
  print nl2br($results);
  print "</pre>";
?>
```

Figure 9-2 shows the output from running the PHP example with the uptime command.

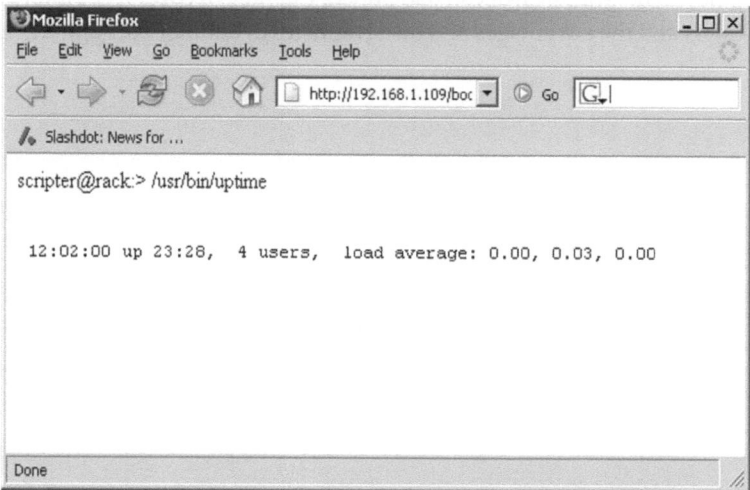

Figure 9-2. *Output of a simple SSH/PHP application*

Web applications that utilize SSH to perform commands and gather data are both useful and dangerous. Planning is the key to success with this type of scripting implementation. Also, remember to restrict the commands that a public key can use by using the command options. The web front end provides an easy-to-use SSH client for users on Windows systems without another client installed. Additionally, many web applications can now be run from cell phones and PDAs. This can really help out when being onsite is not an option.

Summary

Scripts are without a doubt my favorite thing that a proper OpenSSH architecture can provide. While OpenSSH does not have a whole lot to do with scripting, it enables so much work to be automated and repeated with consistency that otherwise would be difficult, if not impossible, to achieve.

Once I started using scripts in conjunction with OpenSSH and keys, I was amazed at how much more work I could get done. I went from managing around 30 servers poorly to managing hundreds with little incident. Of course, if you are migrating from a remote shell environment, you are used to these types of luxuries, but I was normally working with Telnet and FTP, which lack the scripting capabilities provided by OpenSSH.

You also might have noticed that I did not use SFTP once during the scripts in this chapter. There is certainly nothing stopping you from using SFTP in shell, bash, or on the Web, but I often find it cumbersome in comparison to SCP. I find that SFTP is nice for interactive users, but normally from a script, SCP will perform the task in fewer steps.

Scripts take time to develop and tune to your setup and environment. I encourage you to try a few of the examples provided in this chapter, and then modify them to provide the functionality you need. My script directories normally have dozens of scripts in development and usage, with dozens more archived. Scripts and OpenSSH can make UNIX/Linux administration a very rewarding career.

If you happen to be running an SSH product other than OpenSSH, you will see that your scripts and actions might not all be working like you had hoped. Chapter 10 covers SSH interoperability between products and the advantages and disadvantages of another SSH option, SSH Tectia Server.

CHAPTER 10

■ ■ ■

SSH Tectia Server

OpenSSH, while certainly the most popular SSH protocol implementation, is not the only option. Perhaps the most notable of alternatives is SSH Tectia Server, a product offered by SSH creator Tatu Ylönen's company, SSH Communications Security (`http://www.ssh.com`). Over the years, this product has evolved from supporting just a few operating systems to supporting nearly every commonly used operating system including IBM AIX, Sun Solaris, HP-UX, Red Hat Linux, SUSE Linux, Microsoft Windows, and more recently, mainframe operating systems.

Note The main product that replaces SSH Secure Shell for Servers is now called SSH Tectia Server (A). This naming convention changed when SSH Secure Shell for Servers reached the 4.0 release. The Tectia line of products is an implementation of the SSH-2 protocol.

If you are familiar with OpenSSH, switching to and from the Tectia line of products is initially very frustrating. After some experience with both, however, you will see that each has its own advantages and disadvantages.

When discussing SSH and implementation of product options between OpenSSH and SSH Tectia Server, questions will come up as to why one should be used over another. The main focus of this chapter is not about making that choice for you, but to illustrate some examples of advantages, disadvantages, and interoperability scenarios that should help you make an informed decision.

The Pros and Cons of SSH Tectia Server

Before installation and interoperability are covered, it is a good idea to briefly discuss possible advantages and disadvantages of SSH Tectia Server when compared with OpenSSH.

Advantages Over OpenSSH

The commercial SSH Tectia product has some distinct advantages over the OpenSSH implementation of the SSH protocol. Some organizations find these benefits to be great enough to justify the cost of the product, while others find that OpenSSH provides the security and connectivity required.

Standard Microsoft Windows Client

In most environments, workstations run a Microsoft Windows operating system. While OpenSSH has no official client for Windows, SSH Communications Security does. Their client offers profile saving, key caching, and a really nice feature that allows opening a file transfer session via SFTP to a machine you are already connected to.

■**Note** SSH connectivity clients, including the SSH Tectia Client, are covered in Appendix A.

This client does not provide an X server for X11 applications. To use X applications, you will need a third-party X server such as Cygwin (http://www.cygwin.com), Hummingbird Exceed (http://www.hummingbird.com), X-Win32 (http://www.starnet.com), or AttachmateWRQ Reflection (http://www.wrq.com/products/reflection/win/).

Authentication Options

SSH Tectia Server allows for some authentication methods different from those provided by the stock OpenSSH implementation. The Tectia line supports, in total, Public Key Infrastructure (PKI), RSA Security's SecurID, Kerberos, GSSAPI, public key authentication, PAM, password authentication, and keyboard-interactive methods.

Most often, public key authentication, PAM, and passwords are used, but the other options do provide a strong authentication if your organization has those needs. Typically, RSA Security's SecurID technology is used on perimeter firewalls, VPNs, and for access to highly sensitive systems. PKI requires certificates for users and systems, thus requiring a large infrastructure support and maintenance commitment. Working with some of the unique authentication options presented by SSH Tectia Server can be challenging. Luckily, SSH Communications also provides technical resources, in the form of web documentation, knowledge banks, and consultants, to help your organization meet these challenges.

Management Options

SSH Communications Security has a product called the SSH Tectia Manager, which can manage their SSH software. This web-based application uses encrypted communication to distribute, start, stop, and upgrade SSH Tectia products on remote targets. It also populates all host keys from managed hosts into each host, eliminating the need for end users to do so.

The SSH Tectia Manager can also generate and store SSH server and client configuration files and distribute them to managed end points. The Manager provides a log file of which systems got the updated configuration files and which ones it failed on. License management is also handled by the Manager so an administrator can know how many licenses he or she has in use.

The SSH Communications Security SSH Tectia Manager makes managing SSH easier for less technically oriented support staff, but it comes with a hefty price tag.[1]

---

1. At the time of writing, the SSH Tectia Manager product is not available for direct purchase from http://www.ssh.com. Purchase agreements must be reached with the company.

SSH Tectia Server Disadvantages

Picking the right tool for the right job is critical, and even more so when dealing with information security. Nearly all the knowledge in this book applies to both OpenSSH and commercial products, but because the market is most heavily saturated with OpenSSH, that was the focus for the majority of the book. The Tectia product line can be tuned and made to run better than OpenSSH in some situations, or it can crumble with the wrong type of administration. Just as the Tectia product has advantages over OpenSSH, it also is missing some items of importance compared to OpenSSH.

Package Dependencies

The most frustrating thing I run into when using SSH Tectia Server is the package dependency issues on Linux. Oftentimes, packaging/patching tools (even simple ones such as apt/yum) will not allow a system to be patched without meeting every dependency for every package already installed on the system. These options can be overridden, but not meeting dependencies can cause stability issues. Having to remove packages in the middle of the RPM dependency stack is challenging, and working with holes in that stack can be very difficult over time.

Additionally, when working with support personnel from third-party vendors such as IBM, HP, SUN, and Novell, they normally expect OpenSSH to be installed on the machine. Their documentation will all be geared toward OpenSSH, and you will have to translate it for the support staff and your organization. Sometimes support personnel will even ask you to remove the SSH Tectia Server product and place OpenSSH on the system to prove the problem is not stemming from sshd2.

The dependency issue seems to show itself much less on other flavors of UNIX that do not build upon OpenSSH being installed. Certain clustering software products also have configuration and support documentation geared to OpenSSH. While they can almost always work with SSH Tectia Server, documentation must be adjusted.

Privilege Separation

The sshd2 daemon runs as root, no matter who you connect to the machine as. Although I have not seen an exploit for this, it makes me uncomfortable. Using OpenSSH with privilege separation causes the sshd daemon to spawn a new sshd running with user stahnke's privileges and not with root privileges after successful authentication. Before authentication, OpenSSH uses a restricted environment running as the sshd user (by default) to control privilege.

```
stahnke@www: ~> ps -ef | grep ssh
root      2039     1  0 Mar07 ?  00:00:00 /usr/sbin/sshd
root     31161  2039  0 14:37 ?  00:00:00 sshd: stahnke [priv]
stahnke  31164 31161  0 14:37 ?  00:00:00 sshd: stahnke@pts/0
```

Under the Tectia product, a normal user account connects to an sshd2 daemon that runs as root all the time. This output is using the same scenario, my unprivileged account (stahnke) connected to the machine via the SSH protocol:

```
stahnke@rack: ~> ps -ef | grep ssh
root     30902     1  0 14:41 ?  00:00:00 /usr/local/sbin/sshd2
root     30909 30902  1 14:41 ?  00:00:00 /usr/local/sbin/sshd2
```

Cost

At the time of writing, a license of SSH Tectia Server has a list price of $774.00. This is obviously quite expensive for the home user, but for the enterprise customer, this may not be seen as an unbearable cost. This cost also does not include support and maintenance. Those agreements are reached separately with SSH Communications Security.

When it comes to total cost of ownership (TCO), neither SSH implementation is free. Each requires a learning investment and time devoted to architecture, key management, patching, and technical understanding. While it may seem that saving on licensing costs is simply a benefit for OpenSSH, there is more to it than that. In my experience, OpenSSH is more difficult to configure, explore, and tweak for the exact parameters you require. The Tectia product offers a full range of support options from web-based to 24×7 phone support.

In every SSH implementation I have done, this decision has been the hardest to make. Some companies have policies against open source tools. Some require that commercial support must be available. Others are only concerned about dollars spent, not time—training costs, long-term cost, and such.

Recommendations

I used to recommend the Tectia solution to companies with less technical staff because they could rely on support from SSH Communications Security. However, my more recent implementations have led me to rethink that stance. So much software is documented for, and tested on, OpenSSH, that it still takes a very technical understanding of SSH to make SSH Tectia solutions viable in large environments.

Remember to weigh support costs versus documentation available when making a decision about which implementation of SSH to choose. In general, if you have a more technically oriented staff, OpenSSH will work out very nicely for you. The Tectia line provides some extremely nice management functionality and is very easy to use in most cases, but comes at a higher monetary price and will require some integration to work with third-party tools that rely on SSH.

I have been working with SSH Tectia Server in conjunction with OpenSSH for the past three years at several different levels. As a personal recommendation, if you can keep your environment on one type of SSH, whether it is OpenSSH or a commercial version, the end users, security administrators, and application analysts will all benefit. Working in a hybrid environment presents many challenges including management of upgrades, differences in public key–based authentication, working with operating system support from vendors, and troubleshooting connectivity problems.

Installing SSH Tectia Server

Obtaining SSH Tectia Server can be done by following the download link from http://www.ssh.com. Trial versions are available if you register with the company and validate your e-mail address. Commercial purchases are available online or through a company representative.

The installation files come in binary format for the target operating system. Source files are included when purchasing SSH Tectia; however, if you build your own version, then you may be on your own for support also.

Because the SSH Tectia Server packages are provided in native operating system format, installation is done via the system package manager (rpm, pkg, depot, bff, etc.). Removing existing OpenSSH installations is recommended because it may confuse you, your users, and possibly some scripts if $PATH is set to search the directories with SSH binaries in an order that is not expected.

Removing OpenSSH from a Red Hat or SUSE Linux system will cause other packages to have broken dependencies, which can lead to other problems. Some of the more important packages that rely on OpenSSH in Linux are netdump (http://www.netdump.org), which allows a kernel panic to dump memory to a remote file system; and some kdebase packages, which allows for the popular KDE (http://www.kde.org) desktop to be installed. Both of these packages will work if you are comfortable with not checking dependencies for these RPMs for installations. However, future upgrades of those packages and additional packages that depend on those packages can be a difficult experience. Other operating systems fare better than Linux does when installing the Tectia product because they normally do not ship with OpenSSH installed.

The first notable difference is the requirement for a license file. This can be bothersome because the administrator must either write an installation script around the package provided by SSH Communications Security or have the installation complete, have startup of sshd2 fail, drop in the license file, and then restart the sshd2 daemon. Normally, the /etc/ssh2/ directory can be made and have the license_ssh2.dat file placed in it before installing the package, and everything will work as desired.

■**Caution** When upgrading versions for SSH Tectia, be especially careful to place the latest license file that came with the new package in the /etc/ssh2 directory before installing the new package. Administrators can easily drop SSH connectivity if the license file does not match the version now installed. Starting the sshd2 daemon is not possible without the proper license.

The host keys are stored in /etc/ssh2. During installation, a key is generated that is, by default, 2048 bits in length. The generation of this key can take a very long time (up to one hour) on some systems.

The Tectia product also installs a certd daemon, which enables the usage of PKI. Using PKI is something that the Tectia product does natively, whereas OpenSSH requires patching outside of the official OpenSSH tree to support it (http://roumenpetrov.info/openssh/). If your organization has a significant investment in PKI technology, then the Tectia product line will probably integrate into that infrastructure easier.

Differences Between OpenSSH and SSH Tectia Server

An initial look at SSH Tectia Server shows the Tectia file layout is quite similar to that found in OpenSSH. By default, installation of the binary files occurs in the /usr/local space. The configuration files are in /etc/ssh2. The commands to do almost everything the same as with OpenSSH, except each command now ends in the number 2. If OpenSSH is not installed on the system, links will be created so the applications can be named the same thing. For example, in OpenSSH, ssh is the client program. In SSH Tectia Server, it is ssh2. However, upon installation, SSH Tectia Server will link ssh to ssh2 if ssh does not already exist.

The entropy (randomness used to generate encryption keys) for SSH Tectia is provided by /etc/ssh2/random_seed. This seed file changes a few times an hour to cause variance in the random generation algorithms used for encryption.

Also provided by a default is a file called /etc/ssh2/ssh_dummy_shell.out. The ssh-dummy-shell is a shell that the Tectia product can use to provide only SCP/SFTP capabilities to a user. The contents of /etc/ssh2/ssh_dummy_shell.out are given to any user having the dummy shell as their shell and attempting an interactive ssh2 connection. This is the output when using the dummy shell for an attempted ssh2 client connection:

```
stahnke@rack: ~> cat /etc/passwd | grep dummy
dummy:x:503:503::/home/dummy:/usr/local/bin/ssh-dummy-shell
stahnke@rack: ~> ssh dummy@rack
dummy's password:
Authentication successful.
This is ssh-dummy-shell.  Edit /etc/ssh2/ssh_dummy_shell.out
in order to alter this message.
Press any key to exit.
Connection to rack closed.
```

■**Caution** The output file is called ssh_dummy_shell.out with underscores, but the shell itself is called ssh-dummy-shell, with hyphens. This can be quite confusing.

Public Key Authentication with SSH Tectia Server

Public key authentication is set up a little differently than in OpenSSH. First off, the user's home directory for SSH information is $HOME/.ssh2 rather than .ssh. Additionally, the private key file (1024-bit DSA) is normally called id_dsa_1024_a, and the public key is called id_dsa_1024_a.pub. RSA keys are also supported in the SSH Tectia product line.

The local side should have a file called $HOME/.ssh2/identification, which lists each private key the account will be using, one per line. Each line starts with idkey as the token.

```
stahnke@rack: ~> cat $HOME/.ssh2/identification
idkey id_dsa_1024_a
```

On the remote machine side, the public key needs to be placed in the remote user's .ssh2 directory. Additionally, a file called authorization must exist with the following syntax. This example shows that multiple keys are allowed:

```
stahnke@rack: ~> cat $HOME/.ssh2/authorization
key id_dsa_1024_a.pub
key id_rsa_2048_a.pub
```

For public key authentication to work properly, the file pointed at by the authorization file must exist and have secure permissions (not world accessible). Using separate files for these tasks may seem inconvenient at first, but from a key management prospective, it is much easier. If I want to revoke a key, rather than rebuild an authorized_keys file, the public key file can simply be removed from the remote systems, thus leaving all other keys still intact. This does assume that not all keys are named the same thing.

During my SSH implementations involving the SSH Tectia Server product, I normally recommend a `username.source_node` naming convention for a public key. This is nice because in the logs, `sshd2` reports which public key is used to gain access. This eliminates having to trace key fingerprints if the multiple keys are authorized for an account.

```
stahnke@rack: ~> ssh root@rack
root@rack: ~> cat /var/log/secure
...
Mar 13 13:55:39 rack sshd2[29450]: connection from "192.168.1.101"
(listen iface: *** SSH_IPADDR_ANY ***:22)
Mar 13 13:55:39 rack sshd2[30442]: User authorized by public key:
"1024-bit dsa, stahnke@rack, Sun Mar 13 2005 13:54:03 -0600",
fingerprint: xorid-gisyd-tufan-posiz-sisyb-cubym-ledyv-pepyp-zatup-
nipec-laxox
Mar 13 13:55:39 rack sshd2[30442]: Public key
/root/.ssh2/stahnke.rack authorized for user root, verifying
signature.
Mar 13 13:55:39 rack sshd2[30442]: Public key authentication for
user root accepted.
Mar 13 13:55:39 rack sshd2[30442]: ROOT LOGIN: User root (uid 0),
coming from rack, authenticated.
...
```

From the logs, I can see that `stahnke.rack` was used to authenticate. If I am confident in the naming convention, then I can be fairly sure this was the user stahnke coming from the host named `rack`.

Configuration of SSH Tectia Server

Configuration files for SSH Tectia are stored in `/etc/ssh2`. These work in the same manner as with OpenSSH. The files are called `sshd2_config` and `ssh2_config` for the server and client, respectively. The `sshd2_config` is a well-documented configuration file, and the `man` pages will also assist you in developing a configuration file.

Tip The per-user client configuration is called `$HOME/.ssh2/ssh2_config` and not just `config` as with OpenSSH.

The Tectia Server allows an administrator to tailor the configuration on a per-user and per-host basis. This is bit more granular than OpenSSH. The usage of subconfiguration files, or subconfigs, is supported in `sshd2`. A subconfig can specify that, from a certain host, this configuration for `sshd2` applies, whereas normally it would rely on the system defaults.

SSH Communications provides a few examples for every configuration file they use, which can be a nice baseline for configuration. Their subconfigs provide examples for user-based configurations, host-based configurations, and anonymous examples.

■**Note** The SSH Tectia Server anonymous example for SFTP is not the same as an anonymous FTP site. To use the SFTP anonymous account, a password must be known by all users of the account. With traditional FTP anonymous access, any valid e-mail address can act as a password. This makes anonymous SFTP more like a shared-password account than a true anonymous access account.

SSH Tectia Server gives system administrators the ability to contain users to specific directories that appear to end users, to be at the root (/) level. This prevents users from accessing critical system files or seeing the entire directory structure. This is called *jailing* or *change-rooting* (chrooting) a user. The chrooting options inside of SSH Tectia Server are very nice to use. SSH Tectia Server provides options inside of the sshd2_config file that allow specific users and members of specific groups to be chrooted. Additionally, when using the ssh-dummy-shell, the account is only usable for file transfers and not for interactive shell access. This is ideal for users who only update website content or transfer data from one system to another.

The configuration options are documented in the man pages and the support area of the SSH site (http://www.ssh.com/support). Most of the tokens enable similar functionality or restrictions as compared to the options found in OpenSSH.

Configuration Differences

If you are attempting to maintain pristine configuration files for both of your SSH versions, remember that SSH Tectia uses /etc/ssh2/sshd2_config and OpenSSH uses /etc/ssh/sshd_config. Many administrators forget and might accidentally overwrite a good configuration file with one from a different SSH implementation, which will break the daemon until the configuration file is fixed.

■**Tip** Remember to use sshd -t to verify OpenSSH configuration before starting sshd with the new configuration.

The tokens in the configuration files also have differences. For example, PermitRootLogin in OpenSSH has yes, no, and without-password. In SSH Tectia, it is yes, no, and nopwd, which carries the same meaning.

If you work with both distributions enough, you will find yourself wishing that OpenSSH had some features of the SSH Communications Security product and vice versa.

Patching SSH Tectia Server

SSH Tectia does not rely on OpenSSL for product functionality. This can be a good thing because if a vulnerability is found in OpenSSL, the SSH Tectia Server is not affected because the Tectia line of products provides their own encryption libraries. However, because SSH Tectia Server is bundled with its own encryption libraries, vulnerabilities may be found in those that do not affect the open source products. Purchasing SSH Tectia Server for strictly security reasons is probably not a good justification for the purchase. Any software will require patches and updates.

For a number of years, OpenSSH was on SANS.org's *The Twenty Most Critical Internet Security Vulnerabilities* (http://www.sans.org/top20). This led to OpenSSH getting a bad reputation for needing to be patched several times a year for critical security flaws. The number of security flaws found in OpenSSH has dramatically decreased over the last couple years, so the difference in security vulnerabilities is becoming negligible. Keep in mind, though, that for OpenSSH, OpenSSL also needs to be patched. SSH Communications Security Tectia product provides its own encryption libraries that are patched when the product line is patched.

When using OpenSSH for systems other than Linux provided to you from your operating system vendor, such as OpenSSH for AIX 5L on the AIX Toolbox for Linux Applications website, patching can be difficult. Major UNIX vendors commonly wait weeks or months after the official OpenSSH site releases a patch before incorporating it into a usable OS binary package. This can be extremely frustrating. The quickest and best way to patch these systems is to compile OpenSSH from source, but then you are losing the package management functionality desired in the first place. Time lapse is normally not an issue with Linux distributions, because the packages are normally created within hours of OpenSSH publishing a fix. This time lapse has also been getting better with major UNIX vendors in the last 12 months.

In my experience, I have found patching OpenSSH to be easier than with the Tectia line of products. This is because of license file issues with SSH Tectia Server and because it breaks package dependencies in Linux. Overall, with key-based authentication, any SSH patch (commercial or open source) should have the ability to be rapidly deployed.

Working in a Mixed Environment

Oftentimes, it is difficult to standardize on the SSH Tectia product for various reasons. They could be as simple as not having enough licenses, or technically infeasible because embedded devices frequently ship with OpenSSH as the SSH implementation for secure connectivity.

SCP/SFTP

The worst part about working in a mixed environment, besides trying to remember the differences and manage them, is the inability to use scp from an OpenSSH client to a commercial SSH server. The OpenSSH implementation of scp is basically rcp code ported to run over the SSH protocol. SSH Communications Security chose to implement scp over the SFTP protocol in their protocol 2 implementation. This implies, and rightly so, that using sftp between OpenSSH and SSH Tectia works fine. Additionally, a file can be transferred via scp from a commercial client to an OpenSSH server. If you download the scp1 binary from an older version of SSH Secure Shell for Servers (or OpenSSH), scp can work, utilizing protocol 1.

```
stahnke@www ~> scp foo stahnke@rack:
stahnke@rack's password:
scp: warning: Executing scp1.
scp: FATAL: Executing ssh1 in compatibility mode failed (Check that
scp1 is in your PATH).
lost connection
```

If you are using a gateway architecture as discussed in Chapter 8, it is recommended that the gateway node(s) utilize the commercial SSH solution, so you can use scp for file transfers to all nodes in the environment. Key-based authentication, however, will require some modification.

Tip If you find yourself needing to use scp from an OpenSSH client to a Tectia Server, you can install the OpenSSH version of scp as /usr/local/bin/scp1. This will allow the SSH Tectia Server to accept scp connections from OpenSSH clients. scp1 must be in the same directory as the ssh/ssh2 binary.

SSH Keys

Key authentication differs in both file layout and that SSH Tectia Server is unable to authenticate using a key generated using OpenSSH, at least natively. Working with keys from OpenSSH to Tectia is challenging, but luckily OpenSSH includes some utilities to help manage the differences between the SSH implementations.

The ssh-keygen utility provided with OpenSSH allows private and public keys from SSH Communications Security, which are in the IETF SecSH format, to be imported and exported to and from OpenSSH. In my experience, I have found that using SSH Tectia Server private keys and exporting public keys into OpenSSH works with the least amount of hassle.

Importing private keys that have passphrases from SSH Tectia Server to OpenSSH is not possible. If the private key does not have passphrase, it can be done. The following command will import a passphrase-less private SSH Tectia Server key into an OpenSSH format. The use of a private key without passphrase is not recommended, but is demonstrated in this example for completeness:

```
stahnke@www: ~> ssh-keygen -i -f private_commercial_key > id_dsa
stahnke@www: ~> cat id_dsa
-----BEGIN DSA PRIVATE KEY-----
MIIBvAIBAAKBgQCsTv3n7Ry6/30YnwE/hDZLsIxBB5pWtDLDukuS53OqEXcP8vOQ
r30OZDJjLYzjsZr/9PpRneGrweHRgUGd+n8QDu2wvYPRcKYYJJukK/2S82FUHxCH
JrVFM6JbnrVZnfxK8zKMLOUbjrwwlfZnVEkyU6Eov3/vF5w2MDdN/BnKuwIVAJ1Y
XHFpsx3q+y2pMTKi5C9/BS7NAoGBAKWPd+wVYSG5onkdh5L4QDF89vPto3y5XFQR
58Oo2/Fi87RedXRtK6cS1Oted8qTOrVNMHuZCL/fBIAP28uCJplCXi7rkrDA85X4
qzXiX32KI6En9gzOUhCull8zdCiSFLFnizkKSSAX3oKp7ypT+mql38MrY99q4hIu
vIcqwW84AoGBAKZKn081ZiDyKOjwyqFGiKAXH2HSJmRup6I7VEOLhjb6LxQbKrEi
d676xHjeeDOknJ7BAjZoFgzMoMmcX9UjupCwo7TIEcjRh5L8acSBRmoyjx77Enev
U6YKw+XXiZZPBt1N6tY/XCyMPjyvJ5T2djqqlo4ytAgqDkfDKo62JD7JAhQjGp89
9bROrpyXr/TGLucI57P7hg==
-----END DSA PRIVATE KEY-----
```

Importing private keys from SSH Tectia to OpenSSH is not usually practical because most private keys (I would hope all of them) have passphrases. You can remove the passphrase of a private key, convert the private key, and then add a passphrase. However, the easiest way to work with both implementations is to import public keys from Tectia and put them in OpenSSH format. From there, just append the output to an authorized_keys file, and authentication should work as it normally does using OpenSSH. This code uses ssh-keygen to import commercial public keys and append that key to an OpenSSH authorized_keys file. This authorized_keys file can now be placed on a system running OpenSSH and allow clients using SSH Tectia Server keys to authenticate.

```
stahnke@www: ~> ssh-keygen -i -f commercial_public_key >> \
authorized_keys
stahnke@www: ~> cat authorized_keys
ssh-dss AAAAB3NzaC1kc3MAAACBAKxO/eftHLr/XRifAT+ENkuwjEEHmlaOMsO6S5Lnc6oRdw/
y85CvfQ5kMmMtjOOxmv/O+lGd4avCEdGBQZ36fxAO7bC9g9Fwphgkm6Qr/ZLzY5QfEI
cmtUUzoluetVmd/ErzMowvRRuOvDCV9mdUSTJToSi/f+8XnDYwNO38Gcq7ABAAFQCdW
FxxabMd6vstqTEyouQvfwUuzQAAAIEApY937BVhIbmieR2HkvhAMXz28+2jfLlcVBHn
zSjb8WLztF51dGOrpxLU6153ypM6tUOwe5kIv98EgA/by4ImmUJeLuuqsMDzlfirNeJ

ffYojoSf2DM5SEK6WXzNOGJIUsWeLOQpJIBfegqnvKlP6aqXfwytj32riEi68hyrBbz
gAAACBAKZKnO81ZiDyKOjwyqFGiKAXH2HSJmRup6I7VEOLhjb6LxQbKrEid676xHjee
DOknJ7BAjZoFgzMoMmcX9UjupCwo7TIEcjRh5L8acSBRmoyjx77EnevU6YKw+XXiZZP
Bt1N6tY/XCyMPjyvJ5T2djqqlo4ytAgqDkfDKo62JD7J
```

Agent forwarding also does not work when crossing distributions of SSH. This is not normally a significant problem, because you can simply return to your original connection host to get on the next machine. It can be a minor inconvenience in many instances.

Key Management

Key management when using commercial products and OpenSSH becomes more difficult. Normally, I still use an rpm, as shown in Chapter 8, but to build the rpm, I export all commercial SSH public keys to OpenSSH format and build both .ssh and .ssh2 directories for the accounts that I want the rpm to authorize. This is nice in case there is a need to change versions of SSH, as the user, or even yourself, will still be able to connect. Because RPM is supported on most major UNIX vendors, the same tasks that work on Linux apply to Solaris, AIX, etc.

This script is rather lengthy, but it really helps out administrators who have to deal with multiple SSH implementations. Be sure to have the OpenSSH-provided ssh-keygen on the system where you run this script. The script expects ssh-keygen to be in $BASE_DIR. This rpm generation script, presented in Listing 10-1, will convert all keys dropped in $BASE_DIR/ssh2 to OpenSSH format and make an rpm that has both commercial and OpenSSH public keys in their respective directories.

Listing 10-1. A Script That Creates an RPM with Both OpenSSH and IEF SecSH Format Public Keys

```
#!/bin/bash
#CONSTANTS
PATH=/bin:/usr/bin
OPEN_KEY_FILE=authorized_keys
TECTIA_KEY_FILE=authorization
ROOT_HOME=/root
BASE_DIR=/keys
SOURCE_DIR=redhat  #packages on SUSE
# $BASE_DIR/ssh2 is where I have administrators
# (who are authorized to be root on remote systems)
# drop off their public key. This directory should be group-writable.
# It does not need to be readable.
# The box I build this RPM on is VERY secure and is
# only accessible to system administrators.
```

```
# ssh2 is for Tectia
# ssh is for OpenSSH
# $BASE_DIR/ssh-keygen is the ssh-keygen provided with OpenSSH.

#Ensure we start in the correct directory
cd $BASE_DIR

#Remove old RPM if it is there
rm -f *rpm
#If OpenSSH directory does not exist, create it.
if [ ! -d $BASE_DIR/ssh ]
then
  mkdir -p $BASE_DIR/ssh
fi
#Remote Leftovers from last run
rm -f $BASE_DIR/ssh2/$TECTIA_KEY_FILE
chmod 600 $BASE_DIR/ssh2/*

#read in each ssh2 public key from $BASE_DIR/ssh2
#convert to OpenSSH public key
# provide a date for the comment.
dt=`date +%F`
# list ssh2 keys and sort them
for key in `find $BASE_DIR/ssh2 |grep -v ssh2$ |grep -v authorization |sort`
do
  # This step converts SSH.com keys to OpenSSH.
  echo "$key exported to SSH.com on $dt" >> $OPEN_KEY_FILE
  $BASE_DIR/ssh-keygen -i -f $key >> $OPEN_KEY_FILE
done
chmod 600 $OPEN_KEY_FILE
# Put newly created OpenSSH key file in proper place
mv -f $BASE_DIR/$OPEN_KEY_FILE $BASE_DIR/ssh

#build authorization file
cd $BASE_DIR/ssh2
ls -1 $BASE_DIR/ssh2 > $TECTIA_KEY_FILE
sed -e 's/^/key\ /g' $TECTIA_KEY_FILE > tmp
mv -f tmp $BASE_DIR/ssh2/$TECTIA_KEY_FILE
chmod 600 $TECTIA_KEY_FILE

#prepare files for rpmbuild, including spec file, and keys
cd $BASE_DIR
# Make hidden directories to tar up
mkdir $BASE_DIR/.ssh
mkdir $BASE_DIR/.ssh2
cp -pr $BASE_DIR/ssh/* $BASE_DIR/.ssh
cp -pr $BASE_DIR/ssh2/* $BASE_DIR/.ssh2
tar pcf temp_keys.tar .ssh .ssh2
```

```
mv -f $BASE_DIR/temp_keys.tar $ROOT_HOME
cd $ROOT_HOME
# take a backup of what is there
if [ -d $ROOT_HOME/.ssh ]
 then
  mv -f $ROOT_HOME/.ssh $ROOT_HOME/.ssh_rpm
fi
if [ -d $ROOT_HOME/.ssh2 ]
 then
  mv -f $ROOT_HOME/.ssh2 $ROOT_HOME/.ssh2_rpm
fi
# Extract newly created tar ball
# This puts keys in proper location for rpmbuild
tar xf $ROOT_HOME/temp_keys.tar

# Increment the release in spec file
# The first time you run this, this part will fail
# unless you set $rel above.
release=`cat $BASE_DIR/spec | grep Release | cut -d: -f2`
let "rel=$release+1"
echo "Preparing to build public-key-0-$rel.noarch.rpm"
#Create the SPEC file required for RPM build
# Echo the spec file
echo "Name: public-keys
Version: 0
Release: $rel
License: Free
Group: Security
BuildArch: noarch
Summary: Administrator Public SSH Keys
%description
public-keys is the collection of OpenSSH
public keys maintained by the Unix/Linux administration staff.
%pre
# If $ROOT_HOME/.ssh exists, move it.
if [ -d $ROOT_HOME/.ssh ]
then
  mv -f $ROOT_HOME/.ssh $ROOT_HOME/.ssh.rpmsave
  echo "$ROOT_HOME/.ssh saved as $ROOT_HOME/.ssh.rpmsave"
fi
#Package will contain the following files
%files
%defattr(-,root,root)
# OpenSSH files are always the same
%attr(0700,root,root) %dir $ROOT_HOME/.ssh
%attr(0600,root,root) $ROOT_HOME/.ssh/authorized_keys
#SSH Tectia Files require dynamic additions.
%attr(0700,root,root) %dir $ROOT_HOME/.ssh2" > $BASE_DIR/spec
```

```
#Add the dynamic file listing for ssh2.
cd $BASE_DIR/ssh2
echo "ls -1 | grep -v authorization | sed -e \
's/^/%attr(0600,root,root)\ \\$ROOT_HOME\/.ssh2\//g'" | sh  >> \
$BASE_DIR/spec
# cd back to working directory
cd $BASE_DIR
#build the RPM
cp -f $BASE_DIR/spec /usr/src/$SOURCE_DIR/SPECS
rpmbuild -ba /usr/src/$SOURCE_DIR/SPECS/spec
# Replace root's keys with what should be there
if [ -d $ROOT_HOME/.ssh_rpm ]
 then
   rm -rf $ROOT_HOME/.ssh
   mv -f $ROOT_HOME/.ssh_rpm $ROOT_HOME/.ssh
fi
if [ -d $ROOT_HOME/.ssh2_rpm ]
 then
   rm -rf $ROOT_HOME/.ssh2
   mv -f $ROOT_HOME/.ssh2_rpm $ROOT_HOME/.ssh2
fi
# Place new rpm in $BASE_DIR
cp -f  /usr/src/$SOURCE_DIR/RPMS/noarch/public-keys-0-$rel.noarch.rpm $BASE_DIR
# Remove the $BASE_DIR/ssh directory
rm -rf $BASE_DIR/ssh
rm -rf $BASE_DIR/.ssh
rm -rf $BASE_DIR/.ssh2
rm -f $ROOT_HOME/temp_keys.tar
exit 0
```

This script has saved me hours of work when performing key management. Obviously, this script is designed to build a public key setup for the root account on remote systems; however, it can be easily modified to work with any account.

Summary

This chapter provided some information about a primary alternative to OpenSSH, that being SSH Tectia Server from SSH Communications Security. These two solutions are prominent in enterprise environments. Also, because SSH Tectia Server is free for evaluation, home users can explore this option.

The discussion in this book is not intended to be so heavily focused on OpenSSH that working with any other SSH product is like starting over. I am confident you will find your way through any SSH distribution you choose to work with after understanding the material in this book.

The overall advice I would give anyone taking my SSH experience into account would be, if you can avoid creating a hybrid environment, you should ensure that happens. Supporting two different SSH implementations is certainly possible, but it takes away valuable administration time from other important tasks.

APPENDIX A

███

SSH Client Alternatives

The core material of this book is focused on UNIX/Linux-based OpenSSH systems. This involves typing instructions at the command-line prompt to perform an SSH connection. However, sometimes a graphical client offers an ideal alternative to the command-line client because it requires a lower learning curve for end users. Additionally, graphical clients can allow a Microsoft Windows operating system to connect to a UNIX or Linux machine via SSH without involving a command-line interface.

Using the OpenSSH client, the client options are configured through the system-wide ssh_config file and the individual user's $HOME/.ssh/config file. When using graphical clients, the options are managed from within each tool. The configuration options presented by the graphical tools are equivalent to the settings found in an ssh_config file because they attempt to comply with the SSH protocol as a whole. Also note that several clients other than what are covered in this appendix are available.

PuTTY Family

The PuTTY set of SSH client utilities is primarily used on the Microsoft Windows platform, although it is also available for UNIX systems. You can download and use it for free download from http://www.chiark.greenend.org.uk/~sgtatham/putty/download.html. The PuTTY set of tools includes PuTTY for terminal emulation, plink for command-line connectivity, PuTTYgen for key generation and management, Pageant for use as a graphical ssh-agent, PSCP for use as a command-line SCP utility, and PSFTP for use as an SFTP command-line client.

PuTTY

PuTTY is a free connectivity tool used for terminal emulation. PuTTY can be used for SSH connections, supports protocols 1 and 2, and also can connect to machines via rsh/telnet if that is desired.

I commonly recommend PuTTY as an SSH client because of its price and features. PuTTY is a lightweight, yet full-featured client, weighing in at around 415KB. Although an installer is available, you can choose to also download the executable, so getting started is as simple as double-clicking the downloaded executable.

The PuTTY configuration screen, shown in Figure A-1, opens when the executable is started. The more granular configuration options are controlled via the context menus on the left side of the screen. The main session information is controlled on the right side.

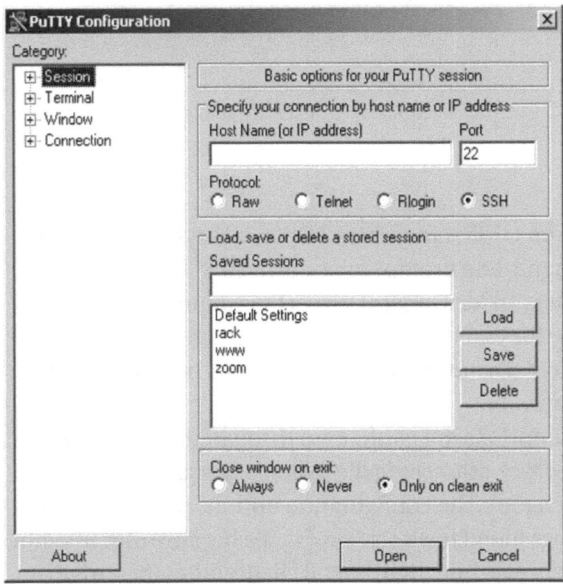

Figure A-1. *The PuTTY configuration screen*

Configuring PuTTY is not all that different from configuring the ssh command-line client. Most, if not all, of the options available to the ssh command-line client are found within the configuration options of PuTTY.

The default configuration for PuTTY is usually adequate for most users; however, there are a few defaults you might consider changing. For instance, sometimes it is necessary to scroll back through many session lines for debugging purposes. To lengthen the history, enable 9999 lines of scrollback capabilities, as shown in Figure A-2.

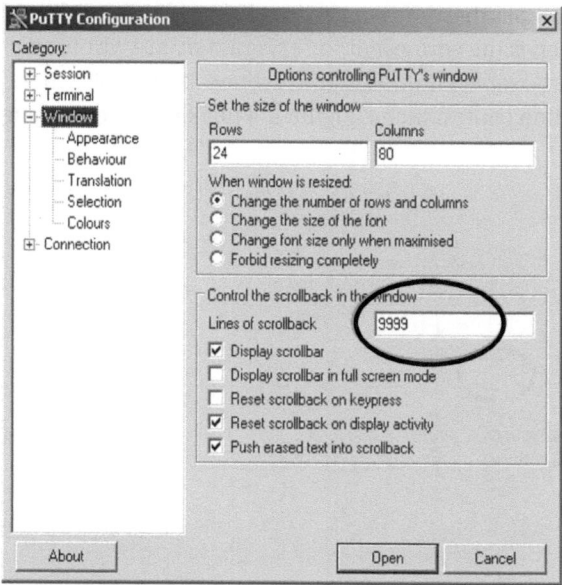

Figure A-2. *Configuring PuTTY with a larger scrollback buffer*

Also, it is quite convenient to be able to run the terminal session in full-screen mode. If this is enabled, pressing Alt+Enter will toggle full-screen mode of a PuTTY session as shown in Figure A-3.

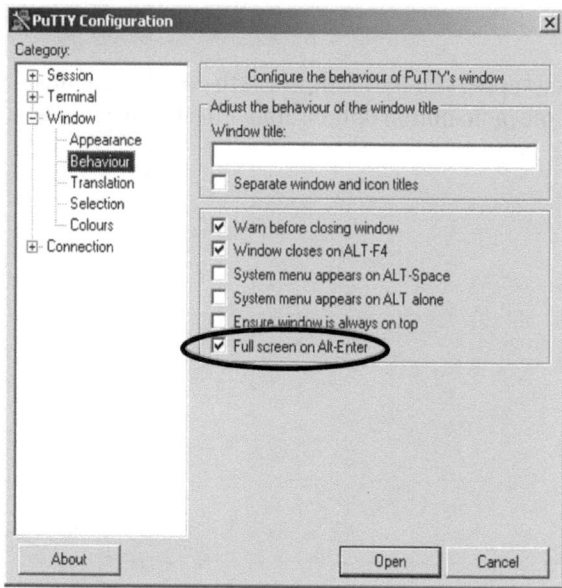

Figure A-3. *Enabling full-screen mode with PuTTY*

When working with SSH servers and firewalls that drop connections if they are idle, enabling the keep-alive feature can be useful, which is the equivalent to `ServerAliveInterval` in the `ssh_config` file. This will communicate to the server/firewall that the connection is still active. This can be configured under the Connection context menu. Figure A-4 highlights the relevant setting.

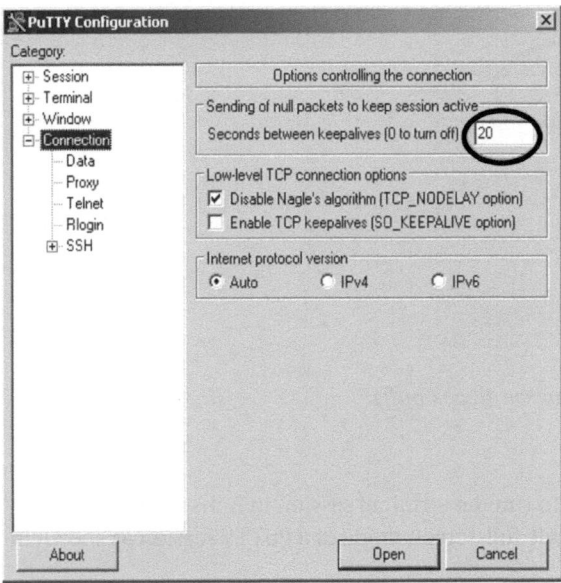

Figure A-4. *Enabling a keep-alive from PuTTY*

For security reasons, consider disabling support for SSH protocol 1. To do this, you must select 2 only, as shown in Figure A-5, from the radio button options under the Connection ➤ SSH context menu.

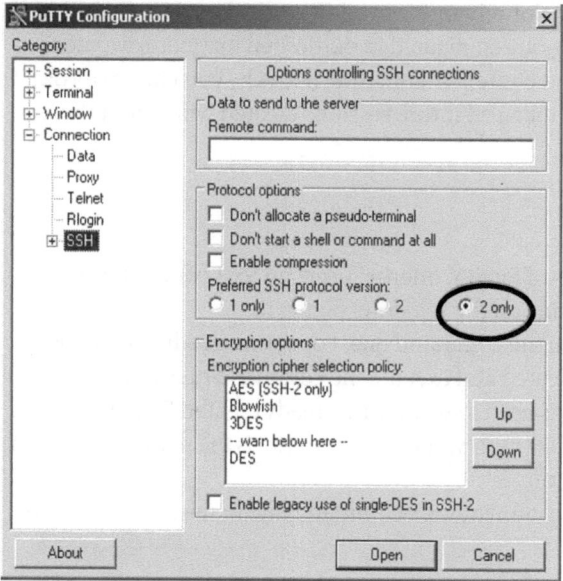

Figure A-5. *Ensuring only protocol 2 is allowed*

Enabling X11 forwarding is a common requirement. PuTTY does not provide an X-Server, so an external program must be used such as Cygwin (see Appendix B). X11 forwarding is configured by going through the Connection ➤ SSH ➤ X11 context menu, to bring up the configuration window shown in Figure A-6. The location for the X display is also configured on this screen.

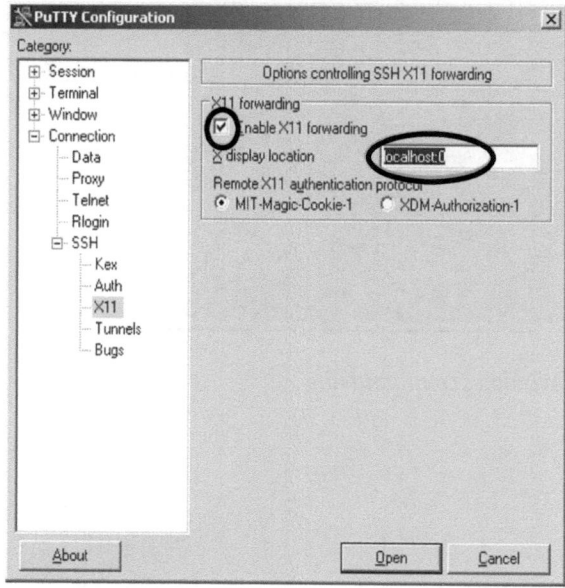

Figure A-6. *Configuration of X11 forwarding is simple with PuTTY.*

Tunnels, automatic usernames, and color schemes can additionally be controlled within the PuTTY configuration. Once your settings are configured in the desired manner, save your session by naming it while under the Session context menu. Alternatively, you can save your session as the Default Session, which will mean all future sessions created will inherit those settings.

plink

plink is another tool from the maintainers of PuTTY, offering users an SSH command-line interface, something not otherwise available on the Windows platform.

plink can be executed directly or from the command line. For command-line execution, navigate to the directory where plink is located and execute the command `plink`, which will display a set of options. Most often, plink is used to work with already created PuTTY sessions. To do this, the syntax is `plink -load session_name`, where `session_name` is the name of a session you have saved in your PuTTY configuration.

For example, to connect via the Microsoft Windows command line to the server www, the command string looks like this:

```
%>plink -load www
```

Figure A-7 depicts a plink connection. Note that because the Windows command line does not handle terminal emulation well, any output attempting to display a control character or colors will be outputted as its ASCII values, rather than interpreted.

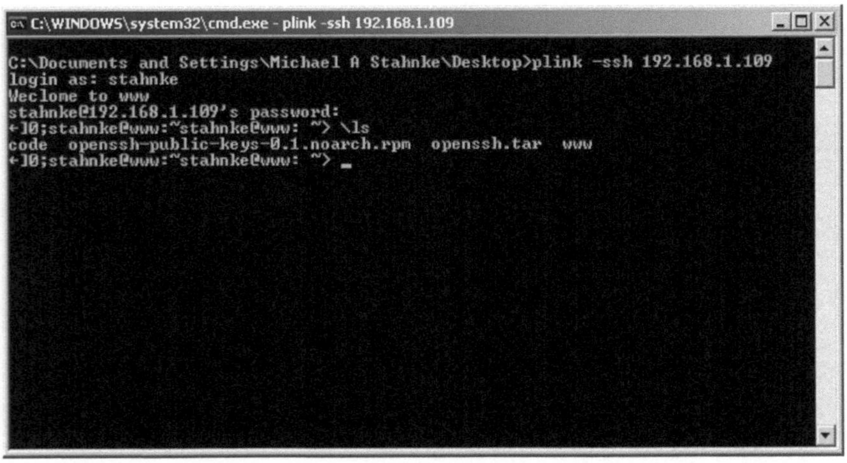

Figure A-7. *Using plink from the Microsoft Windows command line*

PuTTYgen

PuTTYgen is the SSH key generator for PuTTY and its utilities. These keys can be used to connect to remote systems using key-based authentication. PuTTYgen is very similar to its command-line counterpart, ssh-keygen. PuTTYgen can generate RSA and DSA keys for a user, and also has the ability to convert keys from the OpenSSH format to the IETF (Internet Engineering Task Force) SecSH standard, which is used by SSH Communications Security.

To use PuTTYgen, select your key parameters and click the Generate button, as shown in Figure A-8. The generation of the key will require some mouse movement as a source of entropy (randomness) during the generation process. This makes the key more difficult to predict. Upon completion of the generation, enter in a passphrase. PuTTYgen provides the exact text that can be pasted into an authorized_keys file to set up public key authentication, which can be seen in Figure A-9. It can also regenerate public keys from private keys, and change passphrases of private keys.

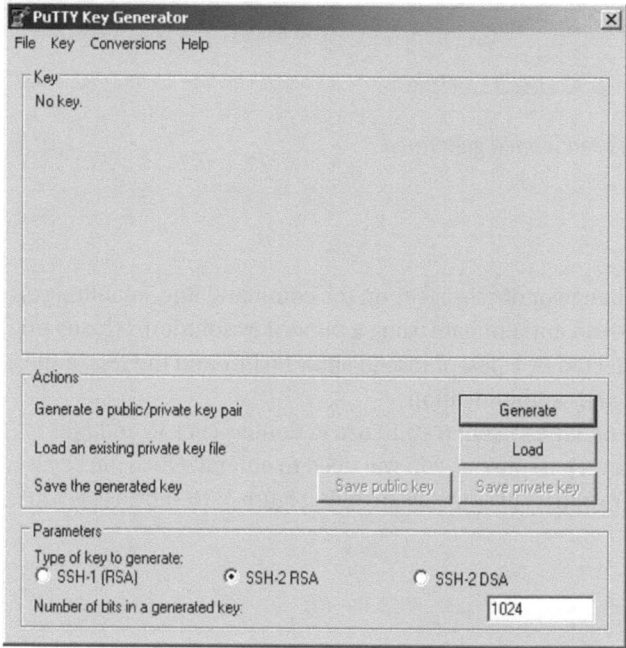

Figure A-8. *The default PuTTYgen screen*

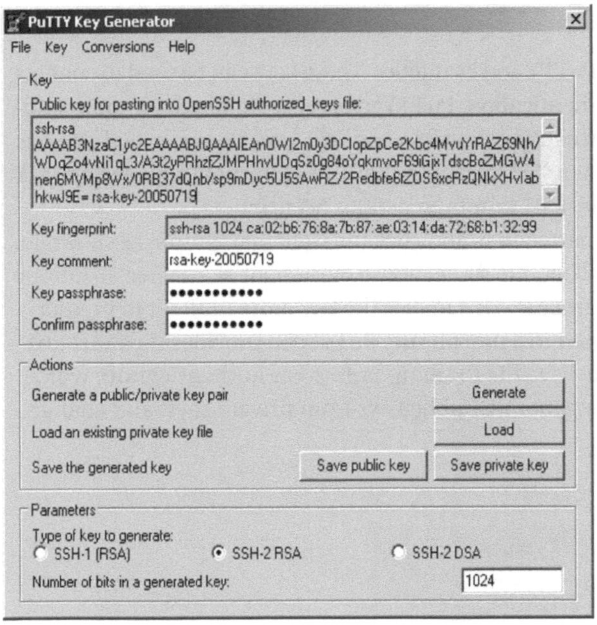

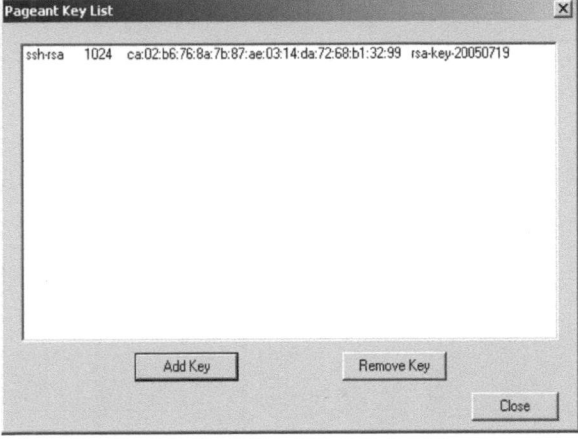

Figure A-9. *PuTTYgen after a key has been loaded/generated*

Pageant

The Pageant program emulates the behavior of `ssh-agent` on the command line, enabling you to log in without a password and instead authenticate using a public key solution. It loads private key files that are optionally protected by a passphrase to allow PuTTY and the rest of the PuTTY utilities to make use of public key authentication.

Upon starting Pageant, it will run in the system tray. To use it, double-click it, and add a private key. If the key is protected by a passphrase, you will need to enter it. Once the key is loaded in the agent, the other PuTTY utilities become aware of it. Figure A-10 shows Pageant listing the private keys loaded into it.

Figure A-10. *Pageant displaying the keys loaded into the agent*

Once the key is loaded, the PuTTY tools will try to authenticate using the key(s) from that agent, as shown in Figure A-11. When a PuTTY connection is attempted, all you need to do is specify the appropriate username, and authentication completes. Optionally, you can instruct PuTTY to use different keys for different saved sessions. Also, usernames can be stored inside of each session, which means that connections can be made without typing a single keystroke once Pageant is loaded.

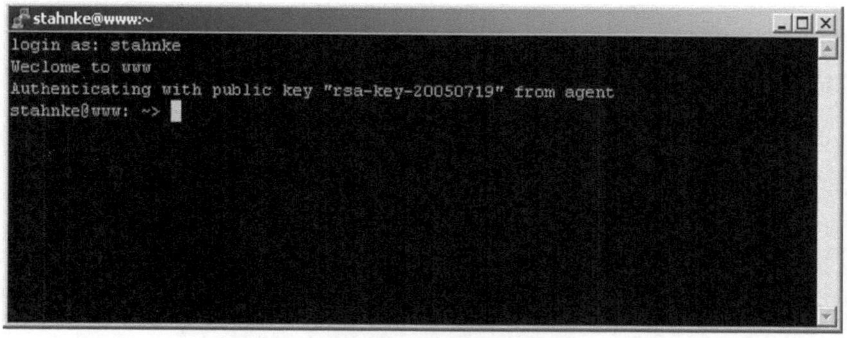

Figure A-11. *Authentication in PuTTY is handled by Pageant.*

PSCP

PSCP is a command-line utility similar to plink, capable of carrying out SCP- and SFTP-based tasks. This is ideal if transferring files to SSH Tectia Server and to OpenSSH servers. PSCP is shown in Figure A-12. PSCP can also use Pageant. PSCP is unable to be executed without supplying the proper arguments.

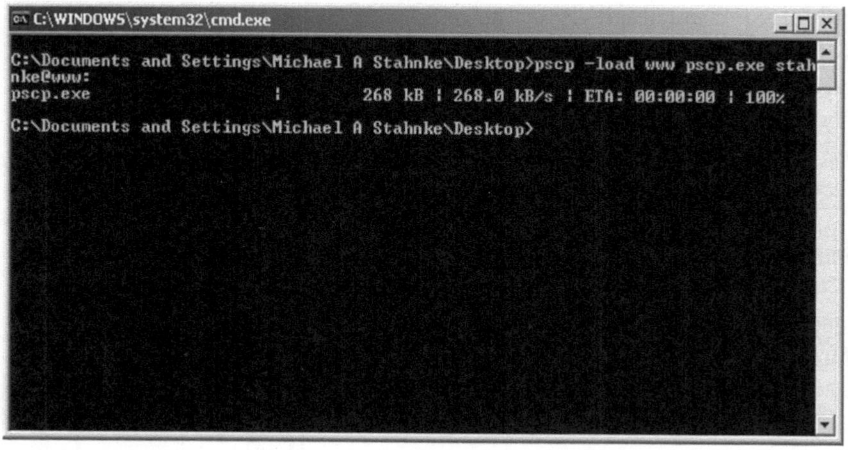

Figure A-12. *SCP connection from the Microsoft Windows command line*

PSFTP

PSFTP is an SFTP client that can be run interactively by double-clicking the executable. At the command line, type **open** and then a hostname, session name from PuTTY, or an IP address. You will then be prompted for a username if your PuTTY session did not define it. Figure A-13 shows a connection established with PSFTP.

Once connected, normal SFTP commands are used such as get, put, and ls.

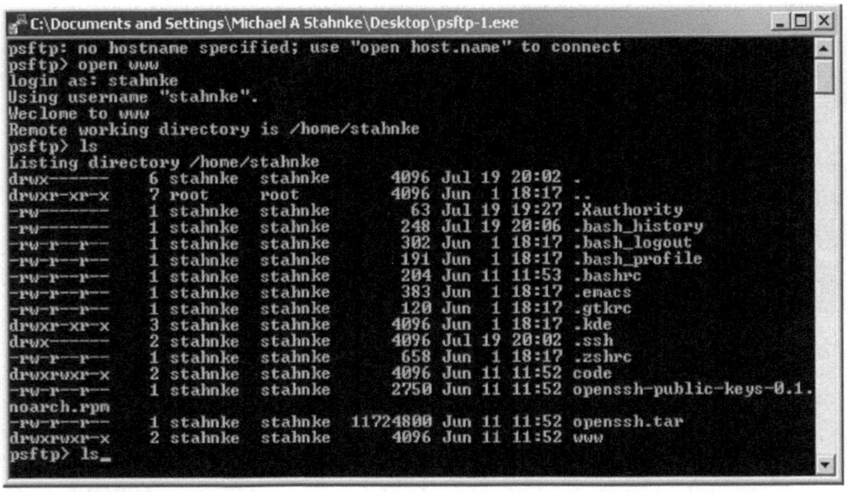

Figure A-13. *PSFTP is an SFTP client for Microsoft Windows.*

PuTTY Summary

The PuTTY family of SSH client utilities is very powerful and does not require installations nor large amounts of disk space to operate. Also, because it is available under the MIT license, it can be used and even incorporated into other projects, without royalties.

I commonly find myself using PuTTY when I arrive at a Microsoft Windows desktop. The PuTTY suite and a few keys can easily fit on a floppy disk or a USB keychain drive. PuTTY even works if my account does not have administrator authority because PuTTY does not have an installer.

As a terminal emulation program, I find PuTTY to be my favorite. However, the command-line utilities for SCP and SFTP are perhaps sometimes too complicated for end users. The next section of this appendix covers some graphical alternatives to PSCP and PSFTP on the Microsoft Windows platform.

WinSCP

WinSCP (http://www.winscp.net/) is my favorite file transfer program for the Windows operating system. WinSCP can be downloaded as a stand-alone application or an installation package, with the difference being the installer adds WinSCP to the Windows Add/Remove Programs menu, adds a desktop and Start menu link, and also optionally will add WinSCP to the Microsoft Explorer Send To Menu.

WinSCP has a similar setup to PuTTY. Options are available on the left side of the screen through expandable context menus. To create a similar environment to the PuTTY environment established in the previous section, navigate to the SSH context menu and specify protocol 2 only by choosing the 2 only radio button option, as shown in Figure A-14.

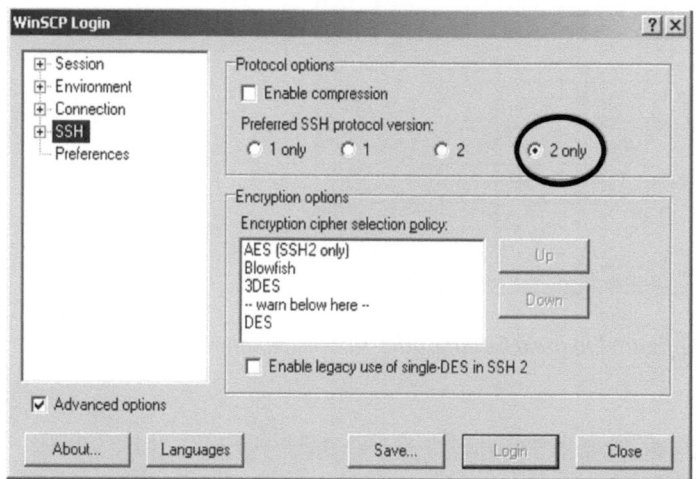

Figure A-14. *Configuring WinSCP for SSH protocol 2 only*

WinSCP can also import PuTTY sessions natively. This is a wonderful feature. To use it, navigate to Sessions ➤ Stored sessions and click Tools, located on the right side of the window. After clicking Import, you can choose which PuTTY session you would like to import. Sessions can also be defined in WinSCP only and saved.

WinSCP has two modes, Commander-like and Explorer-like. These can be changed, as shown in Figure A-15. The Commander-like interface has the local directory structure on the left side and the remote directory structure on the right, as shown in Figure A-16. To transfer files, use drag and drop. The Explorer-like interface, provided in Figure A-17, only shows the remote system. Drag and drop is once again utilized. To configure which mode WinSCP uses, navigate to Preferences in the context menu and make your choice.

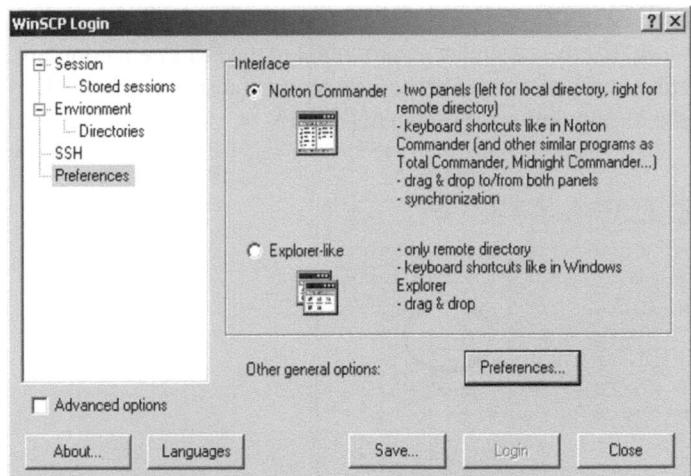

Figure A-15. *WinSCP can be configured to use a Commander-like or Explorer-like interface.*

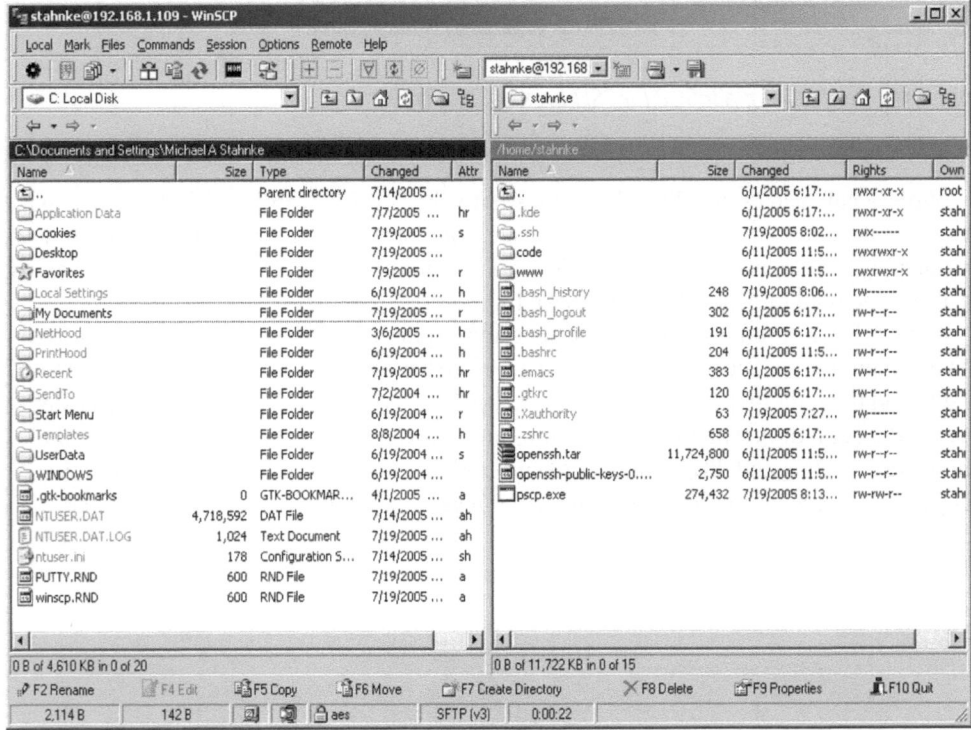

Figure A-16. *WinSCP using the Commander-like interface*

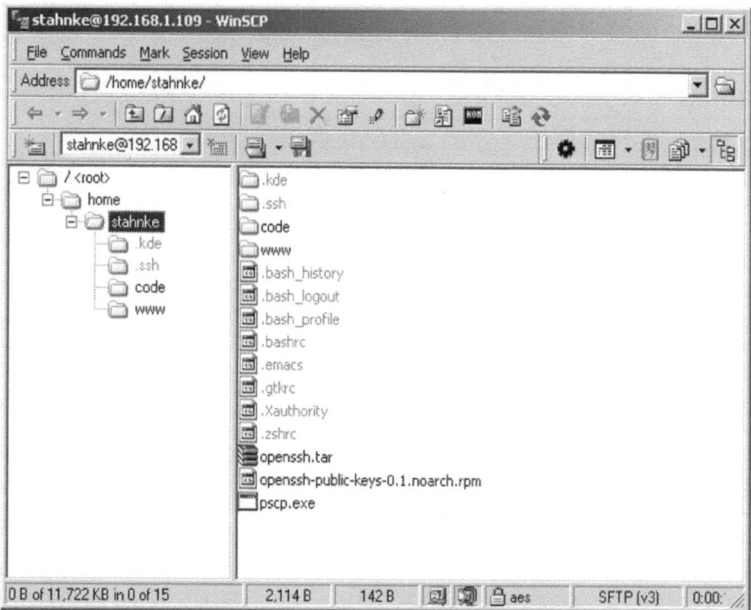

Figure A-17. *WinSCP using the Explorer-like interface*

WinSCP has many other options that can be adjusted to meet your configuration needs. However, in most cases, the default settings will have enough flexibility for end users. Inside the session options of the context menu, a shortcut icon can also be created. This allows for a simple double-click to connect to a remote system.

Caution Although WinSCP can use PuTTYgen private keys, it can also store passwords. This means that commands can be executed through WinSCP using that account and password if access to the desktop compputer is gained. Key-based authentication has the additional security of a passphrase on the private key, providing you choose to protect your private key with a passphrase.

FISH

Files over SSH (FISH) is not an official protocol, but can be utilized from Konqueror when using the K Desktop Environment (KDE, http://www.kde.org). If you are running a KDE desktop, FISH can be used to connect to remote hosts over SFTP.

When using FISH, enter fish://user@hostname from the Konqueror address bar to connect to a remote host, as shown in Figure A-18. All KDE applications are aware of the FISH protocol option, but other applications may not be.

FISH is basically equivalent to using WinSCP to connect to a remote system. Files can be copied via drag and drop.

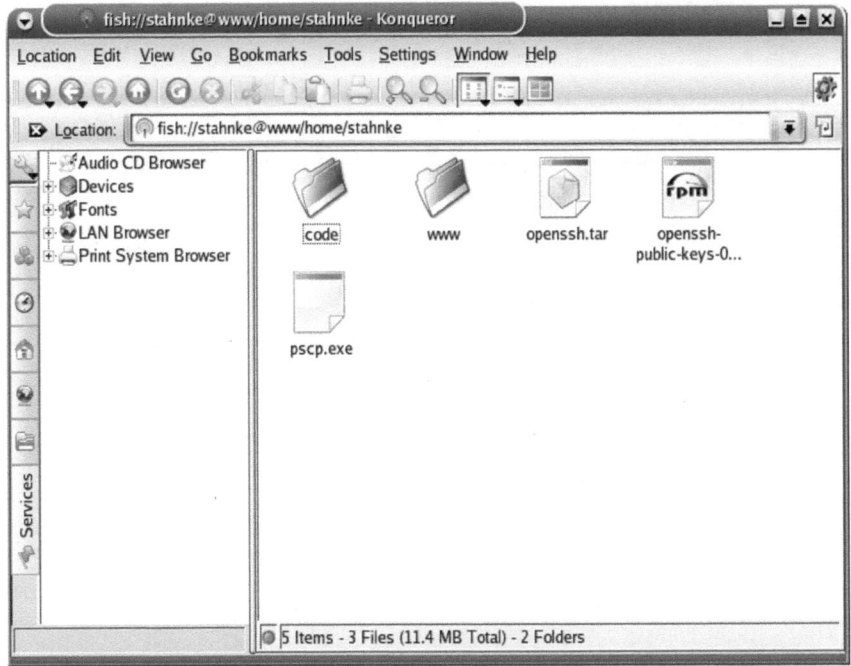

Figure A-18. *Konqueror using the FISH address option*

FileZilla

FileZilla (http://filezilla.sourceforge.net) is a common alternative to WinSCP for secure file transfer. It is very similar to most graphical FTP clients; in fact, it even supports FTP, FTP over SSL, and SFTP. FileZilla is freely available, as it is licensed under the GPL. If your account is not in the administrators group on Windows, FileZilla can be installed without touching the Windows registry.

After installation, a connection must be set up. The initial screen looks very crowded, but most of it is useful. The initial screen is shown in Figure A-19.

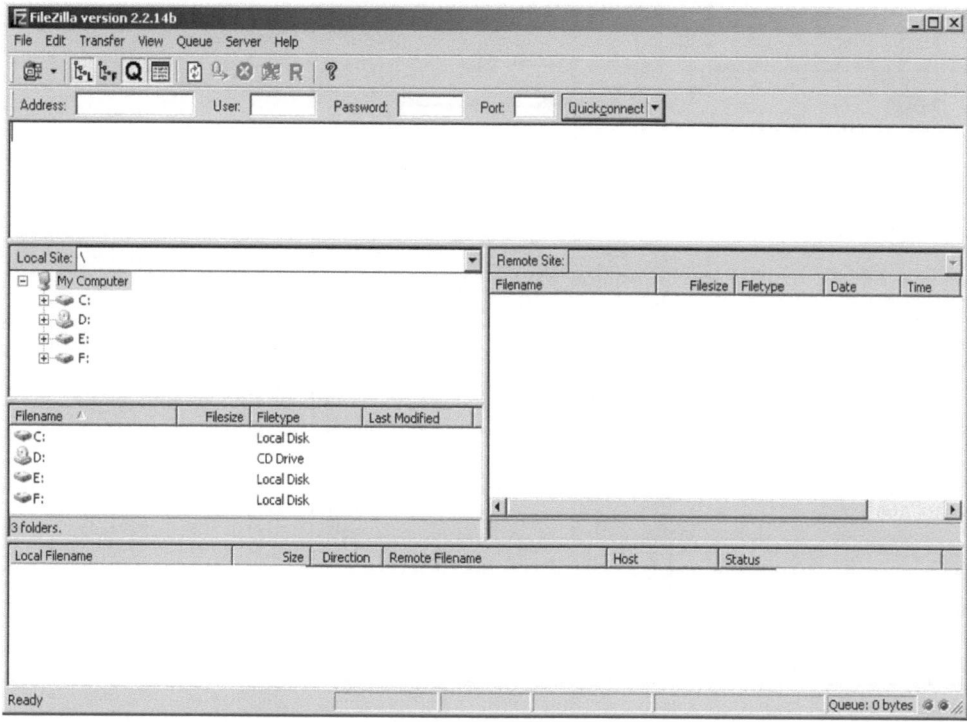

Figure A-19. *The initial FileZilla screen*

To set up a new connection, click File ➤ Site Manager. From there, create your connection. Be sure to change the default ServerType option from FTP to SFTP Using SSH2. You then need to specify a username and password, as anonymous logins are not supported via SFTP. My connection to remote system www looks like what you see in Figure A-20.

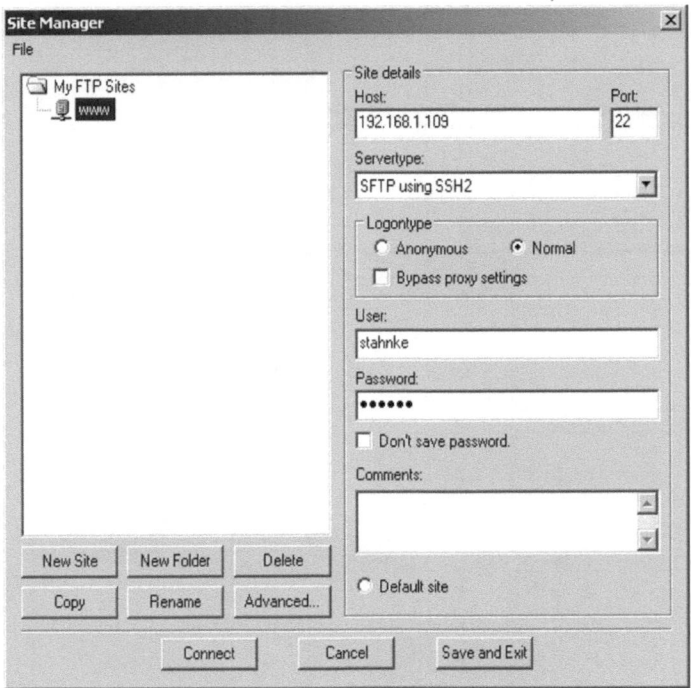

Figure A-20. *A Site Manager window in FileZilla configured for a remote SFTP connection*

After configuring the connection, click the network icon to select your connection. FileZilla provides messages and log information at the top, remote file listing on the right, and local file listing on the left. The bottom of the window is the transfer queue. Files are transferred via double-click or drag and drop. A connection screen via FileZilla is shown in Figure A-21.

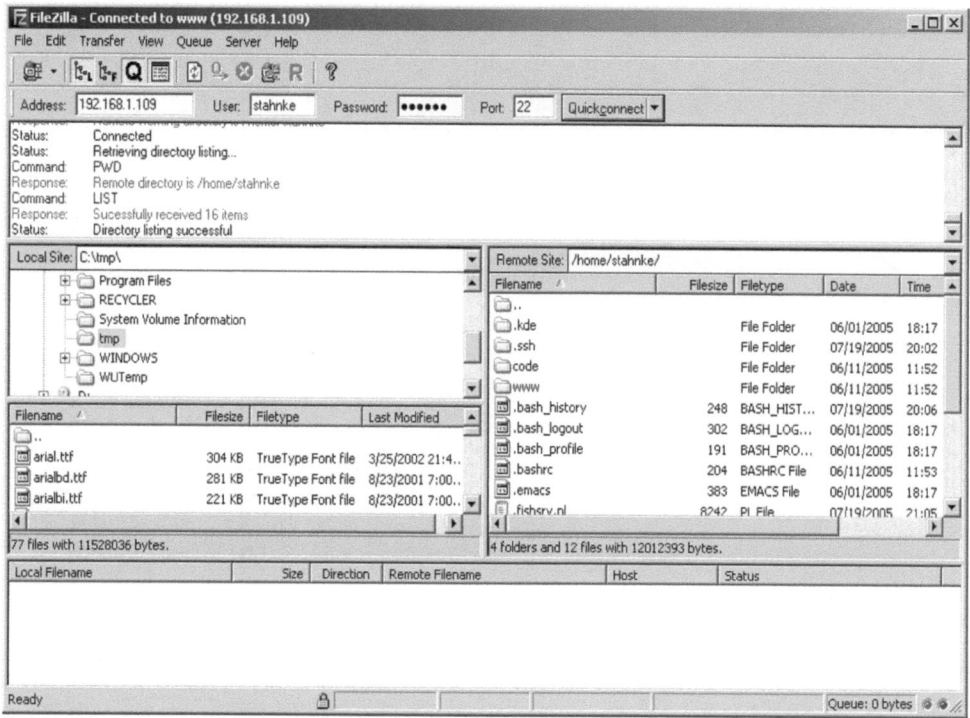

Figure A-21. *An established SFTP connection via FileZilla*

SSH Tectia Client

The SSH Tectia Client from SSH Communications Security is a commercial SSH client that has some nice features. As with the rest of the clients mentioned in this appendix, the Tectia Client can be used in conjunction with both OpenSSH and commercial SSH implementations.

Installing the Tectia Client is a straightforward process. Run the TectiaClient-4.x.x.xx.msi file where the x characters are replaced with the version of the client you are running. An installation wizard will begin. After accepting the license agreement, clicking Next and accepting the defaults will complete the installation.

The SSH Tectia Client is shown in Figure A-22. Connections can be saved in profiles inside of the client. Additionally, ad hoc connection setups can be created using the Quick Connect button. Once a connection is established to a remote system via the Quick Connect option, it can be saved into a profile. By default, the SSH Tectia Client will warn the user if it is making an SSH Protocol 1 connection.

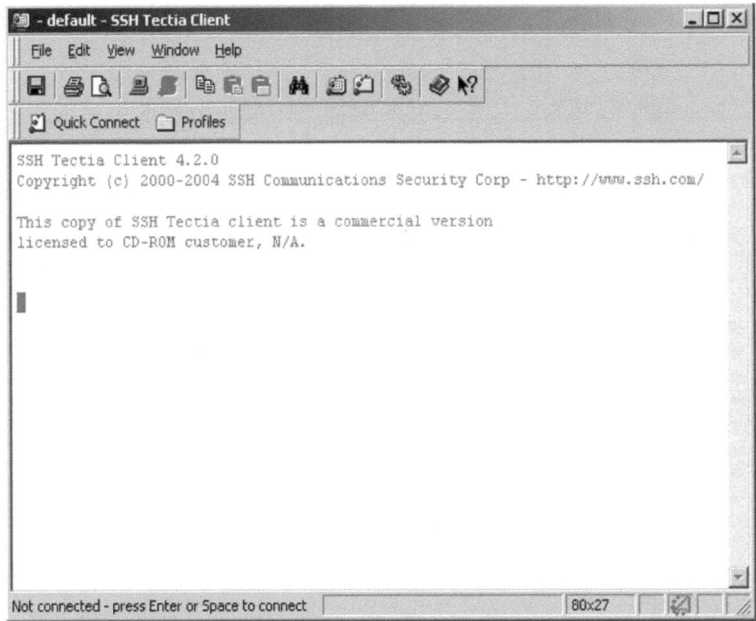

Figure A-22. *The SSH Tectia Client window*

After establishing a connection, the SSH Tectia Client has several very nice options. If you find the need to have more than one connection open to a system, perhaps to edit source in one window and compile/run the source in another, the SSH Tectia Client has the ability to simply open new terminal connections without additional authentication. This is similar to the functionality of ControlMaster and ControlPath with the command-line OpenSSH ssh client.

If you are connected to a system and need to transfer files to it, you can click the New File Transfer Window icon to create a new window with drag-and-drop file transfers, very similar to WinSCP or FileZilla.

Session options similar to those found in the ssh_config can be made for the entire SSH Tectia Client by clicking Edit ➤ Settings. Settings can also be made per connection profile, similar to a $HOME/.ssh/config file using the edit profiles option shown in Figure A-23. Most often, editing the Tunneling tab is enough to make this connectivity client very usable. Check the box for X11 forwarding if that is desired. Figure A-24 shows a configuration with a tunnel already created for Telnet to my remote system www via a localhost connection on port 12345.

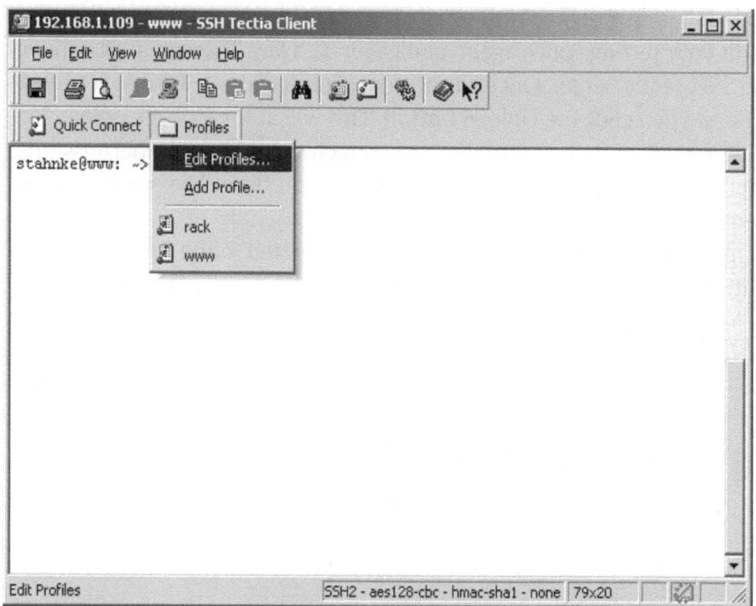

Figure A-23. *Editing Profiles setting in the SSH Tectia Client*

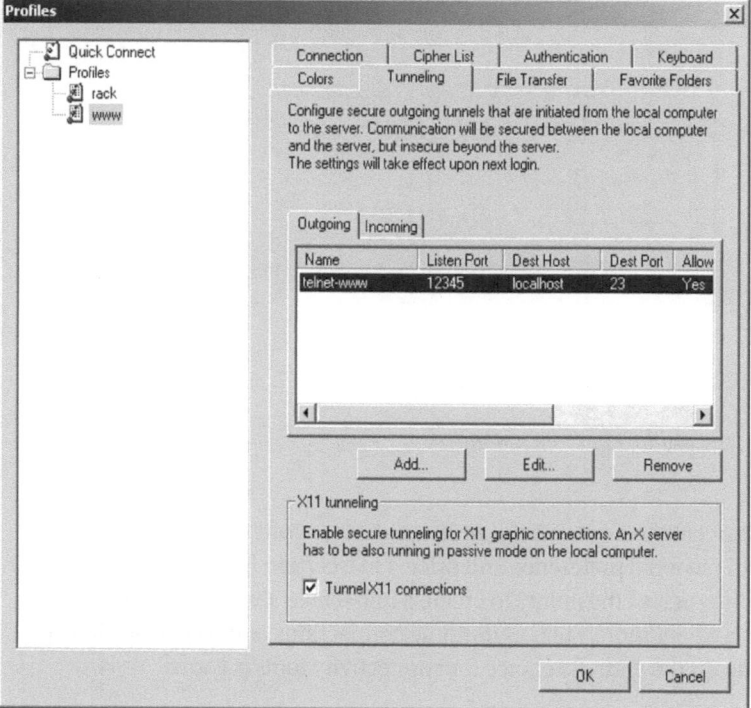

Figure A-24. *Creating and removing tunnels is easy via the SSH Tectia Client.*

Public key authentication is also very easy to set up, if you are using the SSH Tectia Server with the Tectia Client. Edit your settings once again, and generate a key. Then create a connection to a system running SSH Tectia Server. Once connected, click Settings ➤ Global Setting ➤ User Authentication ➤ Keys. Then click the Upload button. This will automatically upload your key, as shown in Figure A-25, and place it in the .ssh2 directory with proper permissions. Then next time a connection is attempted to the remote system, you should be prompted for a passphrase and connect via public key authentication.

If you are utilizing OpenSSH private keys, the key can be converted to the SecSH format by using the OpenSSH utility ssh-keygen as in this example, run from a command line:

stahnma@rack:~> **ssh-keygen -i -f .ssh2/SecSH_rsa**

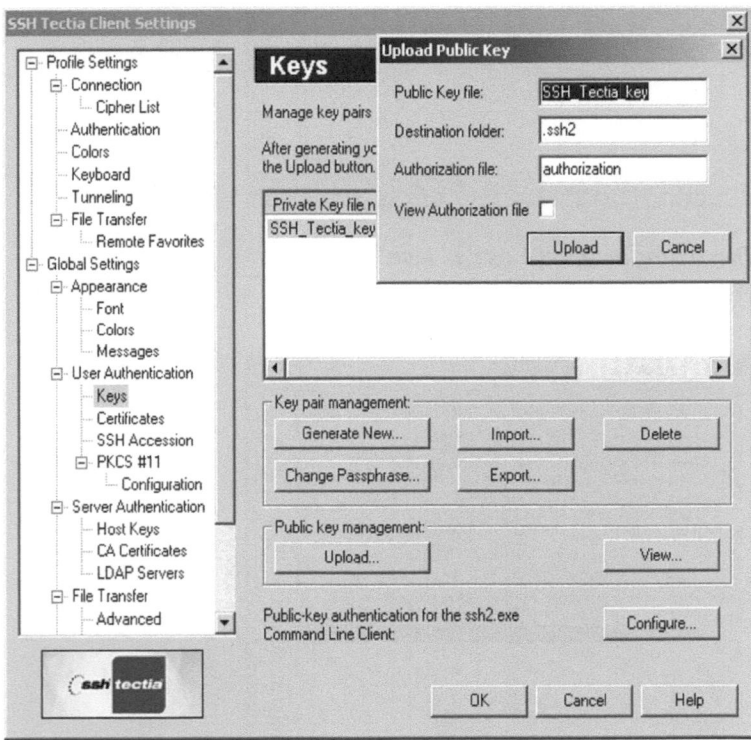

Figure A-25. *Configuring the public key to be uploaded*

The SSH Tectia Client can be a very useful utility, although your personal choice will ultimately come down to personal preference and price. I like certain features of PuTTY more than the SSH Tectia Client, such as the ability to create a full-screen session, and I like some features of the SSH Tectia Client more, such as multiple connections at the click of a button and the ease of tunneling. In the end, the choice for connectivity tools is yours.

Tip The SSH Tectia Client also installs binaries for clients that can be used from the Windows command line. The connectivity binary is called ssh2.

Summary

There are several other options available, both freely and for purchase; however, the software packages introduced in this chapter seem to be the most popular. Improvements will be made on all of these clients over time, and new clients may be developed that leave these looking like legacy connectivity options. Connection tool choices are up to you. Remember that if you are using SSH, regardless of the connectivity tools, you are more secure than when you started.

APPENDIX B

###

OpenSSH on Windows

Information technology architects, integrators, and system administrators often require a multiplatform environment in order to most effectively do their jobs. However, in today's computing world, many home network and data centers alike rely on a blend of Microsoft Windows and UNIX/Linux platforms. As you learned in Appendix A, OpenSSH clients are available for the Windows operating system, making cross-platform communications a trivial matter. Sometimes, however, running an OpenSSH server on Windows can be quite convenient.

While other cross-platform communication solutions are available—Samba (`http://www.samba.org`), for instance—my experience has shown that such solutions require a UNIX administrator to have a wealth of Windows knowledge to make them work efficiently and securely. Thankfully, the SSH protocol works in the same manner regardless of what platform hosts the SSH daemon. This makes working with SSH on Windows systems easier because of the previous understanding of SSH that has been developed on UNIX systems.

OpenSSH via Cygwin

The official OpenSSH website does not offer an OpenSSH binary for Microsoft Windows. It does, however, provide a Cygwin (`http://www.cygwin.com`) implementation. There have been other attempts, most of which are no longer maintained, of porting OpenSSH to Windows, but they relied on Cygwin in some respect.

Introduction to Cygwin

Cygwin provides a UNIX/Linux-type environment inside of a Windows system. It allows for installation of many common UNIX/Linux utilities, including OpenSSH, `rsync`, `perl`, `bash`, `vi`, and many more. The core of Cygwin is implemented as a Windows DLL file with other files included for support. Programs can then be compiled against the Cygwin DLL and libraries to work in a Cygwin environment. Traditional UNIX/Linux binaries will not run on Cygwin without recompiling them from their source inside the Cygwin environment.

Downloading and Installing Cygwin

The first step to installing Cygwin is of course to download it. The Cygwin package is a network-based installer that is only 280K. The installer has hundreds of packages that can be selected for installation. To download the installer, click on a link to the Cygwin `setup.exe` file found throughout the Cygwin home page.

To install Cygwin, run the downloaded setup.exe file by double-clicking on it. The installer will ask if you would like to install from the Internet, download without installing the files, or install from local files. The default Install from Internet option, shown in Figure B-1, is fine for most situations.

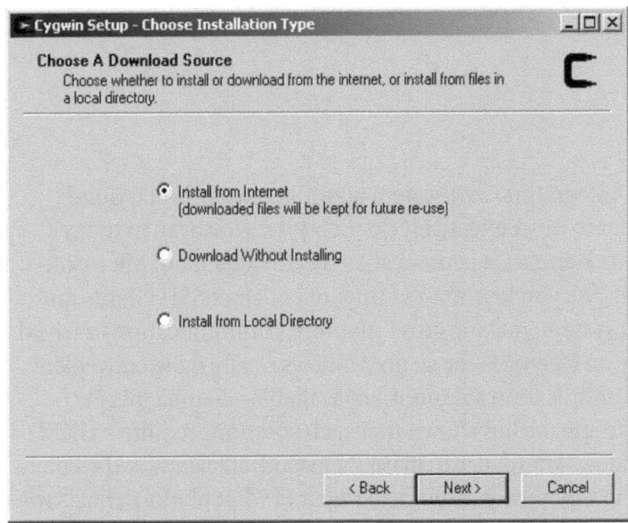

Figure B-1. *Cygwin installation via a direct Internet connection*

Once the package metadata information has been downloaded, you will be presented with a screen that allows for package selection. There are hundreds of packages to choose from. If you are particularly fond of a package, feel free to install it, as it should not conflict with OpenSSH.

OpenSSH is not installed by default. To install it, click the View button. The package selection view will then change to a full package listing. From there, navigate down to openssh under the Package heading, as shown in Figure B-2. The installation value will toggle if the Skip icon is clicked. Click it, and the OpenSSH version will appear. The dependencies for OpenSSH, such as zlib and OpenSSL, will automatically be selected.

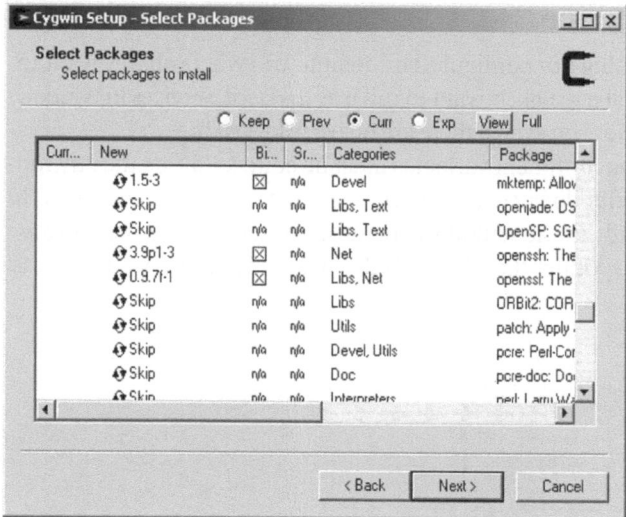

Figure B-2. *Cygwin package selection*

Click Next, and the package download will begin. This may require a considerable amount of time depending on network speed and the amount of packages you selected.

Tip The vi editor is not installed by default, and I find that to accomplish almost anything in a UNIX-type environment, an editor is required. You might want to install the editor of your choosing.

Once installed, click the Cygwin icon that has been placed on your Desktop or in the Start Menu. It will launch a bash shell session, as shown in Figure B-3.

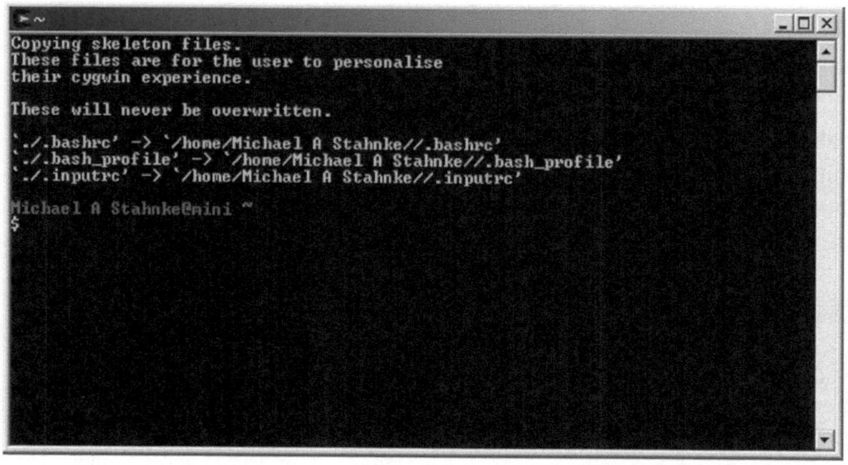

```
Copying skeleton files.
These files are for the user to personalise
their cygwin experience.

These will never be overwritten.

'./.bashrc' -> '/home/Michael A Stahnke//.bashrc'
'./.bash_profile' -> '/home/Michael A Stahnke//.bash_profile'
'./.inputrc' -> '/home/Michael A Stahnke//.inputrc'

Michael A Stahnke@mini ~
$
```

Figure B-3. *A* bash *shell launched from Cygwin*

Configuring sshd as a Service

Once installed, sshd is neither running nor configured by default. You will probably want to change this behavior because you will most likely want to run it as a *service*. Services in Windows are like daemons in UNIX/Linux—they run even if there are no users logged in.

To run sshd as a service, a few environment variables must be edited. Editing the environment variables can be done via a script (located at /usr/bin/ssh-host-config) or manually. To edit environment variables manually in the Windows operating system, right-click the My Computer icon and click Properties. Under the Advanced tab, click Environment Variables, as shown in Figure B-4.

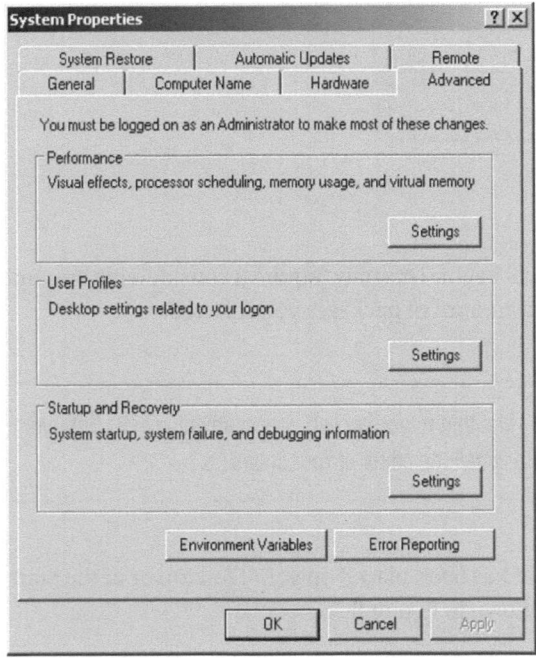

Figure B-4. *Click the* Environment Variables *button.*

A new variable called CYGWIN must be added. This variable will set the Cygwin security mechanism, configuring Cygwin to use the Windows security mechanism for managing user information. The value of this environment variable should be ntsec tty, as shown in Figure B-5.

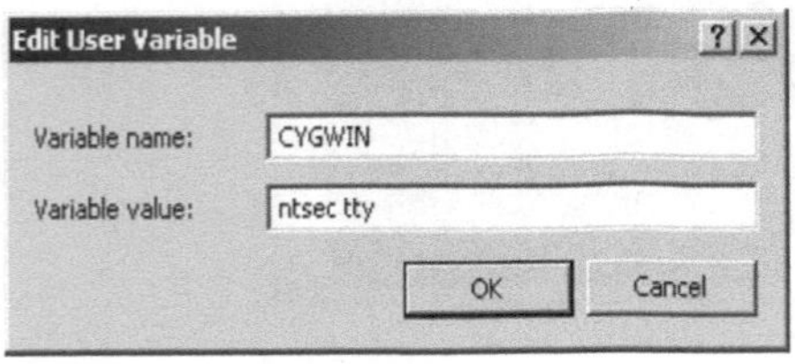

Figure B-5. *Setting the* CYGWIN *environment variable in Windows*

You should also add C:\cygwin\bin (or your Cygwin directory if not at the default location) to the PATH variable. To do this, click on PATH and click Edit.

To start sshd as a service, you can use the command line within Cygwin or a normal Windows command line, and type net start sshd. To stop sshd, type net stop sshd. Starting and stopping sshd as a service is shown in Figures B-6 and B-7.

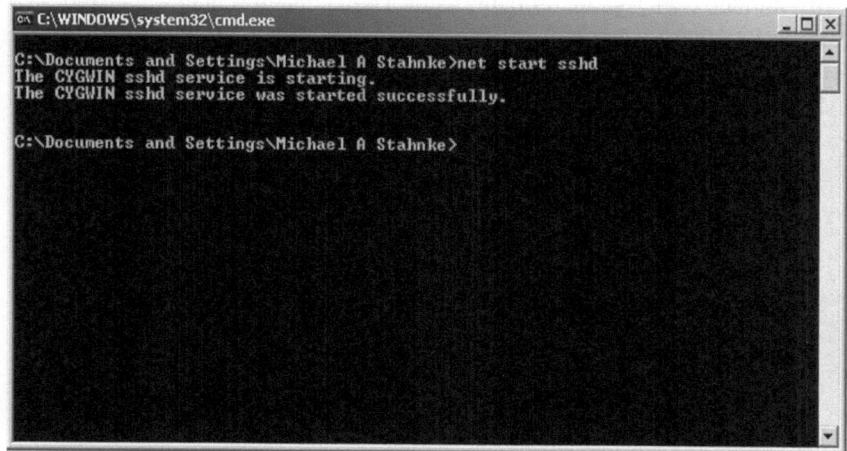

Figure B-6. *Starting the Cygwin* sshd *service*

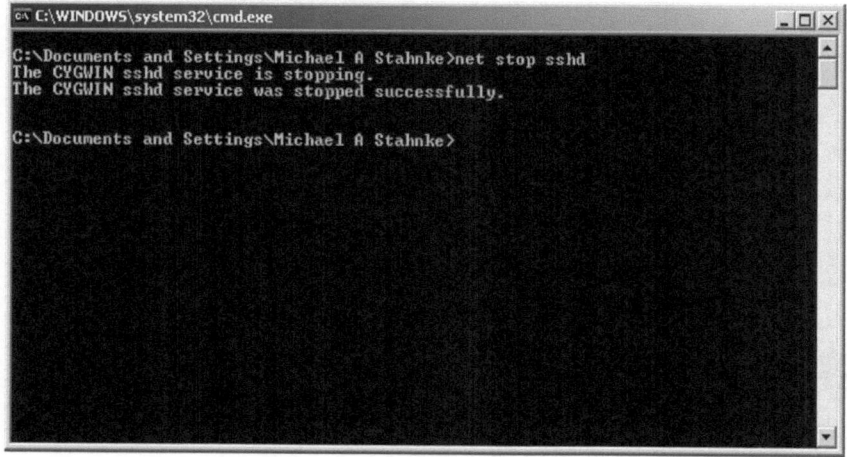

Figure B-7. *Stopping the Cygwin* sshd *service*

Testing the Connection

That's really all there is to getting sshd up and running on a Windows system. The next step is to test your connection via an SSH client.

Windows Firewall

If you are a security-minded user, you are probably using a personal firewall of some kind, whether it is the firewall built into Windows or a third-party solution. In fact, if you are running Windows XP Service Pack 2 or later, the Windows Firewall is enabled by default. To allow SSH connection from other systems, you will need to open TCP port 22 on that firewall.

To enable sshd from the Windows Firewall, navigate to the Windows Control Panel. Click Security Center, and then click the bottom icon that says Windows Firewall, as shown in Figure B-8.

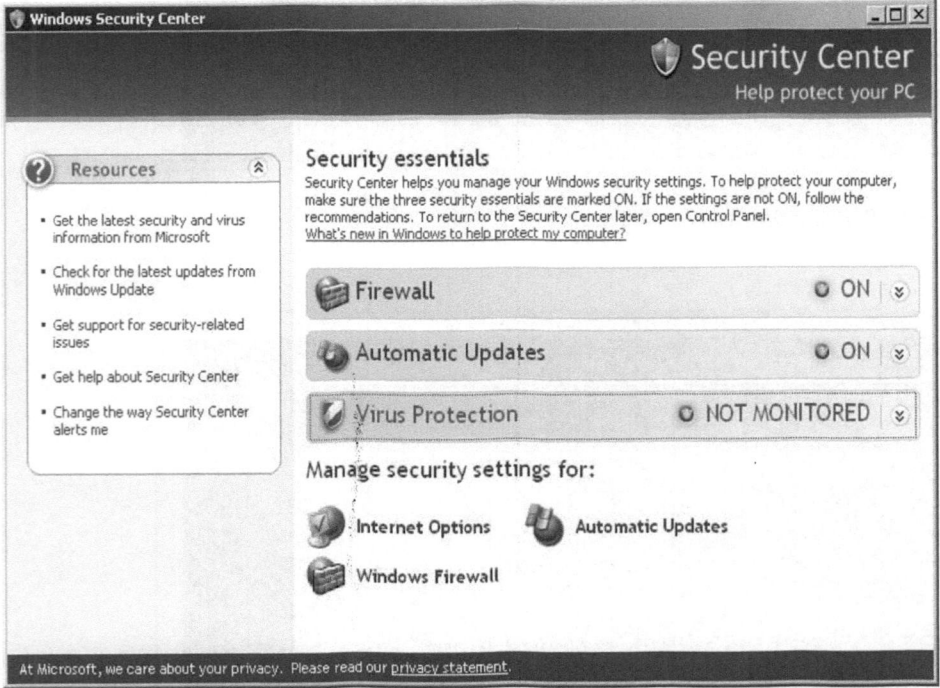

Figure B-8. *Click* Windows Firewall.

Under the Exceptions tab, click the Add Port button, and add an appropriate name along with TCP port number 22. Figure B-9 depicts the process of adding sshd as an allowed application.

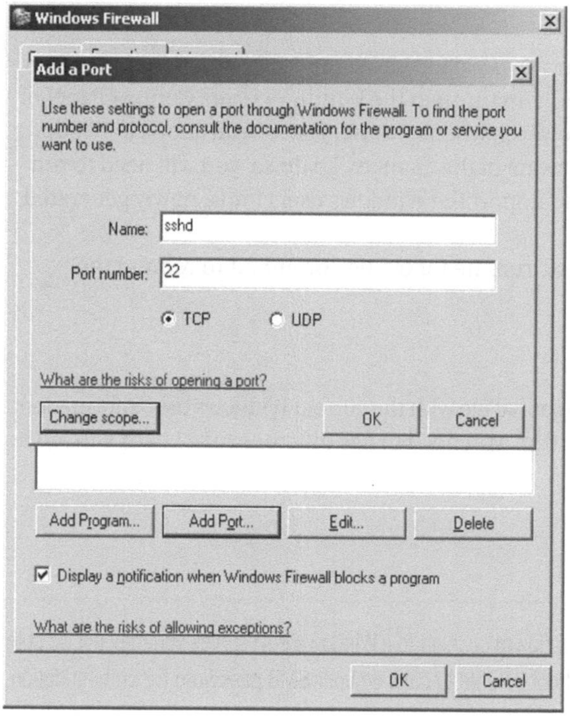

Figure B-9. *Adding* sshd *as an application on TCP port 22*

Establishing the Connection

After configuring your firewall to allow TCP port 22 inbound connections, test the SSH connection from an SSH client. I used PuTTY from my system, but the command line from Cygwin will also work. Remember to use the actual hostname for the Windows system, not localhost, since by default the firewall will not stop connections coming from localhost. If all goes well, you should see something similar to Figure B-10.

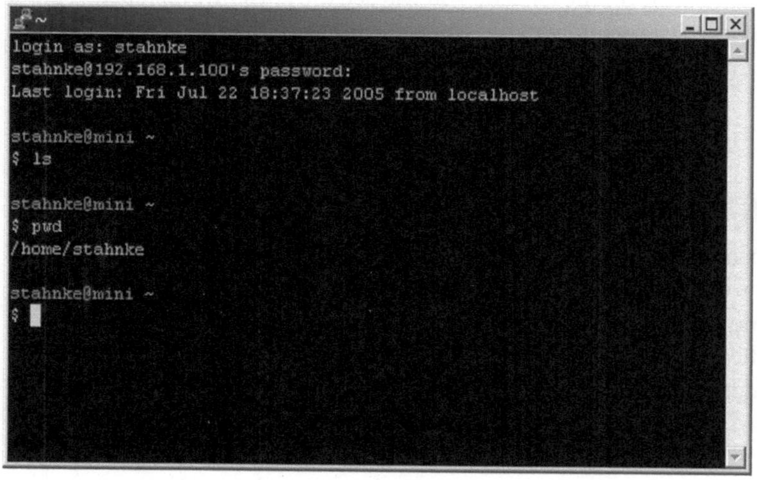

Figure B-10. *A connection has been established with* sshd *running on Windows.*

Cygwin and Users

When Cygwin is installed, it creates an /etc/passwd file based on the current Windows users. If you need to add users, it is best to add them through the Windows Users Control Panel or through the use of a domain controller. However, when new users have been added to Windows in either manner, Cygwin must be made aware of the changes. To do so, you will need to run the Cygwin mkpasswd command in order to import the Windows users into a newly generated /etc/passwd file.

After adding a user through Windows, run the following command to rebuild the /etc/passwd file:

```
$ mkpasswd -l > /etc/passwd
```

This command will create a new /etc/passwd file with the current Windows user information; however, if you are in a domain infrastructure, you need to use different switches. If you are in a domain, run

```
$ mkpassswd -d > /etc/passwd
```

■**Caution** If you are using public key authentication to connect to a Windows SSH server, you may not be able to access network drives because Windows will not be able to pass on your SMB password for authentication.

Upgrading OpenSSH Cygwin Packages

OpenSSH is upgraded on a regular basis. To keep current with these changes, you can download the latest builds from http://www.openssh.com and compile and install them via Cygwin. You will need GNU Make and other utilities (available via the Cygwin installer) to complete the compilation. See the Cygwin documentation for more information about these requirements.

You could also wait for the Cygwin team to release the updated package. To install new updates in this fashion, run the Cygwin setup.exe file (or download a new one). From there, select the Install from Internet option and continue until you are prompted for package selection. Navigate to OpenSSH. On the left side you will see the currently installed version under the Current heading. The second column will show the available new version. If you wish to upgrade, select Install and click Next. The upgraded package will be downloaded and installed.

Configuration

The configuration of OpenSSH on Microsoft Windows is identical to that of sshd and the ssh client on any other platform, with the exception of ControlMaster and ControlPath in the client. The configuration files inside of Cygwin are found in /etc.

Public key authentication, key generation, SSH agents, and file transfers all work the same with OpenSSH on Windows as they do on traditional UNIX/Linux platforms.

Cygwin as an X Server on Windows

Cygwin can also provide a free X server for Windows system. This will accept an X11 connection forwarded through SSH so UNIX/Linux graphical applications can be run from Windows workstations. To create an X server, run the Cygwin `setup.exe` file. Navigate to the X11 category and select `X-start-menu-icons`. This will select everything that is required to make your PC run as an X server. The installation will probably take a few minutes.

Once the X server has been installed, you can use the Start Menu icon to start the X server, or type `startx` from the Cygwin `bash` shell. The default configuration of X from Cygwin is fairly secure. It will allow a forwarded SSH connection to connect to it, but it will not allow other displays to connect without explicitly allowing them via `xhost`.

Index